Publics and Counterpublics

Publics and Counterpublics

Michael Warner

ZONE BOOKS · NEW YORK

2005

ZONE BOOKS
633 Vanderbilt Street
Brooklyn, NY 11218

First Paperback Edition
Fourth Printing 2014

Printed in the United States of America.

Distributed by The MIT Press,
Cambridge, Massachusetts, and London, England

Library of Congress Cataloging-in-Publication Data

Warner, Michael, 1958–
     Publics and counterpublics / Michael Warner.
        p.   cm.
     Includes bibliographical references.
     ISBN 978-1-890951-29-0 (pbk.)
        1. Social Structure. 2. Public interest. 3. Mass society.
 I. Title.
HM706.W37 2002
301—dc21

                                        2001043527

Contents

Introduction

Publics are queer creatures. You cannot point to them, count them, or look them in the eye. You also cannot easily avoid them. They have become an almost natural feature of the social landscape, like pavement. In the media-saturated forms of life that now dominate the world, how many activities are *not* in some way oriented to publics? Texts cross one's path in their endless search for a public of one kind or another: the morning paper, the radio, the television, movies, billboards, books, official postings. Beyond these obvious forms of address lie others, like fashion trends or brand names, that do not begin "Dear Reader" but are intrinsically oriented to publics nonetheless. (There is no such thing as a pop song, for example, unless you hear it as addressing itself to the audience that can make it "pop.") Your attention is everywhere solicited by artifacts that say, before they say anything else, *Hello, public!*

Much of the texture of modern social life lies in the invisible presence of these publics that flit around us like large, corporate ghosts. Most of the people around us belong to our world not directly, as kin or comrades or in any other relation to which we could give a name, but as strangers. How is it that we nevertheless recognize them as members of our world? We are related to them (and I am to you) as transient participants in common publics, potentially addressable in impersonal forms. Most of us would find it nearly impossible to imagine what social life without publics would look like. Each time we address a public, as I am doing now with these words, we draw on what seems like simple common sense. If we did not have a practical sense of what publics are, if we could not unself-consciously take them for granted as really existing and addressable social entities, we could not produce most of the books or films or broadcasts or journals that make up so much of our culture; we could not conduct elections or indeed imagine ourselves as members of nations or movements. Yet publics exist only by virtue of their imagining. They are a kind of fiction that has taken on life, and very potent life at that.

Behind the common sense of our everyday life among publics is an astonishingly complex history. The idea of a public is a cultural form, a kind of practical fiction, present in the modern world in a way that is very different from any analogues in other or earlier societies. Like the idea of rights, or nations, or markets, it can now seem universal. But it has not always been so. Its conditions have been long in the making, and its precise meaning varies from case to case — especially now, as it has found such variable extension in the postcolonial world. There are ambiguities, even contradictions in the idea. As it is extended to new contexts and new media, new polities and new rhetorics, its meaning can be seen to change in ways that we have scarcely begun to appreciate.

This book brings together eight essays on the theme "What is a public?" The essays try to show that this deceptively simple question introduces an immense variety of inquiries. Properly understood, it can reframe the way we understand literary texts, contemporary politics, and the modern social world in general. Perhaps because contemporary life without the idea of a public is so unthinkable, the idea itself tends to be taken for granted, and thus little understood. What discipline or method has a claim to say much about it? How would one go about studying it?

People often speak these days not just of *the public* but of multiple publics. And not without reason, since the publics among which we steer, or surf, are potentially infinite in number. In one way, this makes the analytic question tougher; publics might all be different, making generalization difficult. In another way, to emphasize multiple publics might seem to get rid of the analytic difficulty completely: since publics are all different, why generalize? But to speak in this way only defers the questions of what kind of thing a public is, how publics could be studied, how you know when one begins and another ends, what the different kinds of publics might be, how the differences matter, how the history of the form might be told, and how it might matter differently for different people.

The question "What is a public?" requires, to begin with, an explanation of two apparently contradictory facts. The first is that the category seems to presuppose a contingent history, varying in subtle but significant ways from one context to another, from one set of institutions to another, from one rhetoric to another. The second is that the form seems to have a functional intelligibility across a wide range of contexts. How can both be true at once? How could readers in eighteenth-century London and filmgoers in twenty-first-century Hong Kong belong to publics in the same way? Does it make sense to speak of a form common to both? Can it be described in a way that still does justice to the differences of setting and medium?

A public is inevitably one thing in London, quite another in Hong Kong. This is more than the truism it might appear, since the form must be embedded in the background and self-understanding of its participants in order to work. Only by approaching it historically can one understand these preconditions of its intelligibility.

9

To address a public or to think of oneself as belonging to a public is to be a certain kind of person, to inhabit a certain kind of social world, to have at one's disposal certain media and genres, to be motivated by a certain normative horizon, and to speak within a certain language ideology. No single history sufficiently explains all the different ways these preconditions come together in practice. Yet despite this complexity, the modern concept of a public seems to have floated free from its original context. Like the market or the nation — two cultural forms with which it shares a great deal — it has entered the repertoire of almost every culture. It has gone traveling.

The scope of this translation to new contexts might tempt us to think of publics only in systemic or acultural terms — much the way markets are usually understood. We could understand the globalization of the concept as a shift in the conditions of communication, taking place in ways that participants cannot notice and beyond the control of any merely local culture. Various models already exist for such an analysis, more or less attached to a wide range of political programs, from deterministic theories of media technology to deterministic theories of capitalism, from celebratory accounts of informational rationality to postcolonial skepticism about globalization as ideology. One might, for example, explain the global extension of publics as a result of the West's power in imposing its forms in every context touched by colonialism.

But this explanation, despite all the truth that might lie behind it, is not much of an explanation. Like all the other varieties of acultural explanation, it defers the question of how this form in particular could adapt itself to, or be imposed in, so many contexts. And to identify the form only with its Western articulation might be to block from view some of the most significant points of difference, both in colonial settings and within Western cultures themselves. Filmgoers in present-day Hong Kong might be both enabled and constrained by a form whose genealogy has much to do with the London book trade after the Restoration; but that does not mean that they have been merely passive recipients of the form (nor that modern Londoners have been). Hong Kong films, moreover, now have publics elsewhere, just as English books did then.

Confronted by the local histories and contexts that make the form work, we might be tempted by the opposite approach, treating the idea of a public with nominalist skepticism: it just is whatever people in a particular context think it is. Its meaning depends on its "appropriation." It is all local culture and contingent history. This rather desperate solution, which too often passes as historicism in literary studies, eschews the problem of translation altogether. Obviously, I think the generality of the form in the contemporary world requires more reflection. I suggest below, in fact, that the idea of a public has a metacultural dimension; it gives form to a tension between general and particular that makes it difficult to analyze from either perspective alone. It might even be said to be a kind of engine of translatability, putting down new roots wherever it goes. I have tried to describe both the historical path by which publics acquired their importance to modernity and the interlocking systematicity of some of the form's key features. Though I concentrate on Anglo-America, my hope is to provoke more comparative discussion of a form that has been one of the defining elements of multiple modernities.

To develop the topic exhaustively is beyond the reach of this collection. Here I try to dig below the intuitive sense we have, as members of modern culture, of what a public is and how it works. The argument, as developed in the title essay, is that the notion of a public enables a reflexivity in the circulation of texts among strangers who become, by virtue of their reflexively circulating discourse, a social entity. I hope that the explanation below will render this cryptic formula clearer. What I mean to say about it here is simply that this pattern has a kind of systematicity that can be observed in widely differing contexts and from which important consequences follow. The idea of a public does have some consistency, despite the wide variety of its instances. The social worlds constructed by it are by no means uniform or uncontested, but they are nevertheless marked by the form in common ways.

The paradox is that although the idea of a public can only work if it is rooted in the self-understanding of the participants, participants could not possibly understand themselves in the terms I have stated. Among other reasons, it seems that in order to address a public, one must forget or ignore the fictional nature of the entity one addresses. The idea of a public is motivating, not simply instrumental. It is constitutive of a social imaginary. The manner in which it is understood by participants is therefore not merely epiphenomenal, not mere variation on a form whose essence can be grasped independently.

That is not all. One of the central claims of this book is that when people address publics, they engage in struggles — at varying levels of salience to consciousness, from calculated tactic to mute cognitive noise — over the conditions that bring them together as a public. The making of publics is the metapragmatic work newly taken up by every text in every reading. What kind of public is this? How is it being addressed? These questions and their answers are not always explicit — and cannot possibly be fully explicit, ever — but they have fateful consequences for the kind of social world to which we belong and for the kinds of actions and subjects that are possible in it.

One example is shown on the cover of this book. What kind of public do these ladies make up? Posing for each others' cameras at home, they might seem to be not public at all. They might seem merely to imitate familiar mass media genres: the fashion runway, the Hollywood promotional still, the celebrity profile, advertising. Are their cameras simply signs of media envy, icons for an absent mass public? If so, it is at least interesting that the ambition of publicity matters so much to them. Why should it?

As it happens, the photograph comes from a collection of photo albums compiled by a circle of drag queens who came together, from the mid-fifties to the mid-sixties, in a New Jersey house they called Casa Susanna. (Other snapshots from the series can be seen in the magazine *Nest* [Summer 2000].) The suburban, domestic scene in which we find them—panelled and centrally heated—is being put to an unusual use. It is a space of collective improvisation, transformative in a way that depends on its connection to several publics—including a dominant and alien mass public. To most people in that mass public, of course, these queens would be monsters of impudence, engaged in nothing more than *flaunting*. The private setting protects them from an environment of stigma, but clearly their aspiration is to a different kind of publicness.

The ladies of Casa Susanna are doing *glamour*, which for them is both a public idiom and an intimate feeling. Its thrill allows them to experience their bodies in a way that would not have been possible without this mutual witnessing and display. And not theirs alone: they must imagine that each of their cameras allows the witnessing of indefinite numbers of strangers beyond the confines of the room. The more strangers, the greater the glamour. From other photos in the albums we know that they each competed in local drag balls as well; the cameras are more than merely wishful props. The photo itself must have been taken by another drag queen, presumably captured in turn by the camera in the upper right. All these cameras on the one hand indicate the absent attentions of the mass media; but on the other hand they create publicly

13

circulating images, making possible a different style of embodiment, a new sociability and solidarity, and a scene for further improvisation. Like the She-Romps discussed in chapter 2, the queens of Casa Susanna are revising what it means to be public.

In many ways, the unending process of redefinition — always difficult and always conflicted — can be strategic, conscious, even artful. Much of the art of writing, or of performing in other media, lies in the practical knowledge that there are always many different ways of addressing a public, that each decision of form, style, and procedure carries hazards and costs in the kind of public it can define. The temptation is to think of publics as something we make, through individual heroism and creative inspiration or through common goodwill. Much of the process, however, necessarily remains invisible to consciousness and to reflective agency. The making of a public requires conditions that range from the very general — such as the organization of media, ideologies of reading, institutions of circulation, text genres — to the particular rhetorics of texts. Struggle over the nature of publics cannot even be called strategic except by a questionable fiction, since the nature and relationship of the parties involved in the game are conditions established, metapragmatically, by the very notion of a public or by the medium through which a public comes into being.

As several of the essays try to show, interplay among these different levels can be complex. In some cases, for example, a conscious strategy of style can be seen as struggling to compensate for conditions of circulation, perhaps vainly. "Styles of Intellectual Publics" argues that this often happens when academics try to reach popular audiences through the plain style. In other cases, interactions that seem to have no manifest political content can be seen as attempting to create rival publics, even rival modes of publicness. "Publics and Counterpublics" proposes that queer and other minor publics can be seen in this light, and "The Mass Public and the Mass Subject" suggests that half-articulate struggles over the mediation of publics are general in mass culture. In still other cases, aesthetic effects can be produced by the dialectic between conditions of textuality and the strategies made possible by those conditions, as, for example, by manipulating incommensurable modes of publicness in unfamiliar ways. "Whitman Drunk" reads Whitman's poetry as such an enterprise.

This book proposes, in other words, a flexible methodology for the analysis of publics. It tries to model, through a range of case studies, the sort of multileveled analysis that, I think, is always demanded by public texts. That, at any rate, is the best face that can be put on a collection that is heterogeneous for plenty of other reasons as well. The essays that follow were written for different occasions, over more than a decade. A few of them could be described as queer theory, others as public-sphere theory or simply as literary criticism or cultural history. I do not try to resolve all the generic or methodological unclarity that might result, let alone the conceptual and stylistic shifts from older essays to more recent ones. My consolation for the embarrassment of inconsistency is that the very heterogeneity of the essays might help to suggest the range of projects that can spring from my central theme.

On some points I do think the method is consistent. It is essentially interpretive and form sensitive. I urge an understanding of the phenomenon of publics that is historical in orientation and always alert to the dynamics of textuality. The mode of proceeding in this book will therefore seem strange, possibly silly, to those in the social sciences to whom the public is simply an existing entity to be studied empirically and for whom empirical analysis has to mean something more definite, less interpretive, than attention to the means by which the fiction of the public is made real. This school of thought continues to march along despite all the criticisms that have been leveled against it.[1]

On the other hand, the historical method and literary criticism in their usual modes are in themselves not adequate to the analysis of publics. Analysis can never begin simply with the text as its object, as literary criticism is wont to do. Publics are among the conditions of textuality, specifying that certain stretches of language are understood to be "texts" with certain properties. This metapragmatic background — itself of infinite complexity — must be held up for analysis if we are to understand the mutually defining interplay between texts and publics. Publics are essentially intertextual, frameworks for understanding texts against an organized background of the circulation of other texts, all interwoven not just by citational references but by the incorporation of a reflexive circulatory field in the mode of address and consumption. And that circulation, though made reflexive by means of textuality, is more than textual — especially now, in the twenty-first century, when the texts of public circulation are very often visual or at any rate no longer mediated by the codex format. (One open question of this book is to what degree the text model, though formative for the modern public, might be increasingly archaic.) For all these reasons, the phenomenon of publics requires a disciplinary flexibility. The exigency of such a flexible method might account for the relative invisibility of the form as an object of sustained inquiry in academic thought.

Half of the essays are new; the others I collect here because of their bearing on the theme. One or two have complex histories of their own. "The Mass Public and the Mass Subject" was written for a 1989 conference introducing the English translation of Jürgen Habermas's *Structural Transformation of the Public Sphere*. It addresses a debate in social theory, trying to introduce concerns that we might now associate with queer theory. In 1989, of course, queer theory was not yet a recognizable enterprise. I could not write that essay now. Its emphases might be very different from those of the more recent essays. I have not tried to rewrite it for consistency, partly because I do not know if it could even be done and partly because the essay has been cited by many others and it seemed best to leave it in its original shape. "Sex in Public," on the other hand, was written almost a decade after "The Mass Public and the Mass Subject." Coauthored with my friend and collaborator Lauren Berlant, it, too, owes much to the context that gave rise to it, in particular its attempt to redirect the field of queer studies. Many of its arguments I have pursued elsewhere, in a nonacademic work of political polemic titled *The Trouble with Normal.*[2] It serves in the context of this volume as a case study in struggles over the mediation of publics.

The first two essays stand together as a kind of general introduction of the subject. "Public and Private," which was conceived for a planned volume called *Critical Terms for the Study of Gender and Sexuality*, reviews the conceptual complexity of the terms "public" and "private," traces the major debates of public-sphere theory, and introduces the idea of counterpublics in relation to feminist and public-sphere theory. The next essay, "Publics and Counterpublics," treats the complexities of "public" as a noun. This essay more than any other stands at the heart of the present volume, elaborating the idea of a public as I have presented it in this introduction.

Doubtless there are other stories to be told about the coherence or motivated incoherence of the essays. For some readers, perhaps, the central story here will be one of queer theory. Certainly a major motivation of the essays, without exception, has been to bring some clarity to the process by which people have made dissident sexuality articulate; how they have come together around nonnormative sexualities in a framework for collective world making and political action; how in the process people have challenged the heteronormative framework of modern culture while also availing themselves of its forms; how those forms of collective action and expression mediate the sexualities and identities they represent; and how many of the central aspirations of the resulting queer culture continue to be frustrated by the ideological and material organization of publics, both of dominant culture and of queer culture. The essays are examples of this process, not just analyses of it. They are the means by which I tried to articulate a place in the world. (This is especially true of "The Mass Public and the Mass Subject" and "Sex in Public," both of which were written against what at the time felt like huge blockages in the sayable.)

The way I pursued this project of self-clarification, however, increasingly put me at odds with the identitarian gay rights movement. The period over which these essays were written was one in which the American lesbian and gay movement enjoyed increasing visibility and a considerable measure of success. Yet I became convinced that it had paid a high price in the process. The movement had embraced, as the definition of its own constituency, a privatized notion of identity based in the homo/hetero language of sexual orientation. Along with many other academics who were developing the field of queer theory in the 1990s, I thought this language distorted sexuality and its politics.

Queer theory, meanwhile, got to be very good at redescribing nonnormative sexualities and the flaws of identitarian thinking. But partly because the field relied so heavily on psychoanalytic theory for this purpose, it was somewhat less adept at describing the worldliness of sexuality and the conditions of the social-movement form. As I began speculating on the close relation between sexual cultures and their publics in the modern context, I came to the conclusion that one of the underlying flaws of the gay and lesbian movement was the way it obscured and normalized the most compelling challenges of queer counterpublics.

This is the argument of *The Trouble with Normal*. That book was written in an attempt to reopen some communication between the organized movement and those who were increasingly disaffected from it. It does not use the vocabulary of public-sphere theory explored here. Yet the arguments of that book and this one are, I believe, mutually illustrative. *The Trouble with Normal* is an odd book in many ways, perhaps not least in trying to advance an analysis of publics while also trying to rally a public rhetorically.

The tension between reflective analysis and hortatory position taking will no doubt be seen in a number of these essays as well. It is rather more than the usual theory/practice dilemma, which concerns me very little. The problem in this case is that the preconditions of rhetorical engagement with publics are the object of an analysis that is motivated in large part by a rhetorical engagement with a public. Conceptually, this is like trying to face backward while walking. Preposterousness of this kind is familiar in queer criticism. On the whole, I think the balance in this book tips toward analysis, but I have not tried to eliminate the tension. I do not think that I could do so entirely and am rather persuaded that it is productive on both sides. "Styles of Intellectual Publics" reflects on the two modes and their relation to different publics, making the tension between them itself an object of analysis (and, a bit, of hortatory position taking).

The other motivating subtext of these essays has been the long conversation, now of some fifteen years' duration, with my colleagues in the Center for Transcultural Studies. There, more than anywhere else, I have found not just comprehending readers and tough critics, not just friends whose brilliance was constant inspiration, but a sustained environment for collective thinking. Much of the work in these essays emerged from dialogue, in a way that I cannot do justice to here. More people than I can name took part in the conversation. Obviously, Lauren Berlant has been a collaborator of a special kind; even where she is not named as coauthor (as in *The Trouble with Normal*) she has been a tacit partner. Ben Lee and Dilip Gaonkar have been the organizers and catalysts for the center's discussions; to them I owe an unpayable debt. It is my hope that this book, insofar as it contributes to anything, will direct attention to the distinctive intellectual project of the center, now finding rich realization in the work of so many of my colleagues there: Arjun Appadurai, Craig Calhoun, Vincent Crapanzano, Dilip Gaonkar, Nilüfer Göle, Ben Lee, Tom McCarthy, Mary Poovey, Beth Povinelli, Charles Taylor, Greg Urban, and many others.

CHAPTER ONE

Public and Private

What kind of world would make the values of both publicness and privacy equally accessible to all? This question has often been taken up in modern political philosophy. But that apparently simple question raises, and is made complicated by, another one: How would the experience of gender and sexuality have to be different in such a world?

The link between these two subjects has been noticed for millennia. The story is told of the Greek philosopher Diogenes that whenever he felt sexual need he walked into the central marketplace and masturbated. According to a later Greek commentator, he was in the habit of "doing everything in public, the works of Demeter and Aphrodite alike."[1] This was not usual in Athens in the fourth century B.C.E. Diogenes provoked disgust. His behavior was a kind of "performance criticism," as Foucault has called it, a way of calling attention to the visceral force behind the moral ideas of public and private.[2] Diogenes was attempting, to a degree that has scarcely been rivaled since, to do without the distinction entirely. He evidently regarded it as artificial, contrary to nature, the false morality of a corruption that mistook itself for civilization.

More than two thousand years later, a different challenge to the morality of public and private created an equally queasy sensation.

In the late 1820s, the Scottish-born Frances Wright toured America, lecturing against slavery and for women's rights, birth control, and workers' rights. She provoked nearly universal attack for her public appearances, leading the American Catharine Beecher to write:

> Who can look without disgust and abhorrence upon such an one as Fanny Wright, with her great masculine person, her loud voice, her untasteful attire, going about unprotected, and feeling no need of protection, mingling with men in stormy debate, and standing up with bare-faced impudence, to lecture to a public assembly.... I cannot conceive any thing in the shape of woman, more intolerably offensive and disgusting.[3]

Beecher is offended, eloquently so, by a woman in public. To her, this kind of public behavior — mingling with men, lecturing before audiences, going around with no escort, offering ideas in debate — should be left to men. So deep is this conviction for Beecher that Wright's behavior makes her seem masculine. In fact, the abusiveness in this passage is not so much about Wright's ideas or her acts as about her being: her person is masculine, her voice loud, her attire out of taste; she stands up and is seen. Like her sister Harriet Beecher Stowe, Catharine Beecher did more than simply turn away in disgust. She went on to write several books that articulated, more explicitly than ever before, the theory of separate spheres — that women's place was the home and that women's influence on the world should be moral rather than political. Ironically, in doing so, she became one of the most public women of her day.

In both of these examples, the distinction between public and private comes under an explicit challenge. In both cases, it is not just a distinction but a hierarchy, in which the space of the market or the assembly is given a special importance. In both cases, being in public is a privilege that requires filtering or repressing something that is seen as private. In both cases, too, the transgression is experienced not as merely theoretical, but as a violation of deep instincts about sex and gender. Who can look at it, in Beecher's words, "without disgust and abhorrence"? It is not hard to see, then, why the terms "public" and "private" have often seemed to present a difficulty. The terms are complex enough and shifting enough to allow for profound change; yet in practice they often do not seem theoretical at all. They seem to be preconceptual, almost instinctual, rooted in the orientations of the body and common speech.

The critical literature on public and private is immense, but very seldom does it do justice to the visceral force that the distinction has in these examples. Often the impression seems to be that public and private are abstract categories for thinking about law, politics, and economics. And so they are. But their power, as feminism and queer theory have had to insist, goes much deeper. A child's earliest education in shame, deportment, and cleaning is an initiation into the prevailing meaning of public and private, as when he or she locates his or her "privates" or is trained to visit the "privy." (The word "public" also records this bodily association: it derives from the Latin *poplicus*, for people, but evolved to *publicus* in connection with *pubes*, in the sense of adult men, linking public membership to pubic maturity.) Clothing is a language of publicity, folding the body in what is felt as the body's own privacy. Some bodily sensations — of pleasure and pain, shame and display, appetite and purgation — come to be felt, in the same way, as privacy. Like those of gender, the orientations of public and private are rooted in what anthropologists call habitus: the conventions by which we experience, as though naturally, our own bodies and movement in the space of the world. Public and private are learned along with such terms as "active" and "passive," "front" and "back," and "top" and "bottom." They can seem quasi-natural, visceral, fraught with perils of abjection and degradation or, alternatively, of cleanliness and self-mastery. They are the very scene of selfhood and scarcely distinguishable from the experience of gender and sexuality.

That makes them hard to challenge. In the case of gender, public and private are not just formal rules about how men and women should behave. They are bound up with meanings of masculinity and femininity. Masculinity, at least in Western cultures, is felt partly in a way of occupying public space; femininity, in a language of private feeling. When Diogenes masturbates in the market, the public display of private need may appear disturbing or shameful, but it is not said to throw doubt on his masculinity. His blunt, bold simplicity can be seen as virile integrity in part because it is so very public. When Frances Wright lectures in public, Catharine Beecher perceives her as mannish, even monstrously so. Women, accustomed to being the spectacle displayed to male desire, often experience the visibility of public space as a kind of intimate vulnerability. Men, by contrast, often feel their masculinity challenged when their bodies are on display as objects of erotic desire.[4]

In the case of sexuality, too, not all sexualities are public or private in the same way. Same-sex persons kissing, embracing, or holding hands in public view commonly excite disgust even to the point of violence, whereas mixed-sex persons doing the same things are invisibly ordinary, even applauded. Nelly boys are said to be "flaunting" their sexuality, just by swishing or lisping. They are told to keep it to themselves, even though the "it" in question is their relation to their own bodies. Butch men, meanwhile, can swagger aggressively without being accused of flaunting anything. Just as feminists since Fanny Wright have found that to challenge male domination in public is to change both femininity and the norms of public behavior, lesbians and gay men have found that to challenge the norms of straight culture in public is to disturb deep and unwritten rules about the kinds of behavior and eroticism that are appropriate to the public.

Public and private are bound up with elementary relations to language as well as to the body. The acquisition of language is an education into public and private speech genres and their different social contexts, which are commonly contexts of gender. In one sense, much emphasized by Ludwig Wittgenstein, all language and all thought are public, a feature of the language games that make intelligibility possible. Yet there are degrees of formality in speech and writing that create a continuum of publicness. In many languages, these are sharply divided and lexically distinct, as with the French *tutoyer* and *vouvoyer*. Among the Xavante studied by Laura Graham, the public speech of the morning and evening adult-male convocations is marked by singing styles, polyphonic discourse, and special protocols of pronoun usage and verb conjugations, as well as body posture.[5] In many societies, including the Xavante, classical Athens, and the antebellum United States, these differences are frankly avowed as differences of status and gender: men can speak in public concourse, women cannot. The difference between genres of private and public speech anchors the sense of home and intimacy, on one hand, and social personality, on the other.

The different senses of self and membership mediated by these contexts can seem scarcely comparable. Parents, lovers, strangers, or peers may appear in one context but not the other. In modern culture, where there are so many different genres of speech and writing, each with a different context for one's personality, the felt gap between public selves or roles and private ones has given rise to a Romantic longing for unity — at least among those with the

25

privilege of being public. (The most famous example is Rousseau's *Confessions,* a kind of modern successor to Diogenes.) That longing for unity can also be seen in modes of collective public intimacy such as ecstatic spirituality. Inevitably, identity politics itself magnetizes such longings, affirming private identity through public politics and promising to heal divisions of the political world by anchoring them in the authentically personal realm and its solidarity. In the ideals of ethnic identity, or sisterhood, or gay pride, to take the most common examples, an assertive and affirmative concept of identity seems to achieve a correspondence between public existence and private self. Identity politics in this sense seems to many people a way of overcoming both the denial of public existence that is so often the form of domination and the incoherence of the experience that domination creates, an experience that often feels more like invisibility than like the kind of privacy you value.

Definitions and Contexts

Throughout the Western tradition, private and public have been commonly and sensibly understood as distinct zones. The boundary between bedroom and market, home and meetinghouse can be challenged or violated, but it is at least clear enough to be spatially distinct. Moving from one to another is experienced as crossing a barrier or making a transition — like going from the privacy of one's bedroom to the public room of a convention hall. In medieval thought (which inherited a notion of the *res publica* from Roman law), the public was almost solely a spatial concept, meaning anything open, such as the outside wall of a house. Modern culture has redrawn the spatial distinction, adding new layers of meaning to the term "public" but preserving the idea of physical boundaries. Nineteenth- and twentieth-century middle-class architecture, for example, separates parlors or "living rooms" from family quarters or "withdrawing rooms," trying to erect literal walls between public and private functions even within the home. (Catharine Beecher specialized in this new style of home economics.) Modern American law frequently defines privacy as a zone of noninterference drawn around the home. So strong is this association that courts have sometimes refused to recognize a right to privacy in other spaces.

But this ideology and its architecture represent an ideal or extreme type. Public and private are not always simple enough that one could code them on a map with different colors — pink for private and blue for public. The terms also describe social contexts, kinds of feeling, and genres of language. So although public and private seem so clearly opposed that their violation can produce a sharp feeling of revulsion, the terms have many different meanings that often go unnoticed. However disgusting Catharine Beecher found the idea of a woman lecturing in public, for example, her own writings on the subject were profoundly public: they were published (that is, printed and marketed); they addressed the powerful ideal of public opinion; and they established Beecher as a figure of public fame and authority. Despite the self-evident clarity of the distinction, different senses of public or private typically intermingle in this way. A private conversation can take place in a public forum; a kitchen can become a public gathering place; a private bedroom can be public and commercial space, as in a hotel; a radio can bring public discussion into a bathroom, and so on. American courts, too, have developed other ways of defining public and private in which the terms refer to relationships rather than places. The right to privacy, for example, can be linked to marriage or the right to form intimate associations. Or it can be defined by ideals of autonomy and self-determination, as in the notion of reproductive freedom. In some of these conceptions, publicness and privacy belong to different places; in other conceptions, they belong to different relationships, in still others to persons. These differences can have conflicting implications in law as in theory.[6]

In law as in theory, moreover, public and private can sometimes be used as descriptive, value-neutral terms, simply as a way to make sense of observed practice. At other times, they are used as normative, evaluative terms, naming and invoking ideals that are *not* always observed. And they can have one application outside a context, as analytic or quasi-objective categories, while having quite another inside a context, orienting people to different poles in their own experience: people's private conversations, for example, can be regarded by a third party as public opinion.

To confuse matters further, the terms often seem to be defined against each other, with normative preference for one term; but this is not always the case. The private (from *privatus*, deprived) was originally conceived as the negation or privation of public value. It had no value in its own right. But in the modern period, this has changed, and privacy has taken on a distinctive value of its own, in several different registers: as freedom, individuality, inwardness, authenticity, and so on. Public and private sometimes compete, sometimes complement each other, and sometimes are merely parts of a larger series of classifications that includes, say, local, domestic, personal, political, economic, or intimate. Almost every major cultural change — from Christianity to printing to psychoanalysis — has left a new sedimentary layer in the meaning of the public and the private. (Print culture gave us publication; psychoanalysis, a new sense of the private person.) In modern contexts, the terms have been used in many different and overlapping senses, combining legacies from classical thought and law with modern forms of social organization.

It is no wonder, then, that so many thinkers have sought to sort out the terms, to bring to them a kind of clarity that usage seldom provides, one that might do justice to the visceral conviction that there ought to be a clear distinction. Some thinkers have done so energetically enough that their accounts have become part of the terms' symbolic weight; examples discussed here are Immanuel Kant, Hannah Arendt, and Jürgen Habermas. Yet attempts to frame public and private as a sharp distinction or antinomy have invariably come to grief, while attempts to collapse or do without them have proven equally unsatisfying.

It might be useful, therefore, to consider the range of the often conflicting meanings of public and private. The relation of public to private can take any of the following forms at least:

Public	*Private*
1) open to everyone	restricted to some
2) accessible for money	closed even to those who could pay
3) state-related; now often called public sector	nonstate, belonging to civil society; now often called private sector
4) political	nonpolitical
5) official	nonofficial
6) common	special
7) impersonal	personal
8) national or popular	group, class, or locale
9) international or universal	particular or finite
10) in physical view of others	concealed
11) outside the home	domestic
12) circulated in print or electronic media	circulated orally or in manuscript
13) known widely	known to initiates
14) acknowledged and explicit	tacit and implicit

15) "the world itself, in so far as it is common to all of us and distinguished from our privately owned place in it" (as Arendt puts it in *The Human Condition*).[7]

Matters are further complicated by several senses of private that have no corresponding sense of public, including:

16) related to the individual, especially to inwardness, subjective experience, and the incommunicable
17) discretely or properly comported, in the sense of the French *pudeur* (grasped in English only through its opposite, *impudence,* as when Beecher accuses Fanny Wright of "bare-faced impudence")
18) genital or sexual

There are also a variety of legal contexts, from constitutional law to property law, each with its own inflection of privacy. In the tradition of *Griswold* v. *Connecticut* and *Bowers* v. *Hardwick*, for example, heterosexual marriage is defined as a "zone of privacy" with special protections against state incursion.[8]

"Public," too, is an exceedingly complex noun, and what is meant by "the public" or "a public" or "the public sphere" will require a good deal of explanation below. (See the following essay, "Publics and Counterpublics.") Publicity, too, is a distinct concept, meaning not merely publicness or openness but the use of media, an instrumental publicness associated most with advertising and public relations. None of these terms has a sense that is exactly parallel to or opposite of private. None are simple oppositions, or binaries. Because the contexts overlap, most things are private in one sense and public in another. Books can be published privately; a public theater can be a private enterprise; a private life can be discussed publicly, and so on. Marriage, too, is thought of in modern culture as the ultimate private relation, but every marriage involves the state if it is to carry the force of law. It will be seen below that the public sphere in Habermas's influential account *is* private in several crucial senses. And much work on gender and sexuality in cultural studies has shown that publics in various ways enable privacy, providing resources for interiority and contexts for self-elaboration. "Public" and "private" are crucial terms for understanding these examples. But in each case, the terms need to be understood in more than one context and with some attention to their history.

Although many forms of the public/private distinction have been challenged in feminism and in queer theory, we should not forget that a challenge to one form of the distinction may not necessarily have the same implications for others. None of the versions of public and private listed above can be dismissed as merely archaic, since they are immanent to a host of norms and institutions of modern life and may in many respects be desirable. It remains as difficult now as it was for Diogenes's fellow citizens to imagine a world with neither public nor private.

Public and Private in Feminist Theory

Any organized attempt to transform gender or sexuality is a public questioning of private life, and thus the critical study of gender and sexuality entails a problem of public and private in its own practice. Both the contemporary women's movement and gay liberation took shape as social movements in the 1960s, when counterculture had begun to imagine a politics that would transform personal life across the board, giving public relevance to the most private matters. Other social movements — temperance, abolition, labor, suffrage, antiracism — had also challenged prevailing norms of public and private. A leading defense of racial segregation in the American South, for example, was that private owners of property or businesses had the right to admit whom they chose, just because it was private property. To fight such arguments, it was necessary to advance a strong vision of the public relevance of private life, a vision expressed in the phrase "civil rights." Even more, though, the women's and gay movements represented groups who were by definition linked to a conventional under-standing of private life — gender roles, sexuality, the home and family. They were public movements contesting the most private and intimate matters. Their very entry into public politics seemed scandalous or inappropriate. An understanding of public and private was implied not just in their theories and policy platforms but in their very existence as movements.

In second-wave feminism at the height of identity politics, many took a fairly radical, even draconian solution to the problem of public and private. They argued that the distinction was virtu-ally synonymous with patriarchy. Male was to public as female was to private. In a 1974 essay titled "Woman, Culture, and Society: A Theoretical Overview," Michelle Zimbalist Rosaldo claimed that the gendering of public and private helped to explain the subordi-nation of women cross-culturally. In this context, private meant domestic spaces and functions, and public referred to contexts in which men spoke and made decisions for the community.[9]

There has been much debate about how widely this pattern holds. The women's rights movement had come into being against an especially rigid version of this spatialized and gendered scheme, the separate-sphere ideology of the nineteenth century. But Ros-aldo's theory laid it at the origins of masculinist culture. Jean Bethke Elshtain, concerned with the normative development of the terms in Western thought, was critical of the oversimplifica-tions in this argument. Yet she traced the endurance of a gendered opposition of public and private from Plato and Aristotle to mod-ern thought.[10] Either way, the scale of the problem was enormous. Carol Pateman was able to claim that "the dichotomy between the private and the public is central to almost two centuries of feminist writing and political struggle; it is, ultimately, what the feminist movement is about."[11]

One consequence was to see domestic and private matters,

normally outside the public view, as now being a legitimate area of common concern. In practice, this meant not just public opinion but state intervention in things like marital rape, spousal abuse, divorce, prostitution, and abortion rights. Encountering male domination mainly in the spaces usually called private, notably the home, women could only struggle against that domination by seeing it as a kind of politics. In the words of Catharine MacKinnon, "For women the measure of intimacy has been the measure of the oppression. This is why feminism has had to explode the private. This is why feminism has seen the personal as the political. The private is the public for those for whom the personal is the political. In this sense, there is no private, either normatively or empirically."[12] This is a fairly extreme formulation, and to some degree a contradictory one, since one meaning of privacy is bodily autonomy and its protection from violence; MacKinnon draws on this normative ideal even as she claims to "explode" privacy. She does so because she is writing in the context of *Roe* v. *Wade*, criticizing what she sees as the inadequate liberal logic by which abortion is legitimated only as a private privilege rather than as a public right.

Other feminists put a different emphasis on the critique of public and private. Pateman argued that the practical consequence of the feminist critique would be much broader than women entering public arenas reserved for men, the way Fanny Wright tried to do in the 1820s; rather, it would be an entire transformation of gender roles, for men as well as women, leading to a world in which the differences between women and men would be systematically uncoupled from the divisions between home and public, individual and collective life, personal and political. Most immediately, "If women are to participate fully, as equals, in social life, men have to share equally in child-rearing and other domestic tasks." More generally, "Equal parenting and equal participation in other activities of domestic life presuppose some radical changes

33

in the public sphere, in the organization of production, in what we mean by 'work' and in the practice of citizenship."[13]

These arguments in feminist scholarship are related to the political strategy declared in the famous slogan "The personal is political."[14] This slogan can be taken to mean many different things. The most basic is that the social arrangements structuring private life, domestic households, intimacy, gender, and sexuality are neither neutral nor immutable, that they can be seen as relations of power and subject to transformation. The implications of this insight, I hardly need to add, are still unfolding. In the words of one scholar, it is the "unique and world historical achievement" of the women's movement to have laid bare "the social nature of the family, the 'public' nature of the 'private,' the internal connections that exist between the family and the economy."[15]

For others, "the personal is political" means not that personal life could be transformed by political action but that politics should be personalized; that is, everyone's political views should be read as expressing his or her particular, subjective interests — identities of race, class, gender, and sexuality inevitably color everyone's perspective. This second interpretation of "the personal is political" leads to a sometimes disabling skepticism about any claim to transcendence or any appeal to universal ideals or the common good. Both of these views — the political critique of personal life and the identitarian critique of political life — are often described, confusingly enough, as identity politics.

The very success of the feminist critique of public and private has led to new questions. If "the personal is political," is a distinction between public and private always to be rejected, or exploded, as MacKinnon puts it? The slogan requires a relatively broad sense of "political," to mean contested or shaped by domination; it leaves vague the question whether inequities in "personal life" are to be redressed through private action, non-state

34

public action, or state intervention, all of which can be political in this broad sense. For many, it has been understood to mean that these distinctions should no longer matter.

Perhaps rhetorically, Joan Wallach Scott claimed in *Gender and the Politics of History* (1988) that the politics of gender "dissolves the distinction between public and private."[16] Such rhetoric lumps together the enormous range of the meanings of public and private, and it has therefore been blamed for everything from the rise in confessional memoirs to political correctness and the totalitarian tendencies of some legislative reform programs (hate-speech laws, antipornography statutes, and such). MacKinnon's legal programs, in particular, have been seen as justifying an authoritarian style of state regulation in the way they lead to the criminalization of pornography and sex rather than domination or harassment per se. Should nothing be private? Or, on the other hand, should everything be privatized? Should the state intervene to transform gender relations in the workplace and household?[17]

The answers to these questions have consequence for matters of equity, affirmative action, abortion, birth control, rape, adoption, divorce and child support, palimony, sexual harassment, welfare, health care, day care, segregated education, and so on. In many of these areas, feminism encouraged an activist state to assert the public relevance of private life. Yet the effect was not, as some feminists had hoped (and others feared), to eliminate or "dissolve" the boundary between public and private. Often state action was justified in the name of private right. Ironically, in the United States, it was largely in the contexts of feminist agitation — especially over birth control and reproductive freedom — that privacy came to be fully recognized as a domain of Constitutional law. Some distinctions have eroded, or changed: at the very least, these initiatives of the women's movement, and the understanding of public and private implied by them, enabled a significant expansion of the liberal welfare state into new areas of social life.[18]

Nancy Fraser, for one, has pointed out that some feminists' insistence on an oversimplified distinction between public and private blinded them to these consequences. By using "the public" or "the public sphere" to mean everything outside the home, they blurred together official politics, the state, the market, and other forms of association. Making these distinctions among different meanings of public and private has practical advantages, Fraser writes, "when, for example, agitational campaigns against misogynist cultural representations are confounded with programs for state censorship or when struggles to deprivatize housework and child care are equated with their commodification."[19] In other words, while the personal is "political" in a broad sense, state regulation may not always be appropriate. And while the private realm of the home should often be a matter of public care and concern, the market — like the state and like the majoritarian public of the mass media — has its own destructive tendencies and may be a bad model of "the public."

Scholars have also argued that public and private have always been more than a dichotomy. Some feminist scholars have shown that women have been involved in both public and private realms in most historical periods, often to a surprising degree.[20] Women's networks — of gossip, kinship, affect, and countereconomies — have had important public aspects even at the height of Victorian ideology. We have seen, for example, that while she was criticizing Fanny Wright for violating a boundary between public and private, Catharine Beecher was herself pursuing an active and innovative career in the public sphere. Recent versions of feminism, stressing the diversity of women's positions in different contexts of class, race, religion, or locale, have emphasized that the dominant dichotomies often fail to account for these variations. Other feminists, elaborating deconstructive readings of

36

gender categories that emphasize their uneven deployment or internal incoherence, have tried to conceive public and private in less spatializing, hypostatized ways.[21]

It may be doubted whether any group, even in the most restrictive contexts of power, has been able to monopolize all dimensions of publicness or all dimensions of privacy in the way MacKinnon suggests men have done. At any rate, the distinction is never drawn solely in one way or solely as an antinomy. The gendered division of labor, for example, is a classic and seemingly clear instance of the ideological distinction between public and private — in this case, between public work and private labor. In this system, as many feminists have noted, gender, labor, and publicness are so closely aligned that they seem synonymous. Public work is paid, is performed outside the home, and has long been the realm of men. Private labor is unpaid, is usually done at home, and has long been women's work. Far from being symmetrical or complementary, this sexual division of labor (and division of sexual labor) is unequal. Public work, for example, is understood to be productive, forming vocational identity, and fulfilling men as individuals; private labor is understood as the general reproduction of society, lacking the vocational distinction of a trade or a profession, and displaying women's selflessness. This gendered difference in callings persists, with its unequal mapping of public and private, though the entry of women into trades and professions has weakened it somewhat.

Yet the same separation of spheres has always had other, more complex meanings of public and private besides this direct correlation in gender domination and economic systems. Even the most extreme separation of spheres turns the home and its adjunct spaces into a functional public for women — spaces that can be filled with talk and with the formation of a shared world. There are normative countercurrents as well. In capitalism, paid work came to be understood as private economic life. The workplace lost some of the publicness that had been the hallmark of the guilds and trades. So while men were marking their workplace off more sharply from the increasingly female domestic space, they were also marking it off from the public. Professionalism recuperated some of that publicness for its highly trained classes, in a new rhetoric of expertise — but not for wage labor. Male workers, in other words, underwent a loss of public life as artisanal household economies yielded to new, more modern separations of workplace and home life.[22] The domestic and reproductive functions of the family, meanwhile, acquired ever greater public significance as reform movements made them the objects of so much discourse and as nationalism came to be symbolized through them. Many women, like Catharine Beecher and her sister Harriet, found an entry into public life exactly through these discourses about privacy in reform, in nationalism, in evangelical Christianity, and in antislavery. They could do so in large part because private markets for print linked women as readers and writers.[23] Women in many places also elaborated parallel or informal economies — private, but public in the sense that they lay beyond the home. These developments were simultaneous with the rise of separate-sphere ideology, not simply later reactions against it.

The economic separation of the male public from the female private, in short, was never a static system. It was one normative strand among others in the elaboration of public and private. To say this is not to minimize its power or to underestimate the degree of male domination that it represented. In fact, because the interweaving of gender, labor, and publicness was indirect rather than definitional, it could often go unrecognized, and still does. To see this might help us to understand why inequality persists despite the apparent breakdown of the most static form of the gendered division of labor — why, for instance, so many of the publics of women's culture continue not to recognize themselves as publics because they think of their authenticity and their femininity as rooted necessarily in private feeling and domestic relations; or why so many men failed to understand the privatization of economic life as a loss because they thought of their work as having an extradomestic, vocational publicness.

The Liberal Tradition

Given these complexities, how did the notion of public and private come to be imagined as a binary in need of demolition? The answer lies in the way a whole set of distinctions were powerfully aligned in the liberal tradition, reaching back at least to John Locke but widely institutionalized in politics and law by the nineteenth century. This tradition began as a critique of patriarchy, and one of its unintended consequences was the development of modern feminist thought in the eighteenth century. But by the time of second-wave feminism in the 1960s, this liberal tradition had come to pose serious limitations to both feminist and gay movements.

In liberal thought, private persons, no longer defined by privation or powerlessness, had become the proper site of humanity. They possessed publicly relevant rights by virtue of being private persons. Rights meant no longer the privileges that went with various public legal statuses — fief owner, copyholder, husband, lord of the manor, chief eunuch, citizen, princess — but rather claims that all persons could make on the basis of private humanity. The public, no longer understood as the audience or subjects of the ruler, became a community with independent existence, even sovereign claims and the ability to resist or change rulers. Both public and private were redefined, and both gained enormously in significance following the conception of state power as limited and rights as vested in private persons.[24]

This language for politics also gained in forcefulness from the use of similar terms in arguments for capitalism.[25] The motto of Bernard Mandeville's *Fable of the Bees* (1714) is a famous example: "Private vices, public benefits." According to Mandeville, the competitive pursuit of self-interest ("private vices") could be counted on to yield good effects ("public benefits"), counteracting mere selfishness through the interactions of the market. Such thinking, as later developed by Adam Smith and others, lent powerful support to the idea that economic life, as a realm of private society, should be kept free from state or public interference. In time, capitalist culture would give this distinction between public power and a private economy an additional dimension, remapping social life into distinct arenas of work and "personal life," including the intensified privacies of intimacy, friendship, and the domestic.[26]

Meanwhile, the state was evolving into a modern bureaucracy, with its normative distinction between the public function of office and the private person of the officeholder. And as private persons came to be seen as driven by self-interest, the public came to be defined as disinterested. Those aspects of people's lives that particularize their interests came to be seen as inappropriate to public discussion. To be properly public required that one rise above, or set aside, one's private interests and expressive nature. (This notion of a separation between public voice and private selfhood is often called "bracketing"; a closely related idea in John Rawls's liberal legal theory is called the "veil of ignorance."[27])

All of these characteristically modern developments made possible a vision of freedom as negative liberty, inherent in private persons, and a vision of political life as the restraint of power by a critical public. In these respects, they lent great resources to the development of a critique of gender and sexuality. Early feminism, in writers such as Mary Astell, Mary Wollstonecraft, Judith Sargent Murray, and the Grimké sisters, was articulated through the normative language of the liberal tradition. They were especially enabled by its vision of the rights-bearing private person, its role for a critical public, its principled skepticism about power.[28] Sarah Grimké, for example, was able to take the universal self of reason as an argument for women's access: "When human beings are regarded as *moral* beings, *sex*, instead of being enthroned upon the summit, administering upon rights and responsibilities, sinks into insignificance and nothingness."[29] Having bracketed sex in this way, Grimké goes on to argue for a thorough degendering of social relations: "We approach each other, and mingle with each other, under the constant pressure of a feeling that we are of different sexes; and, instead of regarding each other only in the light of immortal creatures, the mind is fettered by the idea which is early and industriously infused into it, that we must never forget the distinction between male and female."[30] Grimké longs to transcend sex, and in order to do so she declares it irrelevant, something "infused" into the individual, something to "forget." The ideal of the universal voice of reason has allowed her a kind of public participation. But the price she pays is that differences of sex have been ruled out of consideration as merely private.

In this respect, the same liberal tradition that enabled the first wave of the feminist movement also posed immediate obstacles to it as a movement, as it would later to the gay movement. Women such as Wollstonecraft and Grimké argued that their rights as individuals needed new respect. In doing so, they appealed to the ideal of a disinterested, abstract, universal public — just the kind of public in which particularized views and the gendered body would always seem matter out of place, like Fanny Wright's mannish impudence or Diogenes's masturbation. This tension was felt subjectively by many women, including Sarah Grimké's sister, Angelina, who braved the denunciation of relatives, friends, and strangers, as well as the occasional violent mob, in her willingness

to appeal to "the irresistible torrent of a rectified public opinion"
but whose scandalous appearances in public caused her, as she
confessed to her diary, great shame and self-doubt. When she married the abolitionist Theodore Weld, her public speaking tours
ended.[31]

This subjective anxiety over the public display of the body and
the gendered norms of comportment also has a direct equivalent
in liberal notions of what is appropriate for public discussion and
political action. Because the home was the very realm of private
freedom that liberalism had wanted to protect from state intervention, it was off-limits to politics. And the rights of women,
seen as an issue internal to the home, were therefore best left to
the private judgment of each family. They were inappropriate to
politics. Women would have to deal with men in the privacy of
their own families, not in public. But of course the private context of the family was just where men were thought naturally to
rule. As Eli Zaretsky puts it, "The separation between public and
private occluded the perpetuation of relations of domination —
those beyond legitimate authority — into modern society. It did
this politically by rendering those relations 'private.'"[32] The curb-
ing of the state, in the name of private liberty, had entailed a curb
on politics as well, freezing in place all those for whom the private was the place of domination rather than liberty.

This side of the liberal tradition continues to limit the transformative ambitions of feminism, and of the gay movement as
well. For example, the gay writer Andrew Sullivan ends his book
Virtually Normal with an appeal to the liberal distinction between
public and private, arguing for a politics based on "a simple and
limited principle":

> that all *public* (as opposed to private) discrimination against homo-
> sexuals be ended and that every right and responsibility that hetero-

sexuals enjoy as public citizens be extended to those who grow up and find themselves emotionally different. *And that is all.* No cures or re-educations, no wrenching private litigation, no political imposition of tolerance; merely a political attempt to enshrine formal public equality, whatever happens in the culture and society at large.[33]

Everything else, "whatever happens in the culture and society at large," is private, and therefore off-limits to politics. But that includes almost the entirety of homophobia and sexism and the countless daily relations of privilege and domination they entail. Any political attempt to change those conditions is seen, in Sullivan's scheme, as an illegitimate attempt to get government involved in private life, a "political imposition of tolerance." Although this conception of politics is often called neoconservatism, its core ideas derive from the heyday of nineteenth-century liberal thought.[34]

In fact, the liberal distinction between public authority and private freedom has always been in tension with other views, notably with civic humanism since Machiavelli.[35] Liberalism still has powerful contemporary exponents, such as Rawls.[36] But most of the major figures of our time on the subject of public and private have reacted against the liberal tradition. Feminists such as Pateman and MacKinnon, for example, point out that the liberal protection of the private from public interference simply blocked from view those kinds of domination that structure private life through the institutions of the family, the household, gender, and sexuality. Arendt tried to show how many of the strongest conceptions of humanity had been lost or forgotten when freedom was identified with the protection of private life rather than with the give-and-take of public activity. Habermas showed that modern society is fundamentally structured by a public sphere, including the critical consciousness of private people, but that these public ideals and norms are betrayed by modern social organization. And Michel Foucault rendered a strong challenge to the liberal tradition almost without using the terms "public" and "private" by showing in great detail how its key terms and immanent values — public, state, private, freedom, autonomy — fail to account for power relations.

The Public Sphere

A rather different face of liberalism's distinction between public and private can be seen in Kant's celebrated essay "What Is Enlightenment?" (1784). "The *public* use of reason," Kant writes, "must at all times be free, and it alone can bring about enlightenment among men; the *private* use of reason, however, may often be very narrowly restricted without the progress of enlightenment being particularly hindered." Kant's has been called a "two hats" theory; he imagines men (not women) moving constantly between these two contexts, having different freedoms and different relations to power in each.[37] But the surprising turn comes in his definition of public and private uses of reason: "I understand, however, under the public use of his own reason, that use which anyone makes of it *as a scholar* [*Gelehrter*] before the entire public of the *reading world*. The private use I designate as that use which one makes of his reason in a certain *civil post* or office which is entrusted to him."[38]

To most readers, this will seem counterintuitive. The holder of a civil post would in most senses be a public figure — paid by the state, working for the common good, accountable to the community, acting in full view. The scholar or writer would commonly be thought of as private — unofficial, not supported by the state, speaking on behalf of no one but himself, perhaps unknown except through his writings. Yet to Kant the telling fact is that the holder of a civil post cannot simply follow his own will; he must

44

obey rules established by his role. He may disagree with something he is required to say; but his thoughts remain private whether he agrees or not. The scholar or writer makes his views known as widely as possible. He is not limited to his role but speaks "as a member of the entire commonwealth, or even of cosmopolitan society." He can freely criticize church or state. Kant makes it clear that this reasoning takes place in a print public, "the entire public of the *reading world*," and that it is more than national; but a clergyman speaking officially to his congregation addresses "only a domestic assembly, no matter how large it is; and in this respect he is not and cannot be free, as a priest, because he conforms to the orders of another."[39]

A striking feature of this account is Kant's emphasis on the different publics to which thought can be relevant, ranging from inner freedom to domestic assemblies, commonwealths, cosmopolitan society, the transnational public of scholars, and even "the entire public of the *reading world*." Some publics are more public than others. They give greater scope to criticism and exchange of views. But by the same token, they may be less directly political, perhaps not anchored in a state or locality.

With this conception, Kant articulates a key distinction — though one that continues to be confused or overlooked even in sophisticated theoretical accounts — between public and political. These are often thought to be synonymous. They are very nearly so, for example, in Arendt, where the model of the public is clearly the polis (the Greek city-state); and equally (or oppositely) in the slogan "the personal is political." What belongs to the polity is by definition of public relevance. But Kant recognizes that there are publics, such as the reading world, that do not correspond to any kind of polity. They enable a way of being public through critical discourse that is not limited by the duties and constraints of office or by loyalties to a commonwealth or nation.

45

These critical publics may, however, be political in another or higher sense. They may set a higher standard of reason, opinion, and freedom — hence the subversive potential in his picture of enlightenment. (In later years, Kant was forced to hedge on this implication; as he ran afoul of the censors, he narrowed the definition of *Gelehrter* to the scholar per se rather than the reader in general.)[40] Locke, too, had recognized the existence of a critical public not limited to the official politics of the state and having all the freedom from authority of private right. But in Locke this public tends to be imagined as the national people, endowed with the sovereign ability to change rulers. It is in a sense a back-projection from the state. Kant's publics, though less literally revolutionary, range more widely, at least in print.

The difference between the public and the political has been taken up, closer to our own day, by Habermas in *The Structural Transformation of the Public Sphere* (1962).[41] Subtitled "An Inquiry into a Category of Bourgeois Society," the book reflects the Frankfurt School tradition of "immanent critique"; Habermas does not set out to invent or celebrate a putatively lost ideal of the public (though he has sometimes been read this way); he wishes to show that bourgeois society has always been structured by a set of ideals that were contradicted by its own organization and compromised by its own ideology. These ideals, however, contained an emancipatory potential, Habermas thinks, and modern culture should be held accountable to them. But far from moving toward a more radical realization in practice, modern culture has compromised the ideals further. "Tendencies pointing to the collapse of the public sphere are unmistakable," Habermas declares at the beginning of the book, "for while its scope is expanding impressively, its function has become progressively insignificant."[42]

The main structural transformation of the title is the historic shift that Habermas assigns to the late seventeenth and the eighteenth century. Habermas begins with an aristocratic or monarchical model that he calls the "representative public sphere," in which power is displayed before a public (and in which Louis XIV was able to say, "L'état, c'est moi"). The publicity of the court was embodied and authoritative. The monarch's presence was always public, and courtliness always had an audience. This kind of publicity yielded to a newer model of publicness in which the public is composed of private persons exercising rational-critical discourse in relation to the state and power. (The "sphere" of the title is a misleading effect of English translation; the German *Öffentlichkeit* lacks the spatializing metaphor and suggests something more like "openness" or "publicness." The French translation, *L'Espace public*, is worse.)

This shift came about, Habermas claims, through a wide range of cultural and social conditions that developed in the seventeenth and eighteenth centuries, including the rise of newspapers, novels, and other private forms of print; coffeehouses, salons, and related private contexts of sociability in which argument and discussion could take place; the rise of critical discussion of art, music, and literature; the reorientation of domestic architecture; the development of an idea of the family and intimate life as the proper seat of humanity, from which persons could come together to form a public; and the development of a notion of the economy, beyond the household, as a realm of civil society that could be taken as the object of discussion and debate. Through these developments, a public that "from the outset was a reading public" became "the abstract counterpart of public authority" and "came into an awareness of itself as the latter's opponent, that is, as the public of the now emerging *public sphere of civil society.*"[43]

The public in this new sense, in short, was no longer opposed to the private. It *was* private. As the self-consciousness of civil society, it was opposed to the state:

47

The bourgeois public sphere may be conceived above all as the sphere of private people come together as a public; they soon claimed the public sphere regulated from above against the public authorities themselves, to engage them in a debate over the general rules governing relations in the basically privatized but publicly relevant sphere of commodity exchange and social labor. The medium of this political confrontation was peculiar and without historical precedent: people's public use of their reason.[44]

The public sphere in this sense is "a category of bourgeois society," as the subtitle maintains, not just because its members are mostly bourgeois but also because the reorganization of society around the institutions of public criticism was one of the means by which bourgeois society came into being, conscious of itself as "society." Habermas cites Kant's "What Is Enlightenment?" and its ideal of a private citizen as a scholar "whose writings speak to his public, the world." This "world" is both broad, stretching notions of cosmopolitanism and world progress to include "the communication of rational beings," and particularized, being grounded in "the world of a critically debating reading public that at the time was just evolving within the broader bourgeois strata. It was the world of the men of letters but also that of the *salons* in which 'mixed companies' engaged in critical discussion; here, in the bourgeois homes, the public sphere was established."[45]

As Craig Calhoun points out, a radical reversal has taken place between the bourgeois conception traced by Habermas and the Greek conception of public freedom: "Unlike the Greek conception, individuals are here understood to be formed primarily in the private realm, including the family. Moreover, the private realm is understood as one of freedom that has to be defended against the domination of the state."[46]

Habermas shows that this understanding of the public sphere

had its early critics. Chief among these was the young Karl Marx, who objected to the nature of this new private freedom leading "every man to see in other men, not the *realization*, but rather the *limitation* of his own liberty."[47] Noting the contradiction between the universal claims of public reason and its particular basis in bourgeois society, Marx wanted to imagine "the social conditions for the possibility of its utterly unbourgeois realization."[48] Indeed, workers and excluded groups of many kinds were beginning to grasp this possibility, as the explosion of nineteenth-century social movements makes clear. Labor, Chartism, temperance, and other movements were enabled by the new conditions of the public sphere. But liberal critics, such as Alexis de Tocqueville and John Stuart Mill, saw this expansion of critical discussion as a threat to the public sphere and began to treat the public as a force of unreason. Habermas thinks that at this juncture liberal thought began to betray its own best ideals: "The liberalist interpretation of the bourgeois constitutional state was reactionary: it reacted to the power of the idea of a critically debating public's self-determination, initially included in its institutions, as soon as this public was subverted by the propertyless and uneducated masses."[49]

Habermas does not here mention the playing out of the same contradiction regarding gender, an omission for which he has been taken to task by feminist critics and which he has since acknowledged.[50] The important point for him is that the emancipatory potential of the public sphere was abandoned rather than radicalized and that changing conditions have now made its realization more difficult than ever. Habermas stresses especially two such conditions: the asymmetrical nature of mass culture, which makes it easier for those with capital or power to distribute their views but harder for marginal voices to talk back; and the growing interpenetration of the state and civil society, which makes it harder to conceive of the private public sphere as a limitation on state power. These tendencies amount to what Habermas calls a "refeudalization" of the public sphere — in effect, a second "structural transformation." They produce a public that is appealed to not for criticism but for benign acclamation. Public opinion comes less to generate ideas and hold power accountable and more simply to register approval or disapproval in the form of opinion polls and occasional elections. "Publicity once meant the exposure of political domination before the public use of reason; publicity now adds up the reactions of an uncommitted friendly disposition," Habermas writes. "In the measure that it is shaped by public relations, the public sphere of civil society again takes on feudal features."[51] Even the bourgeois conjugal family, which had in theory served as the basis of private humanity (an appearance that, according to Habermas, had always been contradicted by its real functions), now finds most of its functions taken over by mass culture and by other institutions such as schools. As a result, it "has started to dissolve into a sphere of pseudo-privacy."[52]

Habermas's analysis has been the subject of a voluminous debate, much of it marred by reductive summaries and a naive confidence that highly capitalized mass media can be defended and celebrated as "popular culture." Three themes from this debate are important enough to warrant some comment here. First, the public-sphere environment Habermas describes can be seen as the context of modern social movements, including identity politics. Social movements take shape in civil society, often with an agenda of demands vis-à-vis the state. They seek to change policy by appealing to public opinion. They arise from contexts of critical discussion, many of them print-mediated. The question for debate, then, is to what extent the environment for critical social movements is becoming more undemocratic, "refeudalized," or colonized by changing relations among the state, mass media, and the market. This is not a simple issue. It has to do with the increasingly transnational nature of publics, of civil-society structures such as corporations or nongovernmental organizations, and of interstate regulatory apparatuses.[53] It has to do as well with the apparently conflicting trends of an ever higher capitalization of media, which are increasingly controlled by a small number of transnational companies, and the apparent decentralization of new media.

Second, movements around gender and sexuality do not always conform to the bourgeois model of "rational-critical debate," especially as that model has been subsequently elaborated by Habermas. In *The Structural Transformation of the Public Sphere*, Habermas speaks of "people's public use of their reason." But what counts as a use of reason? In later works, he has put forward a highly idealized account of argumentative dialogue.[54] But movements around gender and sexuality seek to transform fundamental styles of embodiment, identity, and social relations — including their unconscious manifestations, the vision of the good life embedded in them, and the habitus by which people continue to understand their selves or bodies as public or private. Because this is the field that people want to transform, it is not possible to assume the habitus according to which rational-critical debate is a neutral, relatively disembodied procedure for addressing common concerns, while embodied life is assumed to be private, local, or merely affective and expressive. The styles by which people assume public relevance are themselves contested. The ability to bracket one's embodiment and status is not simply what Habermas calls making public use of one's reason; it is a strategy of distinction, profoundly linked to education and to dominant forms of masculinity.

Just as the gendered division of public and private kept women from challenging their role in any way that might have been political, public interactions are saturated with protocols of gender and sexual identity. Just as Diogenes's masturbating in the market will be seen by some as philosophy, by others as filth, the critically relevant styles of publicness in gay male sexual culture are seldom recognized as such but are typically denounced as sleaze and as crime. For modern gay men and lesbians, the possibilities of public or private speech are distorted by what we call the closet. "The closet" is a misleading spatial metaphor. As Eve Kosofsky Sedgwick has shown so well, it is a name for a set of assumptions in everyday life as well as in expert knowledge: assumptions about what goes without saying; what can be said without a breach of decorum; who shares the onus of disclosure; what can be known about a person's real nature through telltale signs, without his or her own awareness; and who will bear the consequences of speech and silence.[55] Speech is everywhere regulated unequally. Yet ironically, common mythology understands the closet as an individual's lie about him- or herself. We blame people for being closeted. But the closet is better understood as the culture's problem, not the individual's. No one ever created a closet for him- or herself. People find themselves in its oppressive conditions before they know it, willy-nilly. It is experienced by lesbians and gay men as a private, individual problem of shame and deception. But it is produced by the heteronormative assumptions of everyday talk. It feels private. But in an important sense it is publicly constructed.

In such a regime of sexual domination, publicness will feel like exposure, and privacy will feel like the closet. The closet may seem to be a kind of protection. Indeed, the feeling of protection is one of the hallmarks of modern privacy. But in fact the closet is riddled with fear and shame. So is publicity under the conditions of the closet. Being publicly known as homosexual is never the same as being publicly known as heterosexual; the latter always goes without saying and troubles nothing, whereas the former carries echoes of pathologized visibility. It is perfectly meaningless to "come out" as heterosexual. So it is not true, as common wisdom would have it, that homosexuals live private lives without a secure public identity. They have neither privacy *nor* publicness, in these normative senses of the terms. In the United States, the judiciary, along with the military and its supporters in Congress and the White House, has gone to great lengths to make sure that they will have neither.[56] It is this deformation of public and private that identity politics — and the performative ritual known as coming out — tries to transform.

In some ways, a more daunting version of the same problem faces the transgendered, who do not always wish to appeal in the same way to a private identity as the basis for a public revaluation. Often it is the most private, intimate dimension of sex assignment and self-understanding that must be managed at the same time with the public and social presentations, though these may move at different rates and to different degrees. The task of managing stigma may often present itself as being like the closet; and it may display a similar inequality in claims to knowledge. The epistemological leverage of medical experts, for example, appears as a very public kind of knowledge and authority, objective and neutral where the patient's claims are understood to be subjective and interested, perhaps even pathological. Transgendered people typically have to struggle against that superior claim to know what's good for them or what their true nature is, even while they are dependent on those same experts for assistance, care, and public legitimacy. But of course a sex transition is not something that can be managed privately, and because it is a transition rather than a newly revealed prior condition, "coming out" is not an entirely helpful analogy.

A notion of privacy as a right of self-determination may prove in many contexts to be extremely valuable to the transgendered. A merely naturalized privacy, on the other hand, might block access to the health services and other kinds of publicly available assistance that self-determination might require. The private facilities of public institutions — locker rooms, bathrooms, and such — can be the most public of battlegrounds, especially for FTMs. And the transgendered routinely have to cope with the public, institutional, and state dimensions of such otherwise "personal" and private issues as naming, sex classification, health, and intimate associations. Transgender activism continually points to the public underpinnings of privacy, and probably nowhere more so than in its own practice, which seeks to put into circulation a new publicly available language for self-understanding.

As these examples illustrate, the meaning of gender and sexuality in dominant culture is only partly determined in domestic or familial life. It is also constantly being shaped across the range of social relations, and perhaps especially in the mass media, with their visual language of incorporation and desire. The public sphere as an environment, then, is not just a place where one could rationally debate a set of gender or sexual relations that can in turn be equated with private life; the public sphere is a principal instance of the forms of embodiment and social relations that are themselves at issue.

This is a reason for skepticism about the reigning protocols of what counts as rational-critical debate, including the idea that one need's to bracket one's private self in order to engage in public discussion. But the same reciprocity between public and private is also an advantage to public-sphere analysis in relation to some other critical methods, notably psychoanalysis. Psychoanalysis as a cultural phenomenon, as Zaretsky points out, has contributed profoundly to the twentieth-century revaluation of personal and private life. But as a method, psychoanalysis has been limited in its ability to deal with issues of public and private. Most psychoanalytic analyses of gender and sexuality focus on intrasubjective dynamics and familial relations, generalizing from these to abstract levels of culture such as the Symbolic and the law of the father. In so doing, they methodically embed the equation of gender and sexuality with the realm of the family and the individual —blocking from view the mediation of publics and the multiple social, historical, and political frames of privacy. Freud himself struggled to overcome this limitation in *Group Psychology*, and some later reconstructions of psychoanalytic method, from Frantz Fanon to feminist film theory, have further revised his vocabulary with the aim of incorporating social contexts of domination into our understanding of psychic life and vice versa. Yet the distance between psychoanalytic generality and the complex histories of public and private remains great.[57]

Finally, there is some tension between the publics of gender or sexuality and the public sphere as an ideal. On this point, there has been some confusion; critics commonly accuse Habermas of having adopted a false ideal of a unitary public.[58] But Habermas does not imagine a public unified in reality, as a constituency or a single media context. "Nonpublic opinions are at work in great numbers," he writes, "and 'the' public opinion is indeed a fiction."[59] From the beginning, his account stressed many different kinds of public discourse, from tavern conversation to art criticism. The ideal unity of the public sphere is best understood as an imaginary convergence point that is the backdrop of critical discourse in each of these contexts and publics — an implied but abstract point that is often referred to as "the public" or "public opinion" and by virtue of that fact endowed with legitimacy and the ability to dissolve power. A "public" in this context is a special kind of virtual social object, enabling a special mode of address. As we saw in Kant's "What Is Enlightenment?" it is modeled on a reading public. In modern societies, a public is by definition an indefinite audience rather than a social constituency that could be numbered or named.[60] *The Structural Transformation of Public Sphere* can be read as a history of the construction of this virtual object and its mode of address, where a key development is the fiction of "public opinion" as the ideal background of all possible publics. Habermas did not describe it in these terms, and in his later work on communicative rationality he increasingly collapsed public reason into the model of face-to-face argumentative dialogue — thus making the special context of publics disappear from the analysis. But there is no necessary conflict between the public sphere and the idea of multiple publics.

Counterpublics

The stronger modification of Habermas's analysis — one in which he has shown little interest, though it is clearly of major significance in the critical analysis of gender and sexuality — is that some publics are defined by their tension with a larger public. Their participants are marked off from persons or citizens in general. Discussion within such a public is understood to contravene the rules obtaining in the world at large, being structured by alternative dispositions or protocols, making different assumptions about what can be said or what goes without saying. This kind of public is, in effect, a counterpublic: it maintains at some level, conscious or not, an awareness of its subordinate status. The sexual cultures of gay men or of lesbians would be one kind of example, but so would camp discourse or the media of women's culture. A counterpublic in this sense is usually related to a subculture, but there are important differences between these concepts. A counterpublic, against the background of the public sphere, enables a horizon of opinion and exchange; its exchanges remain distinct from authority and can have a critical relation to power; its extent is in principle indefinite, because it is not based on a precise demography but mediated by print, theater, diffuse networks of talk, commerce, and the like. Counterpublics are often called "subaltern counterpublics," but it is not clear that all counterpublics are composed of people *otherwise* dominated as subalterns. Some youth-culture publics or artistic publics, for example, operate as counterpublics, even though many who participate in them are "subalterns" in no other sense. At any rate, even as a subaltern counterpublic, this subordinate status does not simply reflect identities formed elsewhere; participation in such a public is one of the ways by which its members' identities are formed and transformed.

Habermas's rich historical account of the norms and practices of publicness in modernity can thus reopen the relations between the personal and the political. A public, or counterpublic, can do more than represent the interests of gendered or sexualized persons in a public sphere. It can mediate the most private and intimate meanings of gender and sexuality. It can work to elaborate new worlds of culture and social relations in which gender and sexuality can be lived, including forms of intimate association, vocabularies of affect, styles of embodiment, erotic practices, and relations of care and pedagogy. It can therefore make possible new forms of gendered or sexual citizenship — meaning active participation in collective world making through publics of sex and gender.

Such a model of citizenship or public personhood would be very different indeed from the bourgeois public sphere, though deeply indebted to it as a background set of conditions. The bourgeois public sphere consists of private persons whose identity is formed in the privacy of the conjugal domestic family and who enter into rational-critical debate around matters common to all by bracketing their embodiment and status. Counterpublics of sexuality and gender, on the other hand, are scenes of association and identity that transform the private lives they mediate. Homosexuals can exist in isolation; but gay people or queers exist by virtue of the world they elaborate together, and gay or queer identity is always fundamentally inflected by the nature of that world. The same could be said of women's counterpublics, or those of race, or youth culture. These public contexts necessarily entail and bring into being realms of subjectivity outside the conjugal domestic family. Their protocols of discourse and debate remain open to affective and expressive dimensions of language. And their members make their embodiment and status at least partly relevant in a public way by their very participation.[61]

It is in part to capture the profound difference between the conception of citizenship made possible in such counterpublics and the one prevailing in the bourgeois public sphere that so many critics in gender and sexuality studies have recently turned to the long-unfashionable work of Hannah Arendt. Arendt was especially unfashionable in second-wave feminism. Far from "dissolving the distinction between public and private," Arendt insists on it. For many feminist readers, what stood out was that "when Hannah Arendt defines politics in terms of the pursuit of public happiness or the taste for public freedom, she is employing a terminology almost opposite to that adopted within the contemporary women's movement."[62] Both Adrienne Rich, in *On Lies, Secrets, and Silence,* and Mary O'Brien, in *The Politics of Reproduction*, interpreted Arendt as embracing the system in which male is to public as female is to private. They dismissed her as an essentially masculinist thinker. Lately, however, an impressive range of feminists and other thinkers have begun a reconsideration. They argue that for Arendt public and private refer less to the norms of gender than to the different conditions for action that define humanity. For those who think that gender and sexuality are defined through action in relation to others, and that they can be made subject to transformation for that reason, Arendt can be read as prescribing what Bonnie Honig calls "an agonistic politics of performativity."[63]

In *The Human Condition*, Arendt tries to reconstruct dimensions of humanity put at risk by the world alienation of the modern age. Against the current of her time, in which privacy and personal life came to be viewed as the realm of individuality and freedom, Arendt sees both freedom and individuality in the world-making public activity of the polis, because it is a common framework of interaction that is needed to allow both a shared world of equals and the disclosure of unique agency. The private, by contrast, is the realm of necessity and the merged viewpoints of family life. Arendt believes that the necessities of private life are inappropriate to politics. But she does not say this out of a prudish morality; her ideal of political life is a creative fashioning of a common world, and she understands the word "private" to refer to those conditions — including love, pain, and need in general — that she thinks of as not being defined or transformed by such creative fashioning. As Mary Dietz emphasizes, both public and private in this usage are existential categories, not social descriptions. They are different contexts for personhood. The public that Arendt values so much is the scene of world making and self-disclosure; it is therefore to be distinguished both from the prevailing system of politics and from any universalist notion of rational debate. It is a political scene, necessarily local because the self and the shared world disclosed through it emerge in interaction with others.[64]

Arendt sees at least three great ruptures separating our own time from the classical culture in which the world-making dimension of public action was understood. The first is Christianity, with its eternal private person and devaluation of the public world; the second, Romantic individualism, which leads us to see the private not as the privation of publicness but as an originary value in its own right; the third, what she calls the rise of the social. By "the social" she means the modern way of understanding human relations

59

not as the medium of action and speech but as behavior and regulation. Fundamental human capacities of world making are restricted in scope and consequence by mass society, administration, and instrumentality.

In the context of the Cold War (*The Human Condition* was published in 1958), this was a bold argument, fundamentally criticizing both totalitarianism and liberalism. Because Arendt's public is an action context for speech and an agonistic scene of interaction, it is the realm of rhetoric, not command; there is an implicit contrast here to the totalitarianism that Arendt had treated in her previous book, as well as to juridical models of power generally.[65] But Arendt also offers her description of public and private as a contrast to the distinction between state and society with which it is often made synonymous, especially in liberalism.[66]

The difference between Arendt's pragmatic sense of the public and the liberal universalist sense is sharp. It also occasions unforeseen tensions in Arendt's own thought, and thus opportunities for reading her against the grain. The women's movement and queer culture would represent model cases of public world making, and for the same reason that they are generally understood to be opposed to "family values":

> Being seen and being heard by others derive their significance from the fact that everybody sees and hears from a different position. This is the meaning of public life, compared to which even the richest and most satisfying family life can offer only the prolongation or multiplication of one's own position with its attending aspects and perspectives. The subjectivity of privacy can be prolonged and multiplied in a family, it can even become so strong that its weight is felt in the public realm; but this family "world" can never replace the reality rising out of the sum total of aspects presented by one object to a multitude of spectators.[67]

Familialist conceptions of national or public membership come in for such withering remarks in part because Arendt has in mind the background of fascism; but this analysis has not lost its relevance in the post–Cold War period. Arendt writes that in mass society "people suddenly behave as though they were members of one family, each multiplying and prolonging the perspective of his neighbor."[68] While mass society might seem to be in many respects the opposite of the family, the commodity-ridden waste against which the intimacy of the hearth is usually contrasted, for Arendt these two models of social space share a basic limitation on action and speech. (The point might be illustrated through the mid-1990s phenomenon of the Promise Keepers movement, or "family values" rhetoric generally.) Of course, some feminists (especially in what is called "difference feminism") and some queer theorists might take a more expansive view of the family. Arendt clearly has in mind a classic middle-class model of family life, with its ideals of property interest, ethnic subjectivity, primary allegiance, and undisputed will.

Much of the energy currently being derived from Arendt's work by feminist and queer thought lies in the possibility of reading the slogan "The personal is political" with an Arendtian understanding of the political. This entails the working assumption that the conditions of gender and sexuality can be treated not simply as the given necessities of the laboring body but as the occasion for forming publics, elaborating common worlds, making the transposition from shame to honor, from hiddenness to the exchange of viewpoints with generalized others, in such a way that the disclosure of self partakes of freedom.

The challenge facing this project in transgender activism, feminism, and queer theory is to understand how world making unfolds in publics that are, after all, not just natural collections of people, not just "communities," but mediated publics. Arendt's language of "speech" and "action in view of others" sounds, in this context, fairly antiquated — an unfortunate faithfulness to the metaphor of the polis rather than a complex understanding of how politics happens. Habermas, meanwhile, has a more careful attention to the practices and structures that mediate publics, including print, genre, architecture, and capital. But he extracts from them such an idealized image of persuasion that the world-disclosing activity of a counterpublic falls out of view. Both thinkers share a strong sense that the utopian ideals of public and private have been contradicted by the social conditions for realizing them in modern mass culture.

What remains, then, is a need for both concrete and theoretical understandings of the conditions that currently mediate the transformative and creative work of counterpublics. Counterpublics of sex and gender are teaching us to recognize in newer and deeper ways how privacy is publicly constructed. They are testing our understanding of how private life can be made publicly relevant. And they are elaborating not only new shared worlds and critical languages but also new privacies, new individuals, new bodies, new intimacies, and new citizenships. In doing so, they have provoked visceral reactions, and necessarily so, since the visceral meaning of gender and sexuality is the very matter that they wish to disclose as publicly relevant. It is often thought, especially by outsiders, that the public display of private matters is a debased narcissism, a collapse of decorum, expressivity gone amok, the erosion of any distinction between public and private. But in a counterpublic setting, such display often has the aim of transformation. Styles of embodiment are learned and cultivated, and the affects of shame and disgust that surround them can be tested, in some cases revalued. Visceral private meaning is not easy to alter by oneself, by a free act of will. It can only be altered through exchanges that go beyond self-expression to the making of a collective scene of disclosure. The result, in counterpublics, is that the visceral intensity of gender, of sexuality, or of corporeal style in general no longer needs to be understood as private. Publicness itself has a visceral resonance.

At the same time, these counterpublics are encountering — without always recognizing — limitations in their public media, their relation to the state and to official publics, their embeddedness in larger publics and larger processes of privatization, and their reliance on distorting models of privacy and intimacy. One doesn't "go public" simply as an act of will — neither by writing, nor by having an opinion, nor by exposing oneself in the marketplace. The context of publicness must be available, allowing these actions to count in a public way, to be transformative. How does that come about? Habermas would have us ask whether it is even possible to be public in the validating sense when the public media are mass media, and to some extent this remains a question for counterpublics as well. Counterpublics are, by definition, formed by their conflict with the norms and contexts of their cultural environment, and this context of domination inevitably entails distortion. Mass publics and counterpublics, in other words, are both damaged forms of publicness, just as gender and sexuality are, in this culture, damaged forms of privacy.[69]

Chapter Two

Publics and Counterpublics

This essay has a public. If you are reading (or hearing) this, you are part of its public. So first let me say: welcome. Of course, you might stop reading (or leave the room), and someone else might start (or enter). Would the public of this essay therefore be different? Would it ever be possible to know anything about the public to which, I hope, you still belong? What is a public? It is a curiously obscure question, considering that few things have been more important in the development of modernity. Publics have become an essential fact of the social landscape; yet it would tax our understanding to say exactly what they are.

Several senses of the noun "public" tend to be intermixed in usage. People do not always distinguish even between *the* public and *a* public, though in certain contexts the difference can matter a great deal. *The* public is a kind of social totality. Its most common sense is that of the people in general. It might be the people organized as the nation, the commonwealth, the city, the state, or some other community. It might be very general, as in Christendom or humanity. But in each case, the public, as a people, is thought to include everyone within the field in question. This sense of totality is brought out by speaking of *the* public, even though to speak of a national public implies that others exist;

there must be as many publics as polities, but whenever one is addressed as *the* public, the others are assumed not to matter.

A public can also be a second thing: a concrete audience, a crowd witnessing itself in visible space, as with a theatrical public. Such a public also has a sense of totality, bounded by the event or by the shared physical space. A performer onstage knows where her public is, how big it is, where its boundaries are, and what the time of its common existence is. A crowd at a sports event, a concert, or a riot might be a bit blurrier around the edges but still knows itself by knowing where and when it is assembled in common visibility and common action.

I will return to both of these senses of the term public, but what I mainly want to clarify in this essay is a third sense: the kind of public that comes into being only in relation to texts and their circulation — like the public of this essay. (Nice to have you with us, still.)

The distinctions among these three senses are not always sharp and are not simply the difference between oral and written contexts. A text public can be based in speech as well as writing. When an essay is read aloud as a lecture at a university, for example, the concrete audience of hearers understands itself as standing in for a more indefinite audience of readers. And often, when a form of discourse is not addressing an institutional or subcultural audience like a profession, its audience can understand itself not just as *a* public but as *the* public. In such cases, different senses of audience and circulation are in play at once. They suggest that it is worth understanding the distinctions better, if only because the transpositions among them can have important social effects.

The idea of *a* public, as distinct from both *the* public and any bounded totality of audience, has become part of the common repertoire of modern culture. Everyone intuitively understands

66

how it works. On reflection, however, its rules can seem rather odd. I would like to bring some of our intuitive understanding into the open in order to speculate about the history of the form and the role it plays in constructing our social world.

1. A public is self-organized.
A public is a space of discourse organized by nothing other than discourse itself. It is autotelic; it exists only as the end for which books are published, shows broadcast, Web sites posted, speeches delivered, opinions produced. It exists *by virtue of being addressed.*

A kind of chicken-and-egg circularity confronts us in the idea of a public. Could anyone speak publicly without addressing a public? But how can this public exist before being addressed? What would a public be if no one were addressing it? Can a public really exist apart from the rhetoric through which it is imagined? If you were to put down this essay and turn on the television, would my public be different? How can the existence of a public depend, from one point of view, on the rhetorical address and, from another point of view, on the real context of reception?

These questions cannot be resolved on one side or the other. The circularity is essential to the phenomenon. A public might be real and efficacious, but its reality lies in just this reflexivity by which an addressable object is conjured into being in order to enable the very discourse that gives it existence.

A public in this sense is as much notional as empirical. It is also partial, since there could be an infinite number of publics within the social totality. This sense of the term is completely modern; it is the only kind of public for which there is no other term. Neither "crowd" nor "audience" nor "people" nor "group" will capture the same sense. The difference shows us that the idea of a public, unlike a concrete audience or the public of a polity, is text-based — even though publics are increasingly organized around visual or audio texts. Without the idea of texts that can be picked up at different times and in different places by otherwise un-related people, we would not imagine a public as an entity that embraces all the users of that text, whoever they might be. Often the texts themselves are not even recognized as texts — as, for example, with visual advertising or the chattering of a DJ — but the publics they bring into being are still discursive in the same way.

The strangeness of this kind of public is often hidden from view because the assumptions that enable the bourgeois public sphere allow us to think of a discourse public as a people and therefore as a really existing set of potentially numerable humans. A public, in practice, appears as *the* public. It is easy to be misled by this appearance. Even in the blurred usage of the public sphere, a public is never just a congeries of people, never just the sum of persons who happen to exist. It must first of all have some way of organizing itself as a body and of being addressed in discourse. And not just any way of defining the totality will do. It must be organized by something other than the state.

Here we see how the autotelic circularity of the discourse public is not just a puzzle for analysis but also the crucial factor in the social importance of the form. A public organizes itself inde-pendently of state institutions, laws, formal frameworks of citi-zenship, or preexisting institutions such as the church. If it were not possible to think of the public as organized independently of the state or other frameworks, the public could not be sovereign with respect to the state. So the modern sense of the public as the social totality in fact derives much of its character from the way we understand the partial publics of discourse, like the public of this essay, as self-organized. The way *the* public functions in the public sphere (as the people) is only possible because it is really *a* public of discourse. The peculiar character of *a* public is that it is a space of discourse organized by discourse. It is self-creating

68

and self-organized; and herein lies its power, as well as its elusive strangeness.

In the kind of modern society that the idea of publics has enabled, the self-organization of discourse publics has immense resonance from the point of view of individuals. Speaking, writing, and thinking involve us — actively and immediately — in a public, and thus in the being of the sovereign. Imagine how powerless people would feel if their commonality and participation were simply defined by pre-given frameworks, by institutions and laws, as in other social contexts they are through kinship. What would the world look like if all ways of being public were more like applying for a driver's license or subscribing to a professional group — if, that is, formally organized mediations replaced the self-organized public as the image of belonging and common activity? Such is the image of totalitarianism: non-kin society organized by bureaucracy and law. Everyone's position, function, and capacity for action are specified for her by administration. The powerlessness of the person in such a world haunts modern capitalism as well. Our lives are minutely administered and recorded, to a degree unprecedented in history; we navigate a world of corporate agents that do not respond or act as people do. Our personal capacities, such as credit, turn out on reflection to be expressions of corporate agency. Without a faith, justified or not, in self-organized publics, organically linked to our activity in their very existence, capable of being addressed, and capable of action, we would be nothing but the peasants of capital — which, of course, we might be, and some of us more than others.

In the idea of a public, political confidence is committed to a strange and uncertain destination. Sometimes it can seem too strange. Often one cannot imagine addressing a public capable of comprehension or action. This is especially true for people in minor or marginal positions or people distributed across political systems. The result can be a kind of political depressiveness, a blockage in activity and optimism, a disintegration of politics toward isolation, frustration, anomie, forgetfulness. This possibility, never far out of the picture, reveals by contrast how much ordinary belonging requires confidence in a public. Confidence in the possibility of a public is not simply the professional habit of the powerful, of the pundits and wonks and reaction-shot secondary celebrities who try to perform our publicness for us; the same confidence remains vital for people whose place in public media is one of consuming, witnessing, griping, or gossiping rather than one of full participation or fame. Whether faith is justified or partly ideological, a public can only produce a sense of belonging and activity if it is self-organized through discourse rather than through an external framework. This is why any distortion or blockage in access to a public can be so grave, leading people to feel powerless and frustrated. Externally organized frameworks of activity, such as voting, are and are perceived to be poor substitutes.

Yet perhaps just because it does seem so important to belong to a public, or to be able to know something about the public to which one belongs, such substitutes have been produced in abundance. People have tried hard to find, or make, some external way of identifying the public, of resolving its circularity into either chicken or egg. The idea that the public might be as changeable, and as unknowable, as the public of this essay (are you still with me?) seems to weaken the very political optimism that the accessibility of the public allows.

Pollsters and some social scientists think that their method is a way of defining a public as a group that could be studied empirically, independently of its own discourse about itself. Early in the history of research in communications theory and public relations, it was recognized that such research was going to be diffi-

cult, since multiple publics exist and one can belong to many different publics simultaneously. Public-opinion researchers have a
long history of unsatisfying debate about this problem in method.
What determines whether one belongs to a public or not? Space
and physical presence do not make much difference; a public is
understood to be different from a crowd, an audience, or any
other group that requires co-presence. Personal identity does not
in itself make one part of a public. Publics differ from nations,
races, professions, and any other groups that, though not requiring co-presence, saturate identity. Belonging to a public seems
to require at least minimal participation, even if it is patient or
notional, rather than a permanent state of being. Merely paying
attention can be enough to make you a member. How, then, could
a public be quantified?[1]

Some have tried to define a public in terms of a common interest, speaking, for example, of a foreign-policy public or a sports
public. But this way of speaking only pretends to escape the conun-
drum of the self-creating public. It is like explaining the popularity
of films or novels as a response to market demand; the claim is
circular, because market "demand" is entirely inferred from the
popularity of the works themselves. The idea of a common interest, like that of a market demand, appears to identify the social
base of public discourse; but the base is in fact projected from the
public discourse itself rather than external to it.

Of all the contrivances designed to escape this circularity, the
most powerful by far has been the invention of polling. Polling,
together with related forms of market research, tries to tell us what
the interests, desires, and demands of a public are, without simply
inferring them from public discourse. It is an elaborate apparatus
designed to characterize a public as social fact independent of any
discursive address or circulation. As Pierre Bourdieu pointed out,
however, this method proceeds by denying the constitutive role of

polling itself as a mediating form.[2] Habermas and others have further stressed that the device now systematically distorts the public sphere, producing something that passes as public opinion when in fact it results from a form that has none of the open-endedness, reflexive framing, or accessibility of public discourse. I would add that it lacks the embodied creativity and world making of publicness. Publics have to be understood as mediated by cultural forms, even though some of those forms, such as polling, work by denying their own constitutive role as cultural forms. Publics do not exist apart from the discourse that addresses them.

Are they therefore internal to discourse? Literary studies has often imagined a public as a rhetorical addressee, implied within texts. But the term is generally understood to name something about the text's worldliness, its actual destination, which may or may not resemble its addressee. Benjamin Franklin's autobiography, to take a famous example, remained addressed to his son even after Franklin severed relations with that son and decided to publish the text; the public of the autobiography was crucially nonidentical with its addressee. Of course, one can distinguish in such a case between the nominal addressee and the implied addressee, but it is equally possible to distinguish between an implied addressee of rhetoric and a targeted public of circulation. That these are not identical is what allows people to shape the public by addressing it in a certain way. It also allows people to fail if a rhetorical addressee is not picked up as the reflection of a public.

The sense that a public is a worldly constraint on speech, and not just a free creation of speech, gives plausibility to the opposite approach of the social sciences. The self-organized nature of the public does not mean that it is always spontaneous or organically expressive of individuals' wishes. In fact, although the premise of self-organizing discourse is necessary to the peculiar cultural artifact that we call a public, it is contradicted both by material limits — means of production and distribution, the physical textual objects, social conditions of access — and by internal ones, including the need to presuppose forms of intelligibility already in place, as well as the social closure entailed by any selection of genre, idiolect, style, address, and so on. I will return to these constraints of circulation. For the moment, I want to emphasize that they are made to seem arbitrary because of the performativity of public address and the self-organization implied by the idea of a public.

Another way of saying the same thing is that any empirical extension of the public will seem arbitrarily limited because the addressee of public discourse is always yet to be realized. In some contexts of speech and writing, both the rhetorical addressee and the public have a fairly clear empirical referent: in correspondence and most e-mail, in the reports and memos that are passed up and down bureaucracies, in love notes and valentines and Dear John letters, the object of address is understood to be an identifiable person or office. Even if that addressee is already a generalized role — for example, a personnel committee, or Congress, or a church congregation — it is definite, known, nameable, and numerable. The interaction is framed by a social relationship.

But for another class of writing contexts — including literary criticism, journalism, theory, advertising, fiction, drama, most poetry — the available addressees are essentially imaginary, which is not to say unreal: the people, scholarship, the republic of letters, posterity, the younger generation, the nation, the left, the movement, the world, the vanguard, the enlightened few, right-thinking people everywhere, public opinion, the brotherhood of all believers, humanity, my fellow queers. These are all publics. They are in principle open-ended. They exist by virtue of their address.

Although such publics are imaginary, writing to a public is not imaginary in the same way as writing to Pinocchio. All public addressees have some social basis. Their imaginary character is never merely a matter of private fantasy. (By the same token, all addressees are to some extent imaginary — even that of a journal, especially if one writes to one's ideal self, one's posthumous biographers, and so on.) They fail if they have no reception in the world, but the exact composition of their addressed publics cannot entirely be known in advance. A public is always in excess of its known social basis. It must be more than a list of one's friends. It must include strangers.

Let me call this a second defining premise of the modern idea of a public:

2. A public is a relation among strangers.
Other kinds of writing — writing that has a definite addressee who can be known in advance — can, of course, go astray. Writing to a public incorporates that tendency of writing or speech as a condition of possibility. It cannot in the same way go astray, because reaching strangers is its primary orientation. In modernity, this understanding of the public is best illustrated by uses of print or electronic media, but it can also be extended to scenes of audible speech, if that speech is oriented to indefinite strangers, once the crucial background horizon of "public opinion" and its social imaginary has been made available. We've become capable of recognizing ourselves as strangers even when we know each other. Declaiming this essay to a group of intimates, I could still be heard as addressing a public.

The orientation to strangers is in one sense implied by a public's self-organization through discourse. A public sets its boundaries and its organization by its own discourse rather than by external frameworks only if it openly addresses people who are identified primarily through their participation in the discourse and who therefore cannot be known in advance.

74

A public might almost be said to be stranger-relationality in a pure form, because other ways of organizing strangers — nations, religions, races, guilds — have manifest positive content. They select strangers by criteria of territory or identity or belief or some other test of membership. One can address strangers in such contexts because a common identity has been established through independent means or institutions (creeds, armies, parties, and the like). A public, however, unites strangers through participation alone, at least in theory. Strangers come into relationship by its means, though the resulting social relationship might be peculiarly indirect and unspecifiable.

Once this kind of public is in place as a social imaginary, I might add, stranger sociability inevitably takes on a different character. In modern society, a stranger is not as marvelously exotic as the wandering outsider would have been to an ancient, medieval, or early-modern town. In that earlier social order, or in contemporary analogues, a stranger is mysterious, a disturbing presence requiring resolution.[3] In the context of a public, however, strangers can be treated as already belonging to our world. More: they *must* be. We are routinely oriented to them in common life. They are a normal feature of the social.

Strangers in the ancient sense — foreign, alien, misplaced — might of course be placed to a degree by Christendom, the *ummah*, a guild, or an army, affiliations one might share with strangers, making them a bit less strange. Strangers placed by means of these affiliations are on a path to commonality. Publics orient us to strangers in a different way. They are no longer merely people whom one does not yet know; rather, an environment of strangerhood is the necessary premise of some of our most prized ways of being. Where otherwise strangers need to be on a path to commonality, in modern forms strangerhood is the necessary medium of commonality. The modern social imaginary does not make

75

sense without strangers. A nation or public or market in which everyone could be known personally would be no nation or public or market at all. This constitutive and normative environment of strangerhood is more, too, than an objectively describable *Gesellschaft*; it requires our constant imagining.

The expansive force of these cultural forms cannot be understood apart from the way they make stranger relationality normative, reshaping the most intimate dimensions of subjectivity around co-membership with indefinite persons in a context of routine action. The development of forms that mediate the intimate theater of stranger relationality must surely be one of the most significant dimensions of modern history, though the story of this transformation in the meaning of strangers has been told only in fragments. It is hard to imagine such abstract modes of being as rights-bearing personhood, species being, and sexuality, for example, without forms that give concrete shape to the interactivity of those who have no idea with whom they interact. This dependence on the co-presence of strangers in our innermost activity, when we continue to think of strangerhood and intimacy as opposites, has at least some latent contradictions, many of which come to the fore, as we shall see, in counterpublic forms that make expressive corporeality the material for the elaboration of intimate life among publics of strangers.

The oddness of this orientation to strangers in public discourse can be understood better if we consider a third defining feature of discourse that addresses publics, one that follows from the address to strangers but is very difficult to describe:

3. *The address of public speech is both personal and impersonal.*
Public speech can have great urgency and intimate import. Yet we know that it was addressed not exactly to us but to the stranger we were until the moment we happened to be addressed by it. (I

am thinking here of any genre addressed to a public, including novels and lyrics as well as criticism, other nonfictional prose, and almost all genres of radio, television, film, and Web discourse.) To inhabit public discourse is to perform this transition continually, and to some extent it remains present to consciousness. Public speech must be taken in two ways: as addressed to us and as addressed to strangers. The benefit in this practice is that it gives a general social relevance to private thought and life. Our subjectivity is understood as having resonance with others, and immediately so. But this is only true to the extent that the trace of our strangerhood remains present in our understanding of ourselves as the addressee.

This necessary element of impersonality in public address is one of the things missed from view in the Althusserian notion of interpellation, at least as it is currently understood. Louis Althusser's famous example is speech addressed to a stranger: a policeman says, "Hey, you!" In the moment of recognizing oneself as the person addressed, the moment of turning around, one is interpellated as the subject of state discourse.[4] Althusser's analysis had the virtues of showing the importance of imaginary identification and locating it not in the coercive or punitive force of the state but in the subjective practice of understanding. When the model of interpellation is extracted from his example to account for public culture generally, the analysis will be skewed because the case Althusser gives is not an example of public discourse. A policeman who says "Hey, you!" will be understood to be addressing a particular person, not a public. When one turns around, it is partly to see whether one is that person. If not, one goes on. If so, then all the others who might be standing on the street are bystanders, not addressees. With public speech, by contrast, we might recognize ourselves as addressees, but it is equally important that we remember that the speech was addressed to indefinite others, that in singling us out it does so not on the basis of our concrete identity but by virtue of our participation in the discourse alone and therefore in common with strangers. It isn't just that we are addressed in public as certain kinds of persons or that we might not want to identify as that person (though this is often enough the case, as when the public is addressed as heterosexual, or white, or sports-minded, or American). We haven't been misidentified, exactly. It seems more to the point to say that publics are different from persons, that the address of public rhetoric is never going to be the same as address to actual persons, and that our partial nonidentity with the object of address in public speech seems to be part of what it means to regard something as public speech.

It might be helpful to think of public address in contrast to the modes of address that have come to be associated with the genres of gossip, lyric poetry, and sermons. Each of these three genres can be treated as part of public discourse under certain conditions; but each is organized by conventions — of interactive relationship, reading, and hearing — that ordinarily prevent the reflexivity of circulation from being salient in rhetorical address.

Gossip might seem to be a perfect instance of public discourse. It circulates widely among a social network, beyond the control of private individuals. It sets norms of membership in a diffuse way that cannot be controlled by a central authority. For these reasons, a number of scholars have celebrated its potential for popular sociability and for the weak-group politics of women, peasants, and others.[5] But gossip is never a relation among strangers. You gossip about particular people and to particular people. What you can get away with saying depends very much on whom you are talking to and what your status is in that person's eyes. Speak ill of someone when you are not thought to have earned the privilege, and you will be taken as slandering rather than gossiping. Gossip circulates without the awareness of some people, and it must be prevented from reaching them in the wrong way. Intensely personal measurements of group membership, relative standing, and trust are the constant and unavoidable pragmatic work of gossip.[6]

An apparent exception is gossip about public figures who do not belong to the social network made by gossiping, especially when official or unofficial censorship makes scandal unreportable by more legitimate means. About such people it is possible to gossip among strangers, and the gossip often has both reflexivity ("People are saying..."; "Everybody knows that...") and timeliness (hot gossip versus stale news). A public seems to have come about by such means in eighteenth-century Paris. (Did you hear what the queen did with the dauphin? Guess what Mme de Pompadour has said now!) In the Philippines, to take a more recent example, cell-phone text messaging has become the principal medium by which a public reflexively circulates gossip about corruption scandals involving President Joseph Estrada. (The volume of text messaging there is said to exceed that of the European Union sevenfold.) Of course, in such a case, there might still be some of the risk and thrill of ordinary gossip's gamble of trust, since the conditions that make for public gossip also tend to interest police. To tell someone a juicy tidbit or a joke is to show that you trust him not to be an informer. In contemporary mass culture, too, gossip-based genres have proliferated, to the point of creating new professionals (gossip columnists) who can be celebrities and subjects of gossip in their own right. These kinds of talk might be better described as scandal rather than gossip, precisely to the degree that they circulate among strangers. Gossip in the usual sense, by creating bonds of shared secrecy and calibrating highly particularized relations of trust, dissolves the strangerhood essential to public address.

Lyric poetry is in a way the opposite. It appears to take no cognizance of its addressee whatsoever. "Shall I compare thee to a summer's day?" does not exactly address *thee*. (Even the Holly-wood version in *Shakespeare in Love*, which tried to construe "Shall I compare thee to a summer's day?" as literally addressed to Gwyn-eth Paltrow, was forced to show the nominal addressee holding the paper and simpering while reading the text aloud — to her maid!) Lyric conventions, which are automatically in place when-ever we read a text as lyric poetry, allow for very special inter-pretations of things like mode of address and circulation; our mis-recognition of the text seems to be necessary for producing some of lyric's most valued attributes of deep subjectivity. Virginia Jackson shows that many of the features of lyric utterance are ambiguously taken to be indexical to both an (imaginary) speak-ing event and to the (actual) reading event. As Jackson puts it:

> This structure is one in which saying "I" can stand for saying "you," in which the poet's solitude stands in for the solitude of the individ-ual reader — a self-address so absolute every self can identify it as his own.... The "intersubjective confirmation of the self" performed by a reading of lyric based upon the identity between poet and reader must be achieved by denying to the poem any intersubjective econ-omy of its own. On this view, in order to have an audience the lyric must not have one.[7]

Of course, lyric poems are in fact produced by particular persons and addressed to others, and they circulate in public media (even if only in manuscript). But to read them as lyric, we ignore those facts and reinterpret both the speaking event, the boundaries of the text, and all the figures of apostrophe in the text (even, or especially, in love lyrics, which have a special vocabulary of love that allows us to do this). The rhetoric of lyric, including its affects, scenes, and temporality, exploits this reading convention. In read-ing something as lyric, rather than regard the speaking voice as wholly alienated to the text, we regard it as transcendent. Though it could only be produced through the displacement of writing, we read it with cultivated disregard of its circumstance of circulation, understanding it as an image of absolute privacy.

The contrast between lyric and public speech was underscored by John Stuart Mill in a classic 1833 essay. "Eloquence is *heard*, poetry is *overheard*," according to Mill. "Eloquence supposes an audience; the peculiarity of poetry appears to us to lie in the poet's utter unconsciousness of a listener. Poetry is feeling confessing itself to itself, in moments of solitude."[8] There is, as Northrop Frye puts it, "no word for the audience of the lyric."[9] We could, however, refine this contrast. Poetry is not actually overheard; it is read as overheard. And similarly, public speech is not just heard; it is heard (or read) *as* heard, not just by oneself but by others. The contrast may be carried through point by point. Public speech is no more addressed to a particular person than is lyric. Both require a very special apprehension of apostrophe. In the case of lyric, we regard the event not as communication but as our silent insertion in the self-communion of the speaker, constructing both an ideal self-presence for the speaking voice and an ideal intimacy between that voice and ourselves. In public speech, we incorporate an awareness of the distribution of the speech or text itself as essential to its addressee, which we nevertheless take to be in some measure ourselves. Lyric speech has no time: we read the scene of speech as identical with the moment of reading. Public speech, by contrast, requires the temporality of its own circulation — a point to which I will return in a moment.

So closely related are the textualizing practices of these two generic conventions of reading that one seems to be formed by negation of the other. Publics and lyrics both have long histories, in each case reaching to Antiquity.[10] It is an interesting subject for speculation that both come to have a different and much more important role in modernity and that the period in which publics have acquired the full significance of popular sovereignty and the bourgeois public sphere also happens, perhaps not by coincidence, to be the period in which the lyric — now understood as timeless overheard self-communion — displaces all other poetic genres (epic, poems on affairs of state, georgic, elegy, satire). It is now thought of simply as poetry. Where other poetic genres had circulated among courtly circles, in manuscript coteries, or in print media endowed with public relevance, by the end of the eighteenth century such forms had become rare and archaic. Mill and Hegel, of course, delivered their influential characterizations of the genre at the end of this long process of the lyricization of the poetic, a process that also measures the polarization of poetic genres from the prosaic modes of public address.[11] Both the public sphere and the lyric mode found their ascendancy with print; both show signs of stress under the dominance of massified electronic media.

It is very difficult to hybridize these modes without compromising lyric transcendence, though I argue in the final essay of this book that some of Walt Whitman's more problematic texts seem to make such a compromise.[12] Poetry slams also sometimes create a counterpublic hybrid discourse, where poetry is pressured into embracing its scene of address (with, however, a corresponding loss of lyric transcendence).

A final contrast with sermons might be useful in understanding the reading practice necessary to the public. The sermon, after all, is an instance of public eloquence, and in the American tradition at least its cultural importance can hardly be overestimated. But is a sermon preached to a public? Sometimes, certainly: the political sermon has a long history, and in the Anglican tradition especially the sermon has often been understood as a genre of polite discourse. But there is also a long tradition in which political or literary sermons are not really preaching at all. In the

dissenting Protestant tradition that has made the form most powerful, sermonic eloquence and the preacherly role require that the
consciousness of audience be blocked from consciousness in order
for the rhetoric to work.

In "Of Ineffectual Hearing the Word," a 1641 sermon on listening to sermons, Thomas Shepard distinguishes between "external hearing," which anyone can have in ordinary discourse, and
"internal hearing," which marks right listening to sermons. "When
a man heares things generally delivered," he uses external hearing
so long as he "never thinks the Lord is now speaking, and means
me." But if there is internal hearing, "the word is like an exact picture, it looks every man in the face that looks on it, if God speaks
in it.... When the Lord speaks, a man thinks now I have to do
with God, if I resist I oppose a God." A historian might recognize
here Shepard's interest in the Puritan psychology of conversion,
or the influence of Thomas Hooker and John Cotton. But the
point is the effect sermonic language tries to produce. "Hence it
is one man is wrought on in a Sermon, another not," Shepard
continues. "God hath singled out one, not the other that day....
At last he heares his secret thoughts and sins discovered, all his life
is made known, and thinks 'tis the Lord verily that hath done this;
now God speaks."[13]

As a standard of performance, this is a heavy burden for mor-
tal speakers. It is very different from the controversialist's aim of
persuasion; indeed, it resembles shamanistic performance, however much scholarly exposition and clerical debate might also
mark American sermons in their early development. The preacher tries to meet this criterion of eloquence, striving to speak with
something other than his individual voice, and to address the intimate hearer, creating a scene of hearing markedly different from
the speech of one person to others in ordinary time. When it
works, the hearer hears a voice that is more than the preacher's

83

and hears it as addressed to him or her in a way that excludes other congregants, even if they, too, turn out to be having moments of inner revelation. One Puritan sermon-goer of the early eighteenth century, Sarah Osborn, wrote in her memoirs, "Mr. Clap ... told me the very secrets of my heart in his sermon, as plain as I could have told them to him, and indeed more so. His sermon was very terrible to me.... I saw the depravity of my nature; and how I was exposed to the infinite justice of an angry God."[14] The incomparable intensity of this effect is achieved by *not* recognizing sermons as public speech.

Public speech differs from both lyric and sermonic eloquence by construing its addressee as its circulation, not its private apprehension. The most private, inward, intimate act of reading can be converted by the category of the public into a form of stranger relationality. This can even happen with sermons, of course, though when it does the publicness of sermons is in tension with its performance of spiritualized truth. Such a hybridization of the sermon form seems to have become conspicuous, in the American context, in the course of the Great Awakening. In the earlier colonial setting, preaching had been understood within the web of hierarchical and intimate pastoral relationships between clergy and congregation. In the words of one historian, "Speaker and audience were steadily reminded of their *personal* place in the community; in no context were they strangers to one another, for no public gatherings took place outside of traditional associations based upon personal acquaintance and social rank."[15] The rise of itinerant preachers in revivals — which were also public-sphere mediated events, as several recent scholars have emphasized — changed the speaking relationship in preaching.[16] Suddenly men, even women, were preaching to strangers. The revival context and itinerant preaching made the publicness of the sermon much more salient, in a way that was perceived at the time to be scandalous. By the end of the century, as something like a modern sense of denominational confession became current in the United States, all congregations could be understood implicitly as belonging to a churchgoing public of strangers. A profound shift underlies this history. Scholars often emphasize the oral performance essential to revivalism, thinking that revival preaching is therefore a more popular or folk idiom than that of the learned, lettered clergy; in doing so, they miss the way even the most passionately oral preaching, when it addresses strangers as an indefinite audience of ongoing discourse, relies on a text-based sense of its public.[17] Responses like Sarah Osborn's, however, become rarer in the process. The shamanistic intensity of sermonic eloquence also begins to solicit a more public response in revivalism — not the silent inward meditation of Osborn, but responses that will be audible or visible to other members of the congregation. The so-called Second Great Awakening created a proliferation of these markedly public reception devices: weeping, barking, moaning, coming to the altar, and so on.[18] The intensity of revival affect owes much to the fact that intimate emotion is being performed in the presence of strangers, people who come and go in an indefinite ambit of a revival-going world. Yet for all the changes brought about in the revival context, sermonic eloquence continued to be recognized as a product of particular address by deity to sinner and not as an essentially *circulating* form.

The appeal to strangers in the circulating forms of public address thus helps us to distinguish public discourse from forms that address particular persons in their singularity. It remains less clear how a public could be translated into an image of *the* public, a social entity. Who is the public? Does it include my neighbors? The doorman in my building? My students? The people who show up in the gay bars and clubs? The bodega owners down the street from me? Someone who calls me on the phone or sends me an e-mail?

You? We encounter people in such disparate contexts that the idea of a body to which they all belong, and in which they could be addressed in speech, seems to have something wishful about it. To address a public, we don't go around saying the same thing to all these people. We say it in a venue of indefinite address and hope that people will find themselves in it. The difference can be a source of frustration, but it is also a direct implication of the self-organization of the public as a body of strangers united through the circulation of their discourse, without which public address would have none of its special importance to modernity.

Walter Lippmann in a way picked up on the odd nature of public address when he complained that no one could possibly be the sort of creature that is routinely addressed as the public of politics: the fully informed, universally interested and attentive, vigilant, potent, and decisive citizen. "I have not happened to meet anybody, from a President of the United States to a professor of political science, who came anywhere near to embodying the accepted ideal of the sovereign and omnicompetent citizen."[19] But it doesn't follow that politicians and journalists should be more realistic in their address. To think so is to mistake the addressee of public speech for an actual person. Lippmann thought the appropriate response was an honest assessment of the actual reception of public discourse, and therefore a more frankly elite administration:

> We must assume as a theoretically fixed premise of popular government that normally men as members of a public will not be well informed, continuously interested, nonpartisan, creative or executive. We must assume that a public is inexpert in its curiosity, intermittent, that it discerns only gross distinctions, is slow to be aroused and quickly diverted; that, since it acts by aligning itself, it personalizes whatever it considers, and is interested only when events have been melodramatized as a conflict.[20]

86

Interestingly, Lippmann cannot observe his own advice. Even in writing this passage, he writes to an alert and thoughtful public ("we," he calls it) with an assumption of activity. Public discourse itself has a kind of personality different from that of the people who make up a public.

In this passage, Lippmann stumbles across another of the principal differences between a public and any already-existing social group. A public is thought to be active, curious, alert. But actual people, he notices, are intermittent in their attention, only occasionally aroused, fitfully involved. He thinks this is a sad fact about the general character, comparing unfavorably with the greater energies of concentration that elites maintain in their engagement with public questions. But between ideally alert publics and really distracted people there will always be a gap, no matter what the social class or kind of public. This is because publics are only realized through active uptake.

4. *A public is constituted through mere attention.*
Most social classes and groups are understood to encompass their members all the time, no matter what. A nation, for example, includes its members whether they are awake or asleep, sober or drunk, sane or deranged, alert or comatose. Publics are different. Because a public exists only by virtue of address, it must predicate some degree of attention, however notional, from its members.

The cognitive quality of that attention is less important than the mere fact of active uptake. Attention is the principal sorting category by which members and nonmembers are discriminated. If you are reading this, or hearing it or seeing it or present for it, you are part of this public. You might be multitasking at the computer; the television might be on while you are vacuuming the carpet; or you might have wandered into hearing range of the speaker's podium in a convention hall only because it was on your way to the bathroom. No matter: by coming into range, you fulfill the only entry condition demanded of a public. It is even possible for us to understand someone sleeping through a ballet performance as a member of that ballet's public, because most contemporary ballet performances are organized as voluntary events, open to anyone willing to attend or, in most cases, to pay to attend. The act of attention involved in showing up is enough to create an addressable public. Some kind of active uptake, however somnolent, is indispensable.

The existence of a public is contingent on its members' activity, however notional or compromised, and not on its members' categorical classification, objectively determined position in the social structure, or material existence. In the self-understanding that makes them work, publics thus resemble the model of voluntary association that is so important to civil society. Since the early-modern period, more and more institutions have come to conform to this model. The old idea of an established national church, for example, allowed the church to address itself to parish members literate or illiterate, virtuous or vicious, competent or idiotic. Increasingly, churches in a multidenominational world must think of themselves instead as contingent on their members; they welcome newcomers, keep membership rolls, and solicit attention. Some doctrinal emphases, like those on faith or conversion, make it possible for churches to orient themselves to that active uptake on which they are increasingly dependent.

Still, one can join a church and then stop going. In some cases, one can even be born into one. Publics, by contrast, lacking any institutional being, commence with the moment of attention, must continually predicate renewed attention, and cease to exist when attention is no longer predicated. They are virtual entities, not voluntary associations. Because their threshold of belonging is an active uptake, however, they can be understood within the conceptual framework of civil society; that is, as having a free, voluntary, and active membership. Wherever a liberal conception of personality obtains, the moment of uptake that constitutes a public can be seen as an expression of volition on the part of its members. And this fact has enormous consequences. It allows us to understand publics as scenes of self-activity, of historical rather than timeless belonging, and of active participation rather than ascriptive belonging. Under the right conditions, it even allows us to attribute agency to a public, even though that public has no institutional being or concrete manifestation. (More on this later.)

Public discourse craves attention like a child. Texts clamor at us. Images solicit our gaze. Look here! Listen! Hey! In doing so, they by no means render us passive. Quite the contrary. The modern system of publics creates a demanding social phenomenology. Our willingness to process a passing appeal determines which publics we belong to and performs their extension. The experience of social reality in modernity feels quite unlike that in societies organized by kinship, hereditary status, local affiliation, mediated political access, parochial nativity, or ritual. In those settings, one's place in the common order is what it is regardless of one's inner thoughts, however intense their affective charge might sometimes be. The appellative energy of publics puts a different burden on us: it makes us believe our consciousness to be decisive. The direction of our glance can constitute our social world.

The themes I've discussed so far — the self-organization of publics through discourse, their orientation to strangers, the resulting ambiguity of personal and impersonal address, membership by mere attention — can be clarified if we remember their common assumption, which goes a long way toward explaining the historical development of the other four:

5. *A public is the social space created by the reflexive circulation of discourse.*

This dimension is easy to forget if we think only about a speech event involving speaker and addressee. In that localized exchange, circulation may seem irrelevant, extraneous. That is one reason why sender/receiver or author/reader models of public communication are so misleading. No single text can create a public. Nor can a single voice, a single genre, even a single medium. All are insufficient to create the kind of reflexivity that we call a public, since a public is understood to be an ongoing space of encounter for discourse. Not texts themselves create publics, but the concatenation of texts through time. Only when a previously existing discourse can be supposed, and when a responding discourse can be postulated, can a text address a public.

Between the discourse that comes before and the discourse that comes after one must postulate some kind of link. And the link has a social character; it is not mere consecutiveness in time but an interaction. The usual way of imagining the interactive character of public discourse is through metaphors of conversation, answering, talking back. Argument and polemic, as manifestly dialogic genres, continue to have a privileged role in the self-understanding of publics. Indeed, it is remarkable how little work in even the most sophisticated forms of theory has been able to disentangle public discourse from its self-understanding as conversation.[21] In addressing a public, however, even texts of the most rigorously argumentative and dialogic genres also addresses onlookers, not just parties to argument. They try to characterize the field of possible interplay. When appearing in a public field, genres of argument and polemic must accommodate themselves to the special conditions of public address; the agonistic interlocutor is coupled with passive interlocutors, known enemies with indifferent strangers, parties present to a dialogue situation with parties whose textual location might be in other genres or scenes of circulation entirely. The meaning of any utterance depends on what is known and anticipated from all these different quarters. In public argument or polemic, the principal act is that of projecting the field of argument itself—its genre, its range of circulation, its stakes, its idiom, its repertoire of agencies. Any position is reflexive, not only asserting itself but characterizing its relation to other positions up to limits that are the imagined scene of circulation. The interactive relation postulated in public discourse, in other words, goes far beyond the scale of conversation or discussion to encompass a multigeneric lifeworld organized not just by a relational axis of utterance and response but by potentially infinite axes of citation and characterization.

Anything that addresses a public is meant to undergo circulation. This helps us to understand why print, and the organization of markets for print, were historically so central in the development of the public sphere. But print is neither necessary nor sufficient for publication in the modern sense; not every genre of print can organize the space of circulation. The particularly addressed genres I listed earlier — correspondence, memos, valentines, bills — are not expected to circulate (indeed, circulating them can be not just strange but highly unethical), and that is why they are not oriented to a public.

Circulation also accounts for the way a public seems both internal and external to discourse, both notional and material. From the concrete experience of a world in which available forms circulate, one projects a public. And both the known and the unknown are essential to the process. The known element in the addressee enables a scene of practical possibility; the unknown, a hope of transformation. Writing to a public helps to make a world insofar as the object of address is brought into being partly by postulating and characterizing it. This performative ability depends, however, on that object's being not entirely fictitious — not postulated merely, but recognized as a real path for the circulation of discourse. That path is then treated as a social entity.

The ability to address the world made up by the circulation of cross-referencing discourse seems to have developed over a long period, at least from the late sixteenth century to the late eighteenth. In the English case, for example, many of the promotional tracts for colonization of the New World address potential investors or supporters who are understood to have been addressed by competing representations. (That is why so many are called "A True Discourse," "A True Report," and so on.) Yet these same tracts tend to regard this as an unnatural and unfortunate condition that could be righted by properly authoritative and true testimony. Eventually it became possible to thematize circulation, to regard it as an essential fact of common life, and to organize a social imaginary in which it would be regarded as normative.

It is possible to see this cultural formation emerging in England in the seventeenth century. Let me offer a curious example: a 1670 report from the reign of Charles II of the activities in two Whig booksellers' shops. It is an interesting example because the (presumably) royalist author of the report regards those activities with suspicion, to say the least. He describes public discourse without any of the normative self-understanding of public discourse. "Every afternoon," the report says, the shops receive from all over the city accounts of news ("all novells and occurrents so penned as to make for the disadvantage of the King and his affairs"), written reports of resolutions and speeches in Parliament, and speeches on topics of public business. These reports are made available to the booksellers' regular clients, who, according to the report, include young lawyers ("who here generally receive their tincture and corruption"), "ill-affected citizens of all sorts," "ill-affected gentry," and "emissaries and agents of the severall parties and factions about town." The reports and speeches available for these readers were all registered in a central catalog and could be ordered individually from the copyists:

> Against the time of their coming the Masters of those Shops have a grand book or books, wherein are registred ready for them, all or most of the forenamed particulars; which they dayly produce to those sorts of people to be read, and then, if they please, they either carry away copies, or bespeak them against another day.

The circulation of the scribal reports went beyond London, too. "They take care to communicate them by Letter all over the kingdome, and by conversation throughout the City and suburbs. The like industry is used by the masters of those shops, who together with their servants are every afternoon and night busied in transcribing copies, with which they drive a trade all over the kingdome."[22]

The two booksellers of the account were producing a market, in what sounds like a very busy entrepreneurial scene. Some of the elements in the account suggest the norms of the emergent public sphere: the scribal trade promotes private discussion of common concerns; it stands in opposition to power (though here that is regarded as disaffection rather than as a normative role for criticism); and it occupies metatopical secular space.[23] It is not clear from this account whether the participants understood their relation to each other as a relation to a public. (It is somewhat unlikely that they did; one scholar, claiming that "there was as yet no 'public,'" notes that "Dryden always uses the word 'people' where we should now say 'public.'"[24]) The genres circulated in this report are themselves mostly familiar ones of correspondence and speeches, both of which have specific addressees. What is striking, though, is the clarity with which we can see in this account the scene of circulation that is presupposed by the idea of a public. And curiously, it is not simply a scene of print but of scribal copying. That may be one reason why the scene is so scandalous to the informer. The circulatory practices are thought to be illegitimate uses of their genres and modes of address.

In a study published ten years ago, I argued that the consciousness of the public in public address developed as a new way of understanding print, in the context of a republican political language that served as a metalanguage for print, though this consciousness of public address could then be extended to scenes of speech such as political sermons. Reading printed texts in this context, we incorporate an awareness of the indefinite others to whom they are addressed as part of the meaning of their printedness.[25] I now see that in making this argument, I missed a crucial element in the perception of publicness. In order for a text to be public, we must recognize it not simply as a diffusion to strangers but also as a temporality of circulation.

The informer's report makes this clear, calling attention not just to the (possibly seditious) connections forged among strangers but to the punctual circulation that makes those connections a regular scene. Reports are said to come in "every afternoon" and to be indexed promptly. Customers come or send their agents daily for copies, according to rhythms that are widely known and relied on. We are not seeing simply a bookseller distributing copies far and wide; rather, it is a regular flow of discourse in and out, punctuated by daily rhythms and oriented to that punctuality as to news ("novells and occurrents"). Circulation organizes time and vice versa. Public discourse is contemporary, and it is oriented to the future; the contemporaneity and the futurity in question are those of its own circulation.

The key development in the emergence of modern publics was the appearance of newsletters and other temporally structured forms oriented to their own circulation: not just controversial pamphlets, but regular and dated papers, magazines, almanacs, annuals, and essay serials. They developed reflexivity about their circulation through reviews, reprintings, citations, controversies. These forms single out circulation both through their sense of temporality and through the way they allow discourse to move in different directions. I don't just speak to you; I speak to the public in a way that enters a cross-citational field of many other people speaking to the public.

The temporality of circulation is not continuous or indefinite; it is punctual. There are distinct moments and rhythms, from which distance in time can be measured. Papers and magazines are dated and when they first appear are news. Reviews appear with a sense of timeliness. At a longer pace, there are now publishing seasons with their cycles of catalogs and marketing campaigns. The exception might seem to be televisual media, given the enormous significance they attribute to their liveness and "flow" — formally salient features of so much broadcasting, whereby televisual forms arc understood to have a greater immediacy than codex or other text formats. Yet even in televisual media, punctual rhythms of daily and weekly emission are still observed; think of all their serial forms and marked rhythms such as prime time and the news hour.[26]

Reflexive circulation might come about in any number of ways. In France, as in England, it appeared first in print serial forms. *Le Mercure galant*, a newspaper edited by Jean Donneau de Visé, seems to have pioneered many of the devices of reflexive circulation in the late 1670s, including reader letters and a rhetoric of readerly judgment.[27] In this case, the idea that readers participated in the circulation of judgments, thought at the time by Jean de La Bruyère and others to have been a solecism, gradually drew the sense of the term "public" away from the image of a passive theatrical audience.[28] For Abbé du Bos in 1719, "The word *public* is used here to mean those persons who have acquired enlightenment, either through reading or through life in society [*le commerce du monde*]. They are the only ones who can determine the value of poems or paintings."[29] In France, this sense of a critical public did not easily transfer to politics, since legitimate printed news was almost nonexistent under the ancien régime. Yet as Robert Darnton has shown, eighteenth-century Paris gave rise to countless other forms of reflexive circulation. Many of them were known by names that "are unknown today and cannot be translated into English equivalents": *nouvelliste de bouche, mauvais propos, bruit public, on-dit, pasquinade, Pont Neuf, canard, feuille volante, factum, libelle, chronique scandaleuse.* More familiar genres, such as popular songs, seem to have circulated in uniquely Parisian ways.[30] The differences between these genres and their Anglo-American counterparts say much about the difference between the corresponding senses of public life, its legitimacy, and the conditions under which agency might be attributed to a public. Nevertheless, they were forms for giving reflexivity to a field of circulation among strangers in punctual rhythms.

6. *Publics act historically according to the temporality of their circulation.*

The punctual time of circulation is crucial to the sense that discussion is currently unfolding in a sphere of activity. It is not timeless, like meditation; nor is it without issue, like speculative philosophy. Not all circulation happens at the same rate, of course, and this accounts for the dramatic differences among publics in their relation to possible scenes of activity. A public can only act in the temporality of the circulation that gives it existence. The more punctual and abbreviated the circulation, and the more discourse indexes the punctuality of its own circulation, the closer a public stands to politics. At longer rhythms or more continuous flows, action becomes harder to imagine. This is the fate of academic publics, a fact very little understood when academics claim by intention or proclamation to be doing politics. In modernity, politics takes much of its character from the temporality of the headline, not the archive.

Publics have an ongoing life: one doesn't publish to them once for all (as one does, say, to a scholarly archive). It's the way texts circulate, and become the basis for further representations, that convinces us that publics have activity and duration. A text, to have a public, must continue to circulate through time, and because this can only be confirmed through an intertextual environment of citation and implication, all publics are intertextual, even intergeneric. This is often missed from view because the activity and duration of publics are commonly stylized as conversation or decision making. I have already suggested that these are misleading ideologizations. Now we can see why they are durable illusions: because they confer agency on publics. There is no moment at which the conversation stops and a decision ensues, outside of elections, and those are given only by legal frameworks, not by publics themselves. Yet the ideologization is crucial to the sense that publics act in secular time. To sustain this sense, public discourse indexes itself temporally with respect to moments of publication and a common calendar of circulation.

One way the Internet and other new media may be profoundly changing the public sphere is through the change they imply in temporality. Highly mediated and highly capitalized forms of circulation are increasingly organized as continuous ("24/7 instant access") rather than punctual.[31] At the time of this writing, Web discourse has very little of the citational field that would allow us to speak of it as discourse unfolding through time. Once a Web site is up, it can be hard to tell how recently it was posted or revised or how long it will continue to be posted. Most sites are not archived. For the most part, they are not centrally indexed. The reflexive apparatus of Web discourse consists most-ly of hypertext links and search engines, and these are not punc-tual. So although there are exceptions, including the migration of some print serials to electronic format and the successful use of the Web by some social movements, it remains unclear to what extent the changing technology will be assimilable to the tempo-ral framework of public discourse.[32] If the change of infrastruc-ture continues at this pace, and if modes of apprehension change accordingly, the absence of punctual rhythms may make it very difficult to connect localized acts of reading to the modes of agency in the social imaginary of modernity. It may even be nec-essary to abandon "circulation" as an analytic category. But here I merely offer this topic for speculation.

Until recently at least, public discourse has presupposed daily and weekly rhythms of circulation. It has also presupposed an abil-ity — natural to us now, but rather peculiar if one thinks about it — to address this scene of circulation as a social entity. The clearest example, or at any rate the most eloquent, is the *Spectator*, some forty years after the report of the Whig booksellers. Like the booksellers' newsletters, the *Spectator* was a daily form, widely and industriously circulated.[33] "To be Continued every Day," declares the first number, which was designed to look like the newspapers of the day even though, as no. 262 declares, the paper "has not in it a single Word of News." The *Spectator* followed a model worked out by John Dunton, whose *Athenian Mercury* (1691) first began printing regular correspondence from readers, whom it allowed to remain anonymous.[34] The *Spectator* developed a rhetoric that gave a new normative force to Dunton's methods. It ostentatiously avoided political polemic. Unlike the output of the Whig booksellers in the 1670 report, it could not be described as seditious; yet it describes its readers as an active public, a critical tribunal. Readers are called on to pass informed and reflective judgment on fashion, taste, manners, and gender relations. The procedure of impersonal discussion gives private matters full public relevance, while allowing the participants in that discussion to have the kind of generality that had formerly been the privilege of the state or the church. The *Spectator* claims to be general, addressing everyone, merely on the basis of humanity. It is the voice of civil society.[35]

Like Dunton's *Athenian Mercury*, but with a much richer formal vocabulary, the *Spectator* developed a reflexivity about its own circulation, coordinating its readers' relations to other readers. It does not merely assert the fact of public circulation, though it does frequently allude to its own popularity; it includes feedback loops, both in the letters from readers real and imagined and in the members of the club and other devices. Essays refer to previous essays and to the reception of those essays; installments end with, and are sometimes wholly given over to, letters that are or purport to be readers' responses. The fictional persona of the Spectator himself represents the embodiment of a private reader: an observant but perversely mute wanderer ("I am frequently seen in the most publick Places, tho' there are not above half a dozen of my select Friends that know me" [no. 1], the essential stranger, "Mr. *what-d'ye-call-him*" [no. 4], witnessing in dumb privacy the whole social field, combining "all the Advantages of Company with all the Privileges of Solitude" [no. 131]). His club represents a model of the male reception context (constantly in need of supplementation by accounts of and letters from female readers). One is constantly reminded of "this great City inquiring Day by Day after these my Papers."[36] A repertoire of highly temporalized affects and interests — scandal, fascination, fashion, news addiction, mania, curiosity — are projected as the properties not

99

just of individuals but of the scene of circulation itself, without which such affects would lack resonance. This rhetoric represents the subjective mode of being attributed to the public. It describes private and individual acts of reading, but in such a way as to make temporally indexed circulation among strangers the immanent meaning and emotional resonance of those reading acts.

The *Spectator* first perfected the representation of its own circulation. It marks what can now be taken for granted: that public discourse must be circulated, not just emitted in one direction. Even mass media, which because of their heavy capitalization are conspicuously asymmetrical, take care to fake a reciprocity that they must overcome in order to succeed. Contemporary mass media have even more elaborate devices of the kind that Addison and Steele developed: viewer mail, call-in shows, 900-number polling, home-video shows, game-show contestants, town meetings, studio audiences, man-on-the-street interviews, and so on. These genres create feedback loops to characterize their own space of consumption. As with the *Spectator*, too, reflexivity is managed through affect and idiom as well; the *Spectator* essays comment on slang (for example, "jilts") in a way that attributes to folk usage the same historical present tense as the essays' circulation.[37] Mass culture laces its speech with catchphrases that suture it to informal speech, even though those catchphrases are often common in informal speech only because they were picked up from mass texts in the first place. In the United States, sports metaphors are obvious examples, as when politicians describe their speeches or proposals as slam dunks or home runs.

Sometimes the layering of reflexive postures toward circulation can be dizzyingly complex, as happened in 2001 when Budweiser advertisements turned the black street greeting "Whassup?" into a slogan. This "signature catch phrase," as the *New York Times* called it, once broadcast, could subsequently be "joked about on

talk shows, parodied on Web sites and mimicked in other com-
mercials." Ironically, all this repetition of "Whassup?" was understood not as new instances of the street greeting itself but as
references to the commercial. A relation to the mass circulation
of the phrase came to be part of the meaning of the phrase. That
this should happen, moreover, was the deliberate design of the advertising firm that produced the commercial — one DDB Worldwide, part of what is called Omnicom Group:

> The team uses sophisticated research and old-fashioned legwork —
> like checking out new art forms or going to underground film festi-
> vals — to anticipate what is about to become hip to its target audi-
> ence of mostly men in their 20's and 30's. The language, styles and
> attitudes it finds are then packaged in ad campaigns that are broad-
> cast so often that they become part of the public consciousness.[38]

The company sells this circulatory effect to its clients as "talk
value." When office workers use catchphrases to joke around the
coffee machine, they unwittingly realize the talk value that has
already been sold to the corporation whose products were advertised. Indeed, DDB Worldwide has registered the phrase "talk
value" as a trademark. As the phrase suggests, talk value allows a
structured but mobile interplay between the reflexivity of publics
(the talk) and the reflexivity of capital (the value). Neither is re-
ducible to the other, and the DDB strategy only works if the relation between the popular idiom and the sale of beer is indirect, a
process of mutual feedback experienced by individuals as a medium
for improvisation.

Public reflexivity and market reflexivity have been interarticu-
lated in a variety of ways from the beginning. In the case of the
Whig booksellers, consciousness of a public created a new and
expansive circulation for text commodities. In the *Spectator*, a

greater range of dialectical stances opened up as the reflex consciousness of a public turned its critical attention on the reflex consumption of commodities in such forms as fashion. In contemporary mass culture, the play between these different ways of rendering the field of circulation reflexive has created countless nuances for the performance of subjectivity. To take only the most obvious examples, we speak of a "mainstream," of "alternative" culture, of "crossover" trends, naming and evaluating stylistic affinities by characterizing the field in which they circulate.

Talk value has an affective quality. You don't just mechanically repeat signature catchphrases. You perform through them your social placement. Different social styles can be created through different levels of reflexivity in this performance. Too obvious parroting of catchphrases — if, for example, you walk into the office on the morning after Budweiser runs its commercial and grab the first opportunity to say "Whassup?" — can mark you in some contexts as square, unhip, a passive relay in the circulation. In other contexts, it could certify you as one of the gang, showing that you, too, were watching the show with everyone else. Stylistic affinities can perform many functions, of course, but in mass culture they always involve adopting a differential stance toward the field of their circulation. Characterizations of that field are the stuff of performed stances that can range from immersion to irony or aggressivity, in a way that always has some affective charge: hipness, normalcy, hilarity, currency, quaintness, freakishness, and so on. What is called "vernacular" performance is therefore in reality structured by a continually shifting field of artfulness in managing the reflexivity of mass circulation. (Many American critics, seeing only one side of this process, like to interpret such artfulness as evidence of a folk or popular style in the "appropriation" of mass culture; for them, this counts as evidence against the Frankfurt School analysis of mass culture.)

The use of such pseudo vernaculars or metavernaculars helps create the impression of a vital feedback loop despite the immense asymmetry of production and reception that defines mass culture. It helps sustain the legitimating sense that mass texts move through a space that is, after all, an informal lifeworld. That the maintenance of this feedback circuit so often takes the form of humor suggests that, as with all joking, there is a lively current of unease powering the wit. Unease, perhaps, on both sides of the recurring dialectic: to be hip is to fear the mass circulation that feeds on hipness and that in turn makes it possible; while to be normal (in the "mainstream") is to have anxiety about the counterpublics that define themselves through such distinctively embodied performance that one cannot lasso them back into general circulation without risking the humiliating exposure of inauthenticity.

In the *Spectator*, Essay 34 neatly illustrates how these feedback provisions combine with the punctual temporality of the diurnal form and an emergent ideology of polite sociability to produce the understanding of a public structured by its own discourse:

> The Club of which I am a Member, is very luckily compos'd of such Persons as are engag'd in different Ways of Life, and deputed as it were out of the most conspicuous Classes of Mankind: By this Means I am furnish'd with the greatest Variety of Hints and Materials, and know every thing that passes in the different Quarters and Divisions, not only of this great City, but of the whole Kingdom. My Readers too have the Satisfaction to find, that there is no Rank or Degree among them who have not their Representative in this Club, and that there is always some Body present who will take Care of their respective Interests, that nothing may be written or publish'd to the Prejudice or Infringement of their just Rights and Privileges.

Mr. Spectator relates that the members of the club have been relaying to him "several Remarks which they and others had made upon these my Speculations, as also with the various Success which they had met with among their several Ranks and Degrees of Readers." They act as his field reporters, allowing the *Spectator* to reflect on its own reception.

What follows is a fable of reading. Will Honeycomb, the ladies' man, reports that some ladies of fashion have been offended by criticisms of their taste; Andrew Freeport, the merchant, responds that those criticisms were well deserved, unlike those against merchants; the Templar defends those but objects to satires of the Inns of Court; and so on. Every member of the club inflects his reception of the essays with the interests that define the social class of which he is a typification. In the aggregate, each cancels out the others. It is left to the clergyman — a character who scarcely appears anywhere else in the essay series — to explain "the Use this Paper might be of to the Publick" in challenging the interests of the orders and ranks. The result is a sense of a *general* public, by definition not embodied in any person or class but realized by the scene of circulation as the reception context of a common object.

"In short," concludes Mr. Spectator, "If I meet with any thing in City, Court, or Country, that shocks Modesty or good Manners, I shall use my utmost Endeavours to make an Example of it." He continues:

> I must however intreat every particular Person, who does me the Honour to be a Reader of this Paper, never to think himself, or any one of his Friends or Enemies, aimed at in what is said: For I promise him, never to draw a faulty Character which does not fit at least a Thousand People; or to publish a single Paper, that is not written in the Spirit of Benevolence and with a Love to Mankind.

Steele here coaches his readers in the personal/impersonal generic conventions of public address: I never speak to you without speaking to a thousand others. This form of address is tightly knit up with a social imaginary: any character or trait I depict typifies a whole social stratum. Individual readers who participate in this discourse learn to place themselves, as characterized types, in a world of urbane social knowledge, while also ethically detaching themselves from the particular interests that typify them, turning themselves by means of a "Spirit of Benevolence" and "Love to Mankind" into the reading subjects of a widely circulating form.

And not just reading subjects. The achievement of this cultural form is to allow participants in its discourse to understand themselves as directly and actively belonging to a social entity that exists historically in secular time and has consciousness of itself, though it has no existence apart from the activity of its own discursive circulation. In some contexts, it can even be understood to act in the world, to claim moral authority, to be sovereign. A great deal must be postulated for the form to work in the world: not only the material conditions of a circulating medium, but appropriate reading or consuming practices, as well as a social imaginary in which stranger sociability could become ordinary, valuable, and in some ways normative. Such a normative horizon was, by the point of the *Spectator*, well articulated. An ethical disposition, a social imaginary, an extremely specialized set of formal conventions, and a temporality — each could seem to imply and follow from the others.

The discourse of a public is a linguistic form from which the social conditions of its own possibility are in large part derived. The magic by which discourse conjures a public into being, however, remains imperfect because of how much it must presuppose. And because many of the defining elements in the self-understanding of publics are to some extent always contradicted by practice, the sorcerer must continually cast spells against the darkness. A public seems to be self-organized by discourse but in fact requires preexisting forms and channels of circulation. It appears to be open to indefinite strangers but in fact selects participants by criteria of shared social space (though not necessarily territorial space), habitus, topical concerns, intergeneric references, and circulating intelligible forms (including idiolects or speech genres). These criteria inevitably have positive content. They enable confidence that the discourse will circulate along a real path, but they limit the extension of that path. Discourse addressed to a public seeks to extend its circulation — otherwise, the public dwindles to a group — yet the need to characterize the space of circulation means that it is simultaneously understood as having the content and differential belonging of a group, rather than simply being open to the infinite and unknowable potential of circulation among strangers. Reaching strangers is public discourse's primary orientation, but to make those unknown strangers into a public it must locate them as a social entity. Public discourse circulates, but it does so in struggle with its own conditions.

The *Spectator* is understood as circulating to indefinite strangers, but of course the choice of language and the organization of markets for print make it seem natural that those strangers will be English. The closing peroration of the essay coaches its readers in an ethical disposition of impartial publicness; but it is also the ethos of a social class. The essay's style — itself a landmark in the history of English prose — moderates all the interests and characters of its reception context, allowing a speech that can simultaneously address the merchant, the squire, the courtier, the servant, the lady; but it is also the marker of a social type (masculine bourgeois moral urbanity) itself. In these and similar ways, although the language addresses an impersonal, indefinite, and self-organized expanse of circulation, it also elaborates (and masks as unmarked humanity) a particular culture, its embodied way of life, its reading practices, its ethical conventions, its geography, its class and gender dispositions, and its economic organization (in which the serial essay circulates as it does because it is, after all, a commodity on a market).

The *Spectator* is not unusual in having these limitations. If anything, it is unusual in the degree of its social porousness, the range of voices that it makes audible, the number of contexts that it opens for transformation. Even in the best of cases, some friction inevitably obtains between public discourse and its environment, given the circularity in the conventions and postulates that make the social imaginary of the public work. To some degree, this friction is unavoidable because of the chicken-and-egg problem with which I began; the imaginary being of the public must be projected from already circulating discourse.

One result is a special kind of politics that is difficult to grasp in the usual framework of politics as a field of interest-bearing strategic actors in specific relations of power and subordination. In such a framework, the contradiction between the idea of a public and its realization might be said to be more or less ideological. Evidence will not be wanting for such a view. When, in Essay 34, the reading audience is characterized as "Mankind," we have a rather obvious example.[39] Because the positive identity of a public always remains partly covert — given the premises of self-organization through discourse, address to strangers, and membership through mere attention — the limitations imposed by its speech genres, medium, and presupposed social base are always in conflict with its own enabling postulates. When any public is taken to be *the* public, those limitations invisibly order the political world.

Many critiques of the idea of the public in modern thought rest on this covert content. It is one of the things people have in mind when they say, for example, that the public is essentially white or essentially male.[40] It has become customary, in the wake of arguments over Habermas's *Structural Transformation of the Public Sphere*, to lament or protest the arbitrary closures of the publics that came into being with the public sphere as their background. The peculiar dynamic of postulation and address by which public speech projects the social world has mainly been understood as ideology, domination, exclusion. With reason: the history of the public sphere abounds with evidence of struggle for domination through this means and the resulting bad faith of the dominant public culture. What the critiques tend to miss, however, is that the tension inherent in the form goes well beyond any strategy of domination. The projection of a public is a new, creative, and distinctively modern mode of power.

One consequence of this tension in the laws of public discourse is a problem of style. In addressing indefinite strangers, public discourse puts a premium on accessibility. But there is no infinitely accessible language, and to imagine that there should be is to miss other equally important needs of publics: to concretize the world in which discourse circulates, to offer its members direct and active membership through language, to place strangers on a shared footing. For these purposes, language must be concrete, making use of the vernaculars of its circulatory space. So, in publics, a double movement is always at work. Styles are mobilized, but they are also framed as styles. Sometimes the framing is hierarchical, a relation of marked to unmarked. Sometimes the result can be more relativizing. Quite commonly the result can be a double-voiced hybrid. Differential deployment of style is essential to the way public discourse creates the consciousness of stranger sociability. In this, it closely resembles the kind of double-voicing of speech genres classically analyzed by Bakhtin: "For the speakers . . . generic languages and professional jargons are directly intentional — they denote and express directly and fully, and are capable of expressing themselves without mediation; but outside, that is, for those not participating in the given purview, these languages may be treated as objects, as typifactions, as local color."[41] Bakhtin calls this the "critical interanimation of languages."[42]

Perhaps for this reason, the *Spectator* obsessively represents scenes on the margin of its own public, places where its own language might circulate but that it cannot (or will not) capture as its addressee. One example is a hysterical moment in *Spectator* no. 217. Mr. Spectator has received a letter, signed "Kitty Termagant," which turns out to be another of the many letters describing clubs similar to the Spectator's — in this case, the Club of She-Romps. Its members meet once a week, at night, in a room hired for the purpose (in other words, a place that is significantly public, though also secluded from open view). "We are no sooner come together," writes Kitty, "than we throw off all that Modesty and Reservedness with which our Sex are obliged to disguise themselves in publick Places. I am not able to express the Pleasure we enjoy from ten at Night till four in the Morning, in being as rude as you Men can be, for your Lives. As our Play runs high the Room is immediately filled with broken Fans, torn Petticoats, lappets of Head-dresses, Flounces, Furbelows, Garters, and Working-Aprons."[43]

The She-Romps seem to be designed almost as an inverted image of the Spectator's own club. His is all male, theirs female. His is regulated by an ethic of bourgeois moral urbanity — differences of class and self-interest correct each other through the general discussion. Theirs throws off the restraints of decorum. Differences are not balanced through equable conversation but unleashed through raw physical play. It's a bitch fight. And although men might have their own pleasures in fantasizing such a scene, the Spectator more than hints at some antipathy. Kitty Termagant tells

us that the She-Romps refer to the rags and tatters of their dis-
carded clothing as "*dead Men.*" [44]

Women, of course, are hardly excluded directly from the public of the *Spectator*. Quite the contrary. In the fourth paper, Mr.
Spectator announces: "I shall take it for the greatest Glory of my
Work, if among reasonable Women this Paper may furnish *Tea-
Table Talk.*" [45] Women readers are crucial to the *Spectator*'s sense
of its public, and gender relations are made the subject of critical
reflection in a way that must have felt dramatic and transformative. The *Spectator* represents the Club of She-Romps to highlight,
by contrast, the urbanity and restraint of its own social ethic. The
Spectator neither excludes women outright nor frankly asserts
male superiority. He does, however, display what he regards as the
essentially unpublic character of the She-Romps' interaction. He
uses an uneasy mix of mocking humor, male fear, and urbane
scandal to remind the reader of the polite sociability required for
his own confidence in a public composed of strangers.

The She-Romps cannot afford that confidence. For this and
other reasons, the Club of She-Romps cannot really be called a
public at all. It is a finite club of members known to one another,
who would not be able to secure the freedom to meet without the
security of mutual knowledge. Like most gossip, which is strictly
regulated by a sense of group membership and social position, it
is not oriented to strangers. The She-Romps are unpublic not just
in being a closed club; the Spectator's club, after all, is equally
closed. Yet we are given to understand that it cannot open onto
a public, the way the Spectator's club does within his essays. It
expresses a style of sociability too embodied, too aggressional,
and too sexualized to be imagined as the indefinite circulation of
discourse among strangers. These women are not content to be
"reasonable Women" whose highest mode of publicness is "*Tea-
Table Talk*"; they want their publicness to be modeled on some-

thing other than mere private acts of reading. "We are no sooner come together," writes Kitty, "than we throw off all that Modesty and Reservedness with which our Sex are obliged to disguise themselves in publick Places." It is this refusal of any familiar norm for stranger sociability rather than simple femaleness that makes them a counterimage to the public.

The She-Romps, however, clearly want to alter the norms of "publick Places" so as to allow themselves the same physical freedoms as men, as well as an ability to meet with other women who share their history of frustration. They aspire to a public or quasi-public physicality. But dominant gender norms are such that this quasi-public physicality looks like intimacy out of place. It looks most antipublic when it looks like sexuality: "Once a month we *Demolish a Prude*, that is, we get some queer formal Creature in among us, and unrig her in an instant. Our last Month's Prude was so armed and fortified in Whale-bone and Buckram that we had much ado to come at her, but you would have died with laughing to have seen how the sober awkard [*sic*] thing looked, when she was forced out of her Intrenchments."[46] How exactly *did* the queer creature look? Thrilled? Appalled? Or simply speechless? Kitty says no more. The scene can be taken as representing the necessary involvement of strangers in the subjective life of any public, but with its tone raised first to an anxious pitch and then to muteness by the idea that such involvement might also be corporeal and intimate.

Interestingly, it is at just this moment that Kitty invites the Spectator to open her club's scenes to public discourse as he does with his own: "In short, Sir, 'tis impossible to give you a true Notion of our Sport, unless you would come one Night amongst us; and tho' it be directly against the Rules of our Society to admit a Male Visitant, we repose so much Confidence in your Silence and Taciturnity, that 'twas agreed by the whole Club, at our last

Meeting, to give you Entrance for one Night as a Spectator."[47] The women seek, in effect, to open the transformative intent of their coming together onto the critical estrangement of public discourse.

The Spectator refuses. "I do not at present find in my self any Inclination to venture my Person with her and her romping Companions...and should apprehend being *Demolished* as much as the *Prude*." [48] This is a bit of a joke, since Mr. Spectator has only a ghost's body to demolish; he is an allegorical form of the reading eye. But he has something to demolish nonetheless: his own enabling ideology of polite publicness, the norms that offer confidence in circulation among strangers.

The *Spectator* essays contain many odd and diverting moments like this one, but few that say more about its public. One has to read this passage only slightly against the grain to see it as a ghost image of a counterpublic: it is a scene where a dominated group aspires to re-create itself as a public and in doing so finds itself in conflict not only with the dominant social group but with the norms that constitute the dominant culture as a public. The *Spectator* goes so far as to represent the scene in order to clarify the norms that establish its own confidence. It takes the She-Romps as a joke because it considers its own norms of sociability to be obvious and unbreakable. The challenge it so comically imagines against those norms would soon enough find actual expression. Even in the years of the essays' appearance, the public places and stranger sociability of London were already giving rise to clubs of all kinds of she-romps, including the so-called molly houses where something like a modern homosexual culture was developing — though it was not until rather later that such scenes could really articulate themselves through discourse as a freely circulating public.[49]

Over the past three centuries, many such scenes have organized themselves as publics, and because they differ markedly in one way or another from the premises that allow the dominant culture to understand itself as a public, they have come to be called counterpublics. Yet we cannot understand counterpublics very well if we fail to see that there are contradictions and perversities inherent in the organization of all publics that are not captured by critiques of the dominant public's exclusions or ideological limitations. Counterpublics are publics, too. They work by many of the same circular postulates. It might even be claimed that, like dominant publics, they are ideological in that they provide a sense of active belonging that masks or compensates for the real powerlessness of human agents in capitalist society — though I merely leave this question aside. What interests me here is the odd social imaginary established by the ethic of estrangement and social poesis in public address. The cultural form of the public transforms She-Romps and Spectators alike.

In a public, indefinite address and self-organized discourse disclose a lived world whose arbitrary closure both enables that discourse and is contradicted by it. Public discourse, in the nature of its address, abandons the security of its positive, given audience. It promises to address anybody. It commits itself in principle to the possible participation of any stranger. It therefore puts at risk the concrete world that is its given condition of possibility. This is its fruitful perversity. Public discourse postulates a circulatory field of estrangement that it must then struggle to capture as an addressable entity. No form with such a structure could be very stable. The projective character of public discourse, in which each characterization of the circulatory path becomes material for new estrangements and recharacterizations, is an engine for (not necessarily progressive) social mutation.

Public discourse, in other words, is poetic. By this I mean not just that it is self-organizing, a kind of entity created by its own discourse, or even that this space of circulation is taken to be a social entity, but that in order for this to happen all discourse or performance addressed to a public must characterize the world in which it attempts to circulate and it must attempt to realize that world through address.[50]

7. A public is poetic world making.
There is no speech or performance addressed to a public that does not try to specify in advance, in countless highly condensed ways, the lifeworld of its circulation: not just through its discursive claims — of the kind that can be said to be oriented to understanding — but through the pragmatics of its speech genres, idioms, stylistic markers, address, temporality, mise-en-scène, citational field, interlocutory protocols, lexicon, and so on. Its circulatory fate is the realization of that world. Public discourse says not only "Let a public exist" but "Let it have this character, speak this way, see the world in this way." It then goes in search of confirmation that such a public exists, with greater or lesser success — success being further attempts to cite, circulate, and realize the world understanding it articulates. Run it up the flagpole and see who salutes. Put on a show and see who shows up.

This performative dimension of public discourse, however, is routinely misrecognized. Public speech lies under the necessity of addressing its public as already existing real persons. It cannot work by frankly declaring its subjunctive-creative project. Its success depends on the recognition of participants and their further circulatory activity, and people do not commonly recognize themselves as virtual projections. They recognize themselves only as being already the persons they are addressed as being and as already belonging to the world that is condensed in their discourse.

The poetic function of public discourse is misrecognized for a second reason as well, noted above in another context: in the dominant tradition of the public sphere, address to a public is ideologized as rational-critical dialogue. The circulation of public discourse is consistently imagined, both in folk theory and in sophisticated political philosophy, as dialogue or discussion among already co-present interlocutors — as within Mr. Spectator's club. The prevailing image is something like parliamentary forensics. I have already noted that this folk theory enables the constitutive circularity of publics to disappear from consciousness, because publics are thought to be real persons in dyadic author/reader interactions rather than multigeneric circulation. I have also noted that the same ideologization enables the idea that publics can have volitional agency: they exist to deliberate and then decide. Here the point is that the perception of public discourse as conversation obscures the importance of the poetic functions of both language and corporeal expressivity in giving a particular shape to publics. The public is thought to exist empirically and to require persuasion rather than poesis. Public circulation is understood as rational discussion writ large.

This constitutive misrecognition of publics relies on a particular language ideology. Discourse is understood to be propositionally summarizable; the poetic or textual qualities of any utterance are disregarded in favor of sense. Acts of reading, too, are understood to be replicable and uniform.[51] So are opinions, which is why private reading seems to be directly connected to the sovereign power of public opinion. Just as sense can be propositionally summarized, opinions can be held, transferred, restated indefinitely. (The essential role played by this kind of transposition in the modern social imaginary might help to explain why modern philosophy has been obsessed with referential semantics and fixity.) Other aspects of discourse, including affect and expressivity, are not thought to be fungible in the same way. Doubtless the development of such a language ideology helped to enable the confidence in the stranger sociability of public circulation. Strangers are less strange if you can trust them to read as you read or if the sense of what they say can be fully abstracted from the way they say it.

I also suspect that the development of the social imaginary of publics, as a relation among strangers projected from private readings of circulating texts, has exerted for the past three centuries a powerful gravity on the conception of the human, elevating what are understood to be the faculties of the private reader as the essential (rational-critical) faculties of man. If you know and are intimately associated with strangers to whom you are directly related only through the means of reading, opining, arguing, and witnessing, then it might seem natural that other faculties recede from salience at the highest levels of social belonging. The modern hierarchy of faculties and its imagination of the social are mutually implying. The highly conventional understanding of readerly activity, moreover, has now been institutionalized. The critical discourse of the public corresponds as sovereign to the superintending power of the state. So the dimensions of language singled out in the ideology of rational-critical discussion acquire prestige and power. Publics more overtly oriented in their self-understandings to the poetic-expressive dimensions of language, including artistic publics and many counterpublics, lack the power to transpose themselves to the generality of the state. Along the entire chain of equations in the public sphere — from local acts of reading or scenes of speech to a general horizon of public opinion and its critical opposition to state power — the pragmatics of public discourse must be systematically blocked from view.

Publics have acquired their importance to modern life because of the ease of those transpositions upward to the level of the state. Once the background assumptions of public opinion are in place, all publics are part of *the* public. Though essentially imaginary projections from local exchanges or acts of reading and therefore infinite in number, they are often thought of as a unitary space.

This assumption gains force from the postulated relation between public opinion and the state. A critical opposition to the state, supervising both executive and legislative power, confers on countless acts of opining the unity of public opinion; those acts have both a common object and a common agency of supervision and legitimation.

The unity of the public, however, is also ideological. It depends on the stylization of the reading act as transparent and replicable; it depends on an arbitrary social closure (through language, idiolect, genre, medium, and address) to contain its potentially infinite extension; it depends on institutionalized forms of power to realize the agency attributed to the public; and it depends on a hierarchy of faculties that allows some activities to count as public or general and others to be merely personal, private, or particular. Some publics, for these reasons, are more likely than others to stand in for *the* public, to frame their address as the universal discussion of the people.

But what of the publics that make no attempt to present themselves this way? There are as many shades of difference among publics as there are in modes of address, style, and spaces of circulation. Many might be thought of as subpublics, or specialized publics, focused on particular interests, professions, or locales. The public of *Field & Stream*, for example, does not take itself to be the national people or humanity in general; the magazine addresses only those with an interest in hunting and fishing, who in varying degrees participate in a (male) subculture of hunters and fishermen. Yet nothing in the mode of address or in the projected horizon of this subculture requires its participants to cease for a moment to think of themselves as members of the general public; indeed, they might well consider themselves its most representative members.

Other publics mark themselves off unmistakably from any

general or dominant public. Their members are understood to be not merely a subset of the public but constituted through a conflictual relation to the dominant public. In an influential 1992 article, Nancy Fraser observed that when public discourse is understood only as "a single, comprehensive, overarching public," members of subordinated groups "have no arenas for deliberation among themselves about their needs, objectives, and strategies." In fact, Fraser writes, "members of subordinated social groups — women, workers, peoples of color, and gays and lesbians — have repeatedly found it advantageous to constitute alternative publics."[52] She calls these "subaltern counterpublics," by which she means "parallel discursive arenas where members of subordinated social groups invent and circulate counterdiscourses to formulate oppositional interpretations of their identities, interests, and needs."[53]

Fraser here names an important phenomenon. But what makes such a public "counter" or "oppositional"? Is its oppositional character a function of its content alone; that is, its claim to be oppositional? In this case, we might simply call it a subpublic, like that of *Field & Stream*, with the difference that a thematic discussion of political opposition is more likely to be found in it. There would be no difference of kind, or of formal mediation, or of discourse pragmatics, between counterpublics and any other publics. Fraser's description of what counterpublics do — "formulate oppositional interpretations of their identities, interests, and needs" — sounds like the classically Habermasian description of rational-critical publics, with the word "oppositional" inserted. Fraser's principal example is "the late-twentieth-century U.S. feminist subaltern counterpublic, with its variegated array of journals, bookstores, publishing companies, film and video distribution networks, lecture series, research centers, academic programs, conferences, conventions, festivals, and local meeting places."[54] This description aptly suggests the way a public is a multicontextual space of circulation, organized not by a place or an institution but by the circulation of discourse. This is true of any public, including counterpublics. Fraser writes that the feminist counterpublic is distinguished by a special idiom for social reality, including such terms as "sexism," "sexual harassment," and "marital, date, and acquaintance rape." This idiom can now be found anywhere — not always embodying a feminist intention but circulating as common terminology. Is the feminist counterpublic distinguished by anything other than its reform program?

Furthermore, why would counterpublics of this variety be limited to "subalterns"? How are they different from the publics of U.S. Christian fundamentalism, or youth culture, or artistic bohemianism? Each of these is a similarly complex metatopical space for the circulation of discourse; each is a scene for developing oppositional interpretations of its members' identities, interests, and needs. They are structured by different dispositions or protocols from those that obtain elsewhere in the culture, making different assumptions about what can be said or what goes without saying.

In the sense of the term I am advocating here, such publics are indeed counterpublics, and in a stronger sense than simply comprising subalterns with a reform program. A counterpublic maintains at some level, conscious or not, an awareness of its subordinate status. The cultural horizon against which it marks itself off is not just a general or wider public but a dominant one. And the conflict extends not just to ideas or policy questions but to the speech genres and modes of address that constitute the public or to the hierarchy among media. The discourse that constitutes it is not merely a different or alternative idiom but one that in other contexts would be regarded with hostility or with a sense of indecorousness. (This is why the She-Romps seem to anticipate counterpublicness: "We throw off all that Modesty and Reservedness with which our Sex are obliged to disguise themselves in publick Places.") Friction against the dominant public forces the poetic-expressive character of counterpublic discourse to become salient to consciousness.

Like all publics, a counterpublic comes into being through an address to indefinite strangers. (This is one significant difference between a counterpublic and a community or group.) But counterpublic discourse also addresses those strangers as being not just anybody. They are socially marked by their participation in this kind of discourse; ordinary people are presumed not to want to be mistaken for the kind of person who would participate in this kind of talk or be present in this kind of scene. Addressing indefinite strangers, in a magazine or a sermon, has a peculiar meaning when you know in advance that most people will be unwilling to read a gay magazine or go to a black church. In some contexts, the code-switching of bilingualism might do similar work of keeping the counterpublic horizon salient — just as the linguistic fragmentation of many postcolonial settings creates resistance to the idea of a sutured space of circulation.

Within a gay or queer counterpublic, for example, no one is in the closet: the presumptive heterosexuality that constitutes the closet for individuals in ordinary speech is suspended. But this circulatory space, freed from heteronormative speech protocols, is itself marked by that very suspension: speech that addresses any participant as queer will circulate up to a point, at which it is certain to meet intense resistance. It might therefore circulate in special, protected venues, in limited publications. The individual struggle with stigma is transposed, as it were, to the conflict between modes of publicness. The expansive nature of public address will seek to keep moving that frontier for a queer public, to seek more and more places to circulate where people will recognize themselves in its address; but no one is likely to be unaware of the risk and conflict involved.

In some cases, such as fundamentalism or certain kinds of youth culture, participants are not subalterns for any reason other than their participation in the counterpublic discourse. In others, a socially stigmatized identity might be predicated; but in such cases, a public of subalterns is only a counterpublic when its participants are addressed in a counterpublic way — as, for example, African-Americans willing to speak in what is regarded as a racially marked idiom. The subordinate status of a counterpublic does not simply reflect identities formed elsewhere; participation in such a public is one of the ways by which its members' identities are formed and transformed. A hierarchy or stigma is the assumed background of practice. One enters at one's own risk.

Counterpublic discourse is far more than the expression of subaltern culture and far more than what some Foucauldians like to call "reverse discourse." Fundamentally mediated by public forms, counterpublics incorporate the personal/impersonal address and expansive estrangement of public speech as conditions of their common world. Perhaps nothing demonstrates the importance of discursive publics in the modern social imaginary more than this — that even the counterpublics that challenge modernity's social hierarchy of faculties do so by projecting the space of discursive circulation among strangers as a social entity and in doing so fashion their own subjectivities around the requirements of public circulation and stranger sociability.[55]

If I address a queer public, or one of fellow She-Romps, I don't simply express the way my friends and I live. I commit myself, and the fate of my world-making project, to circulation among indefinite others. However much my address to them might be laden with intimate affect, it must also be extended impersonally, available for co-membership on the basis of mere attention. My world must be that of strangers. Counterpublics are "counter" to the extent that they try to supply different ways of imagining stranger sociability and its reflexivity; as publics, they remain oriented to stranger circulation in a way that is not just strategic but constitutive of membership and its affects. As it happens, an understanding of queerness has been developing in recent decades that is suited to just this necessity; a culture is developing in which intimate relations and the sexual body can in fact be understood as projects for transformation among strangers. (At the same time, a lesbian and gay public has been reshaped so as to ignore or refuse the counterpublic character that has marked its history.)[56] So also in youth culture, coolness both mediates a difference from dominant publics and constitutes that difference as the subjective form of stranger sociability. Public discourse imposes a field of tensions within which any world-making project must articulate itself. To the extent I want that world to be one in which embodied sociability, affect, and play have a more defining role than they do in the opinion-transposing frame of rational-critical dialogue, those tensions will be acutely felt.

I cannot say in advance what romping will feel like in my public of She-Romps. Publicness is just this space of coming together that discloses itself in interaction. The world of strangers that public discourse makes must be made of further circulation and recharacterization over time; it cannot simply be aggregated from units that I can expect to be similar to mine. I risk its fate. This necessity of risked estrangement, though essential to all publics, becomes especially salient in counterpublic discourse and is registered in its ethical-political imagination. Dominant publics are by definition those that can take their discourse pragmatics and their lifeworlds for granted, misrecognizing the indefinite scope of their expansive address as universality or normalcy. Counterpublics are spaces of circulation in which it is hoped that the poesis of scene making will be transformative, not replicative merely.

Counterpublics face another obstacle as well. One of the most striking features of publics, in the modern public sphere, is that they can in some contexts acquire agency. Not only is participation understood as active, at the level of the individual whose uptake helps to constitute a public; it is possible sometimes to attribute agency to the virtual corporate entity created by the entire space of circulation. Publics act historically. They are said to rise up, to speak, to reject false promises, to demand answers, to change sovereigns, to support troops, to give mandates for change, to be satisfied, to scrutinize public conduct, to take role models, to deride counterfeits. It's difficult to imagine the modern world without the ability to attribute agency to publics, though doing so is an extraordinary fiction. It requires us, for example, to understand the ongoing circulatory time of public discourse as though it were discussion leading up to a decision.

The attribution of agency to publics works in most cases because of the direct transposition from private reading acts to the sovereignty of opinion. All of the verbs for public agency are verbs for private reading, transposed upward to the aggregate of readers. Readers may scrutinize, ask, reject, opine, decide, judge, and so on. Publics can do exactly these things. And nothing else. Publics — unlike mobs or crowds — are incapable of any activity that cannot be expressed through such a verb. Activities of reading that do not fit the ideology of reading as silent, private, replicable decoding — curling up, mumbling, fantasizing, gesticulating, ventriloquizing, writing marginalia, and so on — also find no counterparts in public agency.

Counterpublics tend to be those in which this ideology of reading does not have the same privilege. It might be that embodied sociability is too important to them; they might not be organized by the hierarchy of faculties that elevates rational-critical reflection as the self-image of humanity; they might depend more heavily on performance spaces than on print; it might be that they cannot so easily suppress from consciousness their own creative-expressive function. How, then, will they imagine their agency? Can a public of She-Romps romp?

It is in fact possible to imagine that almost any characterization of discursive acts might be attributed to a public. A queer public might be one that throws shade, prances, disses, acts up, carries on, longs, fantasizes, throws fits, mourns, "reads." To take such attributions of public agency seriously, however, we would need to inhabit a culture with a different language ideology, a different social imaginary. It is difficult to say what such a world would be like. It might need to be one with a different role for state-based thinking, because it might be only through its imaginary coupling with the state that a public acts. This is one of the things that happens when alternative publics are said to be social movements: they acquire agency in relation to the state. They enter the temporality of politics and adapt themselves to the performatives of rational-critical discourse. For many counterpublics, to do so is to cede the original hope of transforming not just policy but the space of public life itself.

CHAPTER THREE

Styles of Intellectual Publics

In the opening scene of George Orwell's *1984*, the horror of totalitarianism is driven home to the reader by — of all things — the experience of writer's block. The main character, Winston Smith, has just sat down under the glare of the all-seeing tele-screen, intending to begin a diary. He falters. A tremor goes "through his bowels." He feels helpless. "For whom, it suddenly occurred to him to wonder, was he writing this diary?"

Winston's choice of genre, the diary, is perversely apt to illustrate the problem of audience. Perversely, because the addressee of a diary is that unique individual about whom most is known and whose sympathetic response can be taken for granted: oneself. How could anyone, even in the most ruthlessly totalitarian regime, lack an audience for a diary? But even in a diary, one never writes simply to oneself in the present. At the very least, one addresses one's retrospective reading at some point in the future. One therefore addresses oneself as a partial stranger, one who will have forgotten or will have been caught up in a different phase of life and will have become, by consequence, different. And thus oneself comes to stand for posterity, and for a posterity partly brought into being by this act of writing.

It might be that a diary is addressed to others entirely, to an

unborn posterity, and this in fact is how Winston mentally answers his question: "For the future, for the unborn." But this, too,
he finds unsatisfying:

> For the first time the magnitude of what he had undertaken came
> home to him. How could you communicate with the future? It was
> of its nature impossible. Either the future would resemble the pre-
> sent in which case it would not listen to him, or it would be different
> from it, and his predicament would be meaningless.
>
> For some time he sat gazing stupidly at the paper. The telescreen
> had changed over to strident military music. It was curious that he
> seemed not merely to have lost the power of expressing himself, but
> even to have forgotten what it was that he had originally intended to
> say.[1]

Writing in this scene comes to seem impossible because the diary
can have no concretely imagined public, present or future. The
totalitarian state, with its godlike control of media, has eliminated
the civil-society context without which neither public nor private
life can have its modern meaning. The diarist's blockage illustrates
the lack of both. Winston has no privacy because he is visible to
the watching telescreen, and when he puts his notebook away in a
drawer, he knows it is useless to hide it. But he is also deprived of
publicness. That means not only an audience to write for in the
present but, more telling, the sense of a future that might be capable of comprehension, but different. "Either the future would
resemble the present in which case it would not listen to him, or
it would be different from it, and his predicament would be
meaningless." What he requires is a near future, linked to him by a
chain of continuous transformation. Even a diary, the most private
of all forms, requires this hope as its condition of possibility.
Finally, at the end of the scene, Winston arrives at a resolution:

He was a lonely ghost uttering a truth that nobody would ever hear. But so long as he uttered it, in some obscure way the continuity was not broken. It was not by making yourself heard but by staying sane that you carried on the human heritage. He went back to the table, dipped his pen, and wrote:

> To the future or to the past, to a time when thought is free, when men are different from one another and do not live alone.[2]

The public sphere here becomes purely imaginary; or, we might say, internalized as humanity. In order to write even a diary, Winston must imagine the ability to address partial strangers — men who are different and do not live alone. When he turns this ability into an internal freedom, able to dispense with the need to be heard, he begins to speak directly to humanity — in an effect that could aptly be called lyric, since Winston addresses humanity only in the absence of any actual context of address.

Isn't the imaginary character of such a general address necessarily its weakness? The diary has no place to go except into the hands of the police. Its address can only be internal projection. It has no readers, no scene of circulation. It stands for the pure wish that such a scene exist, that it might be oriented — as in fact it cannot be — to a horizon of difference. Its rhetorical addressee is only a placeholder for others and merely marking the idea of a sanity that could be confirmed through the exchange of perspectives.

That this image of writing should be the ghost of freedom makes it a striking image of a frustration that I think is widely felt. Orwell presents it only as a dystopia of totalitarianism. The extreme conditions of the novel would be hard to realize outside the most frozen gulag; 1984 is therefore easier to read as the negative image against which liberal society defines itself than as a plausible critique of existing alternatives. Orwell's dystopia stirs readers because the frustration it asks them to imagine is common enough not just behind the old Iron Curtain but here in the land of freedom, under civil-society conditions, whenever the available genres and publics of possible address do not readily lend themselves to a world-making project. Anyone who wants to transform the conditions of publicness, or through publicness transform the possible orientations to life, is in a position resembling Orwell's diarist.

For whom does one write or speak? Where is one's public? These questions can never be answered in advance, since language addressed to a public must circulate among strangers; neither can they be dismissed, though the answers necessarily remain mostly implicit. One does not stand nakedly to address humanity. Every entry assumes an already recognizable form, a discussion already under way, a discourse already in circulation, a medium, a genre, a style, and, for what counts as politics in modernity, a public to be addressed. People often say, when they are dissatisfied with extant publics, that they write only for themselves; at best, this can be only a lazy, shorthand expression, even for diarists. Every sentence is populated with the voices of others, living and dead, and is carried to whatever destination it has not by the force of intention or address but by the channels laid down in discourse. These requirements often have a politics of their own, and it may well be that their limitations are not to be easily overcome by strong will, broad mind, earnest heart, or ironic reflection. To speak in a certain way is to be typed as a speaker. To publish in a certain venue is to orient oneself to its circulation, as a fate.

It might very well be that extant forms and venues will accommodate many political aims. But what if they do not? What if one hopes to transform the possible contexts of speech? Since such a hope is likely, by its very nature, to be less than fully articulate, I suspect it is more common than anyone imagines. One cannot conjure a public into being by force of will. The desire to have a different public, a more accommodating addressee, therefore confronts one with the circularity inherent in all publics: public language addresses a public as a social entity, but that entity exists only by virtue of being addressed. It seems inevitable that the world to which one belongs, the scene of one's activity, will be determined at least in part by the way one addresses it. In modernity, therefore, an extraordinary burden of world making comes to be borne above all by style.

Recent interest in the idea of the public intellectual suggests, I think, just such a blocked wish, a desire to transform the available contexts of speech and indeed of publicness. So does the ongoing preoccupation, voiced by journalists and academics, with the style of left academic theory. When people complain, as many do, that intellectuals are not writing clearly enough, their yardstick of good style often turns out to be not just grammatical or aesthetic but political. After all, they do not want elegance of just any variety. They do not wish that academics should write beautifully in the mode of, say, Ronald Firbank or Friedrich Nietzsche. The incomparable prose style of Michel Foucault — densely suggestive, both technical and poetic — far from being their ideal of rigorous style, is more likely to serve as an example of writing that is too difficult to be effective. They want language that will bring a certain public into being, and they have an idea of what style will work. The question of style, at any rate, entails a worry about the nature and duties of the intellectual.

The connection is made explicit by many critics of left academics in the humanities, including Pollitt, Martha Nussbaum, Russell Jacoby, and James Miller. Opaque writing is said by these writers to indicate contempt for those whom one might persuade and thus to result in a hollow substitute for political engagement, no matter how radical the claims of the writing. Pollitt, for one, has argued that when intellectuals write for themselves, the result is "a pseudo-politics, in which everything is claimed in the name of revolution and democracy and equality and anti-authoritarianism, and nothing is risked, nothing, except maybe a bit of harmless cross-dressing, is even expected to happen outside the classroom." Pollitt's principal target here is Judith Butler; hence the reference to cross-dressing — though anyone who takes cross-dressing as a metaphor for harmless and risk-free entertainment has never done much drag in public. For the record, I think there is a significant element of truth in Pollitt's argument, and I'll come back to it; for the moment, I am concerned to show how the issue is distorted when it is taken to be one of clarity.

The possibility I would like to raise here is that those who write opaque left theory might very well feel that they are in a position analogous to Orwell's diarist's: writing to a public that does not yet exist, and finding that their language can circulate only in channels hostile to it, they write in a manner designed to be a placeholder for a future public. At stake here is the question of how, by what rhetoric, one might bring a public into being when extant modes of address and intelligibility seem themselves to be a problem.

A small irony of the recent polemics is that Orwell himself has often been cited as the example of writing that is, as all writing should be in the view of some critics, oriented to the largest possible audience. In a recent essay in *Lingua Franca*, James Miller approvingly echoes Pollitt's attack and points out that it has become common among critics who share this view to cite Orwell as a model. Orwell, as they understand him, represents the idea that the writer is obliged to write with the greatest possible transparency, coming as close as possible to an address to all persons. Style, in this argument, is seen as determining the size of the audience, which in turn is seen as determining the potential political result. Orwell illustrates not only the principle of a clear style but the entire chain of reasoning that leads from style to political engagement. "That he was staggeringly successful in reaching the largest possible public, in a way that very few twentieth-century writers have been," Miller writes, is indicated by the "simple" fact that he "has sold, between *Animal Farm* and *Nineteen Eighty-Four*, more than 40 million books in sixty languages which is, according to John Rodden, 'more than any pair of books by a serious or popular postwar author.'"[3] (You can almost hear the Berlin Wall being brought down, like the walls of Jericho, by the chirping of the cash registers at Barnes & Noble.)

Does Orwell really stand for the idea that accessible style leads to mass markets and therefore to effective politics? He himself emphasizes, in "Politics and the English Language," that his ideal of clarity in thought "is not concerned with fake simplicity and the attempt to make written English colloquial." I have my doubts about his definition of precision: "What is above all needed is to let the meaning choose the word, and not the other way about." It is possible to describe the phenomenon that gives force to this idea without the intentionalist semantics to which Orwell here falls prey. Yet he is making a point about the difficulty of precision and not, as is generally implied in current polemic, about the need for a populist idiom in search of a numerically extensive audience.[4]

The image of forty million copies of Orwell's books lighting up the UPC scanners of the free world certainly contrasts oddly with Orwell's own image of Winston's diary, hidden in a drawer, with a speck of dust carefully placed on top so that it will be possible to tell when the police have read it. "It was not by making yourself heard but by staying sane that you carried on the human heritage." Somehow Orwell has come to stand for the opposite of this sentiment — that carrying on the human heritage requires that one be heard by as many people as possible.

We might also read the diary scene, and its intense melancholy, as an unrecognized allegory of the displacement of the writer by the technologies of the mass. There is something unmistakably nostalgic in Winston's fetishization of the cream laid paper, the nib of the pen, writing by hand — a fetishism echoed in that placement of the piece of dust on the cover and by the materiality of every piece of writing described for the remainder of the novel. This is not the image of writing that Orwell's current advocates have in mind; its desperate fetishism suggests that Orwell himself worries about the estrangement of mass publics, which appear in the novel in drag as totalitarianism.

In response to the polemic against the style of left academic theory, Judith Butler has frequently invoked Theodor Adorno's *Minima Moralia* — a much more explicit commentary on the estrangement of mass publics. Her appeal to Adorno is the basis for the conceit of Miller's *Lingua Franca* essay, which discusses the debate over clarity in left academic theory by comparing Orwell and Adorno, contemporaries who, in Miller's view, represent antithetical understandings of the politics of style. Adorno, however, fares no better in this exchange of polemics than does Orwell.

Butler cites Adorno to the effect that common sense is an unreliable standard for intellectual writing. The apparent clarity of common sense is corrupt with ideology and can only be countered by defamiliarization in thought and language. The task of the intellectual is to disclose all the forms of distortion, error, and domination that have been embedded in the current version of common sense. As she points out, views that now strike us as grotesque have often been graced with such immediate comprehension that they hardly needed to be stated at all. The rightness of slavery and the subordination of women are only the most politically salient among many other gruesome examples. Common sense is often enough unjust. Language that takes us outside the usual frame of reference, teaching us to see or think in new ways, can be a necessary means to a more just world. And to the degree that our commonsense perceptions contain distortion, just so far will the effort of reimagining seem difficult, even (to many) unclear.

This is a forceful argument, though one might object that the need for unfamiliar thought is not the same as the need for unfamiliar language. There is a long tradition of argument for both. Dissent from the pressure of unexamined common sense is a cardinal principle of the Enlightenment. For most Enlightenment intellectuals, the idea was to create a new, more reflective — and therefore more just — common sense. And at least since Romanticism, there has also been a long history of skepticism about the possibility of pure and universal clarity, given the arduousness of the vision called for, or about the idea that reflection alone will produce insight.

Indeed, Butler did not need to appeal to so suspiciously foreign an authority as the Frankfurt School on this point; a very similar argument lies at the core of American Transcendentalism. Henry David Thoreau, who is taken in some quarters to be nearly a byword for epigrammatic clarity, had nothing but scorn for common sense and the journalistic demand that one write for it. "It is a ridiculous demand which England and America make, that you shall speak so that they can understand you," he writes at the end of *Walden*. "Why level downward to our dullest perception always, and praise that as common sense? The commonest sense is the sense of men asleep, which they express by snoring."[5] Thoreau had his own reasons for distrusting common sense and its clarity. The commonsensical legitimacy of slavery was one. He also thought that true perceptions must be poetic, transformative, even transgressive; any true thought must wake you out of common sense. This he took to be a demand on style as well as thought.

Thinkers who aspire to expand the realm of the thinkable can hardly be expected to avoid experiments of usage. His call for defamiliarizing language contains both a classic Enlightenment wish (since "men asleep" need to be awakened from the sleep of common sense) and a more Romantic conviction that the result could never look like simple clear reasoning, which would address the rational faculties only. Hence the need for literary language.

Adorno distrusts common canons of clarity for reasons that encompass Thoreau's but go further on the strength of a different kind of argument. "A writer will find that the more precisely, conscientiously, appropriately he expresses himself," writes Adorno, "the more obscure the literary result is thought, whereas a loose and irresponsible formulation is at once rewarded with certain understanding." Adorno did not think this was necessarily or always true; it is true under the conditions of mass culture and an idealization of common sense that is based in commodity culture. "Shoddiness that drifts with the flow of familiar speech is taken as a sign of relevance and contact: people know what they want because they know what other people want."[6] In other words, they embrace the idiom that in its social currency promises them the widest possible belonging. Commodity culture intensifies this desire and distorts it. The producers of mass culture, for obvious reasons of self-interest, take care to make their commodities intelligible to as wide a market as they can. This is one side of the picture, but not what concerns Adorno most. He does not just criticize mass culture as cynical manipulation. He sees the way the expansiveness of mass circulation affects and distorts a desire for social membership on the part of readers; and he thinks this is the root of the problem of style. The wide circulation of language in mass culture is perceived and treasured as a quality of style by those who misrecognize it as clarity and sense.

Adorno is describing the manifestation, in matters of style, of one of the most pervasive and troubling effects in mass society: the phenomenon of normalization. Ideas of the good — and, in this case, the beautiful as well — are distorted in ways that escape nearly everyone's attention, because they have been silently adjusted to conform to an image of the mass. A good style is a normal style. Evaluation depends on distribution; the wider it circulates, the better it must be. The false aesthetic of transparency, in other words, has a powerful social effect. One result is that it will naturally privilege the majority over less familiar views. Equally important to Adorno is that it will distort the judgment of the majority itself, precisely *qua* majority. The tastes and ideas that become those of the majority do so because people need to believe that their tastes and ideas will be widely shared. The result is a kind of invisible power for dominant norms, even though the people who make these normalizing judgments of taste do so not to exercise power (they are not, in other words, simply wielding the tyranny of the majority) but simply to fit in. Adorno implies, with pathos, that people rely on expressions that are precertified for them as common currency out of a kind of defensiveness; they are alienated from the labor of judgment. "Only what they do not need first to understand, they consider understandable; only the word coined by commerce, and really alienated, touches them as familiar."[7]

Now, it does not follow that writing, in order to be valid, must be incomprehensible. Butler, in her op-ed piece in the *New York Times*, comes close to this implication because she stresses the need for defamiliarization.[8] And Miller embraces it outright: "Q.E.D.: The most radical critic of alienation will be the most exquisitely aloof thinker, incomprehensible and unpopular by design, as if enraptured by his unswerving address to an ideal audience of one: a God who may not exist."[9] The picture of an Adorno addressing "an ideal audience of one: a God who may not exist" bears a strong resemblance to the predicament of Orwell's diarist.

Yet here Miller shows himself hasty to score points against Adorno. This position is incoherent except as caricature. You cannot be incomprehensible by design, especially if your audience is yourself. You also cannot be cynically strategic and yet also "enraptured" by an unswerving address.

Adorno does not prescribe incomprehensibility or unpopularity. He prescribes careful, rigorous, precise expression, whether the result is a popular idiom or not — as, for that matter, Orwell does in "Politics and the English Language." In order to present willful incomprehensibility as anyone's considered program, Miller has to present that person as nearly insane. He describes Adorno as "the most exquisitely aloof thinker"; elsewhere, "indistinguishable from a Prussian autocrat," expressing "nothing but contempt," a mandarin, a foreign and inscrutable nerd.[10] Miller does not scruple to produce a personal pathology as the not-so-hidden meaning of Adorno's thought: "*Minima Moralia*," he writes, in an attempt to sound sympathetic, is "the effort of a sensitive introvert."[11]

One of the most amusing moments in Adorno's writing, by the way, is an episode in his autobiographical essay about the years he spent in a research project on the medium of radio in Newark, New Jersey, just after he fled Nazi Germany. One day he was met by a young American researcher who asked him, in what Adorno calls "a completely charming way," "Dr. Adorno, are you an introvert or an extrovert?" He does not tell us his response. Perhaps he was too dumbfounded to make one. When he told this story later, however, it was to illustrate the spread of reified thinking.[12]

Miller, no doubt unaware of this ironic echo, needs to render Adorno an irrational introvert in order to arrive at the question announced by the title of his essay: "Is Bad Writing Necessary?" The question is a false one, an example of polemic rather than real deliberation. To answer the question in the affirmative — bad writing is necessary — entails a contradiction in terms. Any way of writing that could be said to fit necessity cannot be called simply bad. Having posed the issue this way, Miller is able to ensnare the victim in a paradox: "Does this mean that Adorno's and Butler's most challenging ideas, precisely because of their relative popularity among a not-insignificant number of left-leaning intellectuals, have lost their antithetical use value and, by the infernal logic of exchange, been alienated and perhaps even dialectically transformed — turned into something hackneyed and predictable? If one accepts Adorno's position in *Minima Moralia*, there is no escaping the conclusion."[13]

Actually, this conclusion is very easy to escape. Adorno does not infer alienation directly from the number of comprehending readers. He equates alienation with an imitative style of mass comprehension that defensively resists the unpredictability of thought. Numbers of readers are not the issue. The manner of reading is — though Adorno believes that the problem with the currently dominant manner of reading is that its imagination of value is controlled by people's tacit calculations about the numbers of readers with whom they will be in alignment. So no matter how many people read and comprehend his writing, that in itself tells us nothing about its social meaning. Only when the extensiveness of the reading audience is taken into normative consideration in advance by that very reading audience do we have the phenomenon he describes.

I have taken a detour through this episode in Anglo-American polemics partly because it shows how primitive our thinking about publics is. The assumption seems to be that a clear style results in a popular audience and that political engagement requires having the most extensive audience possible. This view is assumed rather than reasoned, which is why anyone who dissents from it can only be heard as proposing inanities: that bad writing is necessary; that incomprehensibility should be cultivated; that speech in order to be politically radical must have no audience. In Miller's summary, Orwell and Adorno are made to share the assumption that clarity of style produces large numbers of readers: Miller's Orwell thinks this is a good thing; Miller's Adorno thinks it is a bad thing.

We begin to normalize intellectual work whenever we suppose a direct equation between value and numbers — imagining that a clear style results in a popular audience and therefore in effective political engagement. So deeply cherished is this way of thinking that to challenge it is to court derision, especially in journalistic contexts. Adorno tried to identify a connection between the mass circulation of discourse and the mode of reading oriented to that circulation.[14] He is heard, instead, as arguing against readability in principle.

Given such confusion, it is perhaps better to return to very basic questions. What kind of clarity is necessary in writing? Clarity for whom?

For some, the answers to these questions are too obvious to need stating. Writing that is unclear to nonspecialists is just "bad writing." This general moral position is implied by Miller's title, as it is by the Bad Writing Award cooked up by the journal *Philosophy and Literature*. People who share this view will be generally reluctant to concede that different kinds of writing suit different purposes, that what is clear in one reading community will be unclear in another, that clarity depends on shared conventions and common references, that one man's jargon is another's clarity, that perceptions of jargon or unclarity change over time. (My students have trouble reading eighteenth-century prose that was a model of clarity in its time, but they take as self-evidently clear such terms as "objective" and "subjective" — denounced as hideous neologistic jargon when Coleridge used them.) People who think the charge of bad writing is self-evident or universally obvious therefore tend to be naive at best and quite often can be shown to be hypocritical. As Butler rightly notes, for example, the charge is almost always reserved for thinkers in the humanities who share certain unpalatable views. Even conservative academics in the humanities who write opaquely are seldom attacked; the hostility of journalists seems reserved not only for certain disciplines but for left thinkers within those disciplines.

Should writing intended for academics in the humanities be readable for everyone when we don't expect the same from writing in physics? Isn't such an expectation tantamount to a demand that there be no such thing as intellectuals in the humanities, that the whole history of the humanistic disciplines make no difference, and that someone starting from scratch into a discussion — of, say, the theory of sexuality — be at no disadvantage compared with someone who has read widely in previous discussions of the issue? When the charge of bad writing comes from journalists, it is hard to avoid the feeling that some hostility to the very idea of scholarly humanistic disciplines is involved.

It is, of course, possible to challenge academic writing on other grounds. It could be argued that the imperative to write clearly is not the same as the need to write accessibly, that even difficult styles can have the clarity of precision. The project of an academic discipline requires a rigor of definition, argument, and debate. One could argue on this basis for clarity, where what would count as clarity might remain highly specialized and inaccessible to lay audiences or journalists. Indeed, to the extent that clarity might require conceptual precision of very unfamiliar kinds, it might compete with accessibility. People adhering to this ideal might feel that clarity is endangered not by the isolation or specialization of the academy but by the failure of humanists to take their own disciplines seriously — either because of the humbug of genteel humanistic piety, or because of the fascination with journalistic authority that besets such professions as history, or because specialized environments like the cultural studies circuit have led academics to think that rigorous argument counts less than a gestural politics of righteousness. An appeal for clarity in this sense would not be an argument about public intellectuals, nor would it apply to left academics more than anyone else.

A third line of thinking is that a special standard of clarity should be applied to just those academics who claim political consequences for their work — which would include almost everyone working in cultural criticism these days. On this view, there might be no need for accessibility in academic disciplines in general, and "bad writing" awards could be dismissed as grandstanding. Yet when academics claim to be furthering justice through their work, this argument goes, they take on obligations that go beyond their own profession. (This is the way the argument has been advanced by Nussbaum and Pollitt, among others.) Even on these terms, it does not immediately follow that *accessibility* is the issue. Nussbaum's critique of Butler's prose style, for example, does not assume that Butler's work should be written for nonspecialists; her more serious charge is that Butler's work is not written for canons of argument among specialists, either in philosophy or in law, and that only the star system of cultural studies accounts for its form of address.[15] Some of the stylistic tics Nussbaum targets, like the tendency to introduce premises in conditional "if...then" clauses and then to treat those premises as givens, have to do with logical argumentation but not necessarily with exposition for nonspecialists such as the presumed readers of the *New Republic*, where Nussbaum was writing.

So a further assumption seems to be required to produce the charge that inaccessible writing is irresponsible, or that good writing must be easy to read. One must hold not only that clarity is a special burden on writers with political aspirations but that the kind of clarity they need is the kind found in journalistic or political publics. This demand seems to me wholly unjustified, for reasons I hope to make clear. In all the attacks on the style of left academic theory, I have not seen a cogent defense of this extra requirement. It tends to be taken for granted, especially by journalists. There is a reason for the silence; those who believe most ardently in the power of journalistic publics tend to believe that those publics are like the air — everywhere, invisible, and permeable to light. It hardly occurs to them to wonder whether a public might be a cultural form predisposed to some ends over others.

Notice, too, that the charge of bad writing carries a corollary assumption: that if only left academics would write accessibly for journalistic publics, they would be more politically effective. This does not obviously follow, and experience suggests it is a mistake. Accessible prose alone gets you nothing, if the ideas are unpalatable for other reasons, or if the public is structured in such a way as to be substantively prejudicial. There are many arguments that will never find their way to the pages of the *New York Times* no matter how clearly expressed. Just as it is a mistake to equate good writing with accessibility, so also is it a mistake to equate an easy style with effectiveness.

We are drawn into these assumptions so insidiously that they can distort the defense of difficult writing as well. It is all very well to argue that some kinds of difficult writing might be good, even politically necessary. But is difficulty a virtue in itself, or an effective strategy for defamiliarizing common sense? To defend academic writing on such grounds is to assume that defamiliarization works all by itself. One falls into the same mistake as those who believe in the effectiveness of transparency, saying nothing about context, audience, ways of reading, or mediation by form. How does writing defamiliarize common sense? If it does so only when read by the protocols of academic discourse — where, for example, it is axiomatic that complexity is to be valued over simplicity — then the arguments of Pollitt and others have some force: the political benefits that flow from this strategy of resistance do so only within the restricted zone of academic culture. Defamiliarization for whom?

Might it not be the case that what might have been defamiliarizing has become, for many in the academy, all too familiar? Many people outside the academy are defensive about using their judgment in the face of difficulty; might it not also be true that many inside it are defensive about giving up the display of difficulty in the surface of writing? There would be nothing surprising in this. Style performs membership. Academics belong to a functionally segregated social sphere, and in the humanities especially that sphere is increasingly marginal, often jeopardized. People use style to distinguish themselves from the mass and its normalized version of clarity. Often, those who do so — especially graduate students, whose role is not institutionally secured — are also trying to mark their own somewhat tenuous membership in a fragile but desperately needed subculture. These social dimensions of style are probably more important to the making of any public than either clarity or defamiliarization considered in the abstract.

At stake in the dispute is not just a difference of views about style but different contexts for writing, different ways of imagining a public. The issues are obscured rather than clarified whenever we assume that a public intellectual is one who writes for large numbers, that an untroubling and familiar idiom is essential to political engagement, that meaningful political work is necessarily performed within the headline temporality of what currently counts as politics, or that political position taking is the only way of being creatively related to a public. What disappears in this view of the politics of prose is the mediation of publics; genres; modes of address; the circulation of cultural forms; ways of reading, including affect; and the social imaginaries that are the background of literate practice.

So we are back where we began: How could one bring a different public into being, transforming the conditions of speech?

The question is blunted by the very ideology that drives much of the talk about public intellectuals in the first place: the dominant ideology of the public sphere, dating at least from the early eighteenth century, according to which the public sphere is simply people making public use of their reason. Citizens, in this commonsense view, form opinions in dialogue with each other, and that is where public opinion comes from. Any address to a public tends to be understood as imitating face-to-face argumentative dialogue or, rather, an idealized version of such dialogue. Public opinion is thought to arise out of a continuum of contexts ranging from common conversation to PTA meetings to parliamentary forensics, op-ed pieces, or critical essays, and at each step the rules of discourse are the same. One proceeds by airing different views in the interest of understanding, making assumptions explicit, and then reaching some decision. The public sphere is critical discussion writ large. A vibrant scene of public-spirited discussion is the motor of democratic culture.

One of the basic points of this book is that publics do not in fact work that way. But if you believe that they do, that there is a continuum from rational dialogue upward to the realm of public opinion, then it might seem obvious that intellectuals are uniquely positioned to address publics publicly. Critical argument is the intellectuals' métier. If public discourse is to be reasonable, who should be better fitted to lead it than intellectuals? If they fail to do so, the thinking goes, then the failure must lie at their own door.

For many people, "public intellectual" has come to mean a quasi-journalistic pundit with a mass following. Older conceptions

— such as that of the intellectual as the conscience of the age, adhering to conviction or historical memory whether anyone listens or not, keeping alive an alternative that may be reanimated in some distant future — have faded into the background. Contemporary culture regards any thought of a distant future as archaic. Given the contracted span of futurity in the headline temporality of politics, which increasingly dominates all thought, we think in horizontal terms: public intellectuals are those who seek socially expansive audiences.

Under the sway of such thinking, one could easily ignore the difference between intellectuals as a class and citizens as a general category. Both use critical reason and articulate considered arguments. Intellectuals are simply those equipped to do this in the greatest degree. John Guillory aptly writes that the idea of an engaged intellectual can be seen as "nostalgia for the very public sphere that functioned historically in the *absence* of a socially identified group of 'intellectuals.'[16] The wish for public intellectuals leads people to speak as though there were a moral imperative to clarity, and a moral imperative to political position taking as well. To the extent that these are moral requirements, they can hardly be expected to result in such a specialized status as the public intellectual. If one were really to argue that everyone should write clearly and that everyone should take political positions publicly, one would be arguing in effect *against* the idea of a public intellectual as a special role.

More to the point, this ideology misrecognizes the fundamental innovation of the public as a cultural form. The public sphere never required a widespread culture of rational discussion. It required the category of a public — an essentially imaginary function that allows temporally indexed circulation among strangers to be captured as a social entity and addressed impersonally. Success in this game is not a matter of having better arguments or more complex positions. It is a matter of uptake, citation, and recharacterization. It takes place not in closely argued essays but in an informal, intertextual, and multigeneric field. There is no reason why intellectuals should be specially positioned for public address in this sense, except where they are packaged as experts. And expert knowledge is in an important way nonpublic: its authority is external to the discussion. It can be challenged only by other experts, not within the discourse of the public itself.

The sociologist Nina Eliasoph has recently published a disturbing study of contexts of discussion that should challenge any idea of the public sphere as a continuum of critical opinion making. Eliasoph examined a wide range of public discussions in local community groups and found that public-minded discussion is systematically inhibited in almost every context. As conversations get closer to public topics, where opinions would have a general relevance and others' views would have to be taken into account, people tend to shut up, deflecting currents of conversation. Even active volunteers in civic groups construct their volunteering so as to avoid risky discussion. They choose topics that allow them to avoid dissent. They frame their motives as prepolitical. Journalists and officials actively conspire to limit public discussion, diverting it into testimony that can be viewed as private passion rather than opinion or argument. They solicit people to regard their public spirit as good feeling, compassion, volunteerism, or anything else that can be divorced from the conflict of views. Journalists report on citizens' feelings or interests rather than on their arguments, keeping for themselves the role of the uncontested mediators of publicness. They profile those who speak as Moms, acting on behalf of their children, rather than as citizens with general views. Officials who respond to citizen involvement tend to invoke expertise or steer discussion into bureaucratic speech protocols in which their own authority can be performed.[17]

Interestingly, Eliasoph herself does not question the assumption that the continuum of public-minded critical discussion is what the public sphere has been or should be about. Her book is driven by a sense of outrage that actual conversations fail to accord with the ideal. But the ideal of critical discussion was itself never sufficient to bring the public sphere into being. The endlessly repeated discovery that public politics does not in fact conform to the idealized self-understanding that makes it work — a discovery made by the Romantics, by Marx, by Lippmann, by Adorno, by Habermas, by Foucault, and *de novo* by Eliasoph — can never generate enough moral passion to force politics into conformity. The image of discussion writ large is necessary to the public sphere as a self-understanding but not as an empirical reality.

That same image, I suspect, fuels the fantasy of the public intellectual as a necessary function for political change, where the intellectual is seen as one especially adept at framing issues for critical discussions and where change results when discussion encompasses the most extensive possible public in its deliberative agency. This conception of the intellectual's relation to politics relies on a language ideology in which ideas and expressions are infinitely fungible, translatable, repeatable, summarizable, and restatable. To the extent that this is what public language is supposed to be about, attention must be deflected away from the poetics of style, as well as from the pragmatic work of texts in fashioning interactive relations. Publics are conjured into being by characterizing as a social entity (that is, as a public) the world in which discourse circulates; but in the language ideology that enables the public sphere, this poetic or creative function of public address disappears from view. Rather than help to constitute scenes of circulation through style, intellectuals are supposed to launch transparently framed ideas into the circulation of an indefinite public. Of course, if intellectuals thought of themselves as involved in world-making projects, it is not clear that intellection would be more effective than, say, corporeally expressive performances. It is not clear that intellectuals would have a naturally leading role in the process at all. And hence it is perhaps not surprising that the professional class of intellectuals should seem reluctant to abandon the conception of public discourse whose inadequacy they continue to discover.

The wish for popularly read intellectuals responds in part to the extreme segregation of journalistic and intellectual publics in the United States. They are segregated not just by attitude and style but by the material conditions of circulation. Publics do not exist simply along a continuum from narrow to wide or from specialist to general, elite to popular. They differ in the social conditions that make them possible and to which they are oriented. The United States is an extreme case. The American strain of anti-intellectualism has made intellectuals feel like exiles for the past two centuries; small wonder that many should dream of vindicating themselves through fame, the only currency of respect that really spends in America. The intense capitalization of mass culture here means that the media that matter are those whose scale and scarcity of access are most forbidding. Meanwhile, the saturation of universities by commercial and state interests makes academic work in some ways less than public, insofar as intellectuals there come to be either marginalized or functionally incorporated into the management culture of expertise. And for the past thirty years or so, trade and academic publishing have been institutionalized as distinct fields of production to a much greater degree than in any other country, while the decentralization of the American university system prevents it from providing the coherent platform of authority that is to be found in more frankly elite systems such as that of France.

University presses and journals are mulish compromises, half professional and half public. Their products are widely available to any stranger who can buy or borrow copies, and in that sense they address publics. But they also take care to maintain a close fit between their circulatory ambit and the private realm of the professions. They select authors from professions; they vet manuscripts (less and less, it is true) with expert readers within fields; they promote works within professional organizations and academic markets. (This is true even of presses like Routledge that have no formal ties to universities.)

The world of strangers to whom this discourse circulates is a world in which strangers are either directly certified in advance by institutions and networks or indirectly limited by the distributional practices of the publisher. Readers share reference points, career trajectories, and subclass interests. They share protocols of discourse, including things like an axiomatic preference for complexity. ("Actually, I believe it's more complicated than that" is, within the academic world, an unanswerable shibboleth; it articulates a professional mode for producing more discourse and for giving it an archivally cumulative character. The same gesture falls hopelessly flat in journalistic settings, where the extensive uptake of audience attention is at a premium.) Writers in this world are inevitably involved in a different language game from journalists.

The private circulation of academic discourse could be all to the good in the routine functioning of a discipline. But when disciplines decline or go into crisis, or when members for their own reasons seek to use the academic platform to address a different public, the existing routes of circulation prove unsatisfactory. Circulation is then controlled by conflicting laws. Journalists, who as a class have an interest in mass circulation and the forms of authority based on it, are only too happy to point out the conflict.

These conditions structure the available publics for thought

148

and writing in the United States. They are not to be overcome by a mere change of attitude, any more than Orwell's diarist could have been expected to generate, out of style alone, "*a time when thought is free, when men are different from one another and do not live alone.*" Left academic theory, mostly from within the jeopardized disciplines of the humanities, has been attempting to reconstitute itself as a public, sometimes with the explicit intention of ceasing to be organized by disciplines. Often enough it seems willing to postulate its own world through style or through idiomatic and topical allusions to mass culture. The result frustrates nearly everyone. Between the academy and the mass, between the disciplines and journalism, the conditions for public circulation do not for the most part now exist.

There are, of course, many ways in which the effort to bring a public into being, to do world-making work in the public sphere, can go wrong. When Pollitt complains that academic intellectuals postulate their own radicalness in a way that entails no risk and reduces to pseudo politics, the strong version of her point is that the public of academic work is being misrecognized. Like most academic expertise, it circulates only in a well-defined path mediated almost entirely by the university system; but it no longer understands itself this way. It seeks to overcome the separation of academic, trade, and political publics by means of its topical content rather than its public circulation. Of course, this perfectly valid point can also be turned around. As Adorno points out, the journalistic public itself can fail to be a scene of risk or world making. When journalists denounce academics for speaking in a way that is not already familiar, they, too, are trying to avoid the risk of truly public circulation.

There are many academics, especially in cultural studies, who distrust the claim of journalists and mass media to represent the only relevant public and who seek public relevance in a different way. Rather than seeking fame or publicity in journalistic publics, they seek to regard all intellectuals as public intellectuals. They aspire to see their own work as politics, either in the general sense of contested culture or in the narrower sense of having a bearing on common action and state policy. Recognizing that academic disciplines, for better or worse, create a functional gap between themselves and political publics, they wish to eschew their disciplines (many of which are in an exhausted state anyway) as the context for their writing and thinking. Yet they do so not by leaving the disciplines entirely, writing for publics and lifeworlds outside the academy, but by adapting work and career within an academic context as much as possible to a political self-understanding.

This experiment has its own dangers. Among them is a loss entailed by imitating the temporality of politics without recognizing the difference of temporality available in these two contexts for circulating discourse. Politicizing thought tends to mean adjusting it to headline temporality. Some kinds of thought, essential to politics but not captured within its terms, might require a different space of circulation. Cultural studies has sometimes attempted a methodical elimination of the apparatus of futurity associated with disciplinarity: cumulative knowledge and field-specific archives, research understood as corrigible inquiry, apprenticeship and expertise, self-reproducing professionalism, and so on. Yet so long as such work continues to circulate only within a metadisciplinary academic framework, its aspirations to political time remain blocked. This contradiction gives force to the objections of journalists.

Any public includes strangers, present or future. The quality of *risk* that Pollitt finds missing in left academic theory is just this orientation to strangers and the submission of discourse to estranging paths of circulation. But that risk can happen over longer as well as shorter durations; it's just that the shorter ones are easier to recognize as politics. Orwell's diarist longs for this risk among strangers when he writes to a time when people "*are different from one another and do not live alone.*" The future scholars of a traditional discipline are also, in this limited sense, semipublic; even quite traditional scholarship is oriented to corrigibility over time by strangers. Neither address to the journalistic public nor the immediate politicization of academic publics, in other words, is the only way to take the necessary risk of publicness. World-making projects require not just intentions, or the moralized postures that are called "having politics," but a set of forms that can articulate the temporality and social space of their circulation.

It is my sense that Foucault was thinking along similar lines toward the end of his career. Foucault must seem an ambiguous figure from the point of view of this essay. His influence has been felt far outside the academy, though he famously refused the role of public intellectual as it had been embodied by Jean-Paul Sartre. His style, notoriously difficult, nevertheless seldom fails to be interesting. Foucault represents as well as any other intellectual the possibility not only of arguing a critical theory but of mobilizing others into a critical stance through the appeal of his writing. In the last ten years of his life, he was conspicuously involved in both local activist projects and a large-scale effort to rethink the nature of politics. What shall we say, then, about his relation to a public?

Foucault once arranged, in effect, to interview himself by having Paul Rabinow ask him questions on which he wanted to set the record aright.[18] The first question was "Why is it that you don't engage in polemics?"[19] I quote Foucault's reply at length because it may strike many as unexpected:

It's true that I don't like to get involved in polemics. If I open a book and see that the author is accusing an adversary of "infantile leftism,"

I shut it again right away. That's not my way of doing things; I don't belong to the world of people who do things that way. I insist on this difference as something essential: a whole morality is at stake, the morality that concerns the search for the truth and the relation to the other.

In the serious play of questions and answers, in the work of reciprocal elucidation, the rights of each person are in some sense immanent in the discussion. They depend only on the dialogue situation. The person asking the questions is merely exercising the right that has been given him: to remain unconvinced, to perceive a contradiction, to require more information, to emphasize different postulates, to point out faulty reasoning, and so on. As for the person answering the questions, he too exercises a right that does not go beyond the discussion itself; by the logic of his own discourse, he is tied to what he has said earlier, and by the acceptance of dialogue he is tied to the questioning of the other. Questions and answers depend on a game — a game that is at once pleasant and difficult — in which each of the two partners takes pains to use only the rights given him by the other and by the accepted form of the dialogue.

The polemicist, on the other hand, proceeds encased in privileges that he possesses in advance and will never agree to question. On principle, he possesses rights authorizing him to wage war and making that struggle a just undertaking; the person he confronts is not a partner in the search for truth but an adversary, an enemy who is wrong, who is harmful, and whose very existence constitutes a threat. For him, then, the game consists not of recognizing this person as a subject having the right to speak but of abolishing him, as interlocutor, from any possible dialogue.[20]

It is somewhat surprising to see Foucault describing his career in print and in publicity as though it were a dialogue. His remarks might seem to be oddly Habermasian: he insists that the orien-

tation to dialogue is a moral issue and that "in the work of reciprocal elucidation, the rights of each person are in some sense
immanent in the discussion. They depend only on the dialogue
situation."

Yet I think Didier Eribon is right to suggest that the passage
represents the closest thing in Foucault's work to a response to
Habermas — we might almost say, a wryly veiled polemic against
Habermas.[21] The question "Why is it that you don't engage in
polemics?" is an opportunity for Foucault to explain why he had
not responded to the frontal assault that Habermas mounted
against him in the lectures that were to be published, a year after
Foucault's death, as *The Philosophical Discourse of Modernity* and
that had been delivered in March 1983 at the Collège de France —
one year before the Rabinow interview. In using this language to
explain his refusal to take up a challenge he disdained, Foucault
out-Habermases Habermas, so to speak. The real substance of his
response comes in the remarks that immediately follow. Here
Foucault offers his view that the morality of the dialogue is to
be grounded not in the transcendental conditions of speech situa-
tions as ideally oriented to understanding and therefore implying
norms of rational morality in general but in the history of polemics and other modes of discourse. Dialogue and polemic are both
genres, with different ethical projects and social relations immanent to them. "Very schematically," Foucault suggests, one could
analyze the language game of polemic through its religious, judiciary, and political antecedents.

In posing the issue this way, Foucault is also trying to explain
why it is difficult to chart the kind of clear path between intellectual work and politics that is currently condensed into the image
of the public intellectual. In a long and eloquent passage dominated by metaphors of war and other forms of violent aggression,
Foucault claims that polemic finds its most powerful model in

politics — even when politics might seem to be about agreement rather than polemic, as when it consists of defining alliances, recruiting partisans, and uniting interests or opinions. So the question "Why is it that you don't engage in polemics?" turns out to be a question about the distinction between Foucault's intellectual project and politics proper.

Foucault says in this context that he prefers to stand back from questions posed within the language of politics in order to pursue problems that cannot entirely be framed as political questions. He cites as examples his work on madness and on sexuality. Sexuality, for example, "doesn't exist apart from a relationship to political structures, requirements, laws, and regulations that have a primary importance for it; and yet one can't expect politics to provide the forms in which sexuality would cease to be a problem."[22] The alternative to polemic, an intellectual program more in keeping with the ethics of dialogue, Foucault calls "problematization." He traces the term to a realization that the Marxist vocabulary was found unsatisfying in 1968 as a way of thinking about the politicization of personal life; that project called for another way of framing what would count as politics.

The term "problematization," awkward enough under the best of circumstances, has become rather confused by its use among post-Foucauldian academics, for whom it often means nothing more than taking something to be problematic. To problematize, in this usage, means to complicate. For Foucault is has a much richer meaning, connected with the argument in volumes 2 and 3 of *History of Sexuality*. There, he treats a problematic not just as an intellectual tangle, but as the practical horizon of intelligibility within which problems come to matter for people. It stands for both the conditions that make thinking possible and for the way thinking, under certain circumstances, can reflect back on its own conditions. Problematization is more than arguing; it is a practical

154

context for thinking. As such, it lies largely beyond conscious strategy.

The "Problematizations" interview can be read in part as Foucault's account of his relation to the gay movement. Despite repeated solicitations from gay journalists and activists, Foucault refused to be set up as the gay intellectual. Of course, he scarcely needed the outlet. But social movements have often been arenas in which professional intellectuals — journalists, lawyers, or academics — have found publics in which their intellectual role could be put to use. Foucault was happy enough to do so on occasion. But when confronted by the rise of a gay movement in his adult life, Foucault, for what were doubtless overdetermined reasons, chose to write a book that corroded the conceptual underpinnings of the gay movement as it was then in formation. *The History of Sexuality* has an extremely vexed and vexing relation to that movement public. There are moments in his interviews, too, in which he anticipates the dead end of identitarian politics of sexual orientation with a lucidity that remains unsurpassed.

More generally, the "Problematizations" interview revises Foucault's earlier account of the public intellectual in "Intellectuals and Politics" (1972). There he argued against the kind of general intellectual embodied by Sartre, in favor of a new "specific" intellectual with expertise relevant to a topical arena. The later account of problematization — as work on the framing of politics — makes it now opposed to any political policy public, whether general or specific. Given such a conception, the relation between problematization and activism must necessarily be unclear, even disturbingly so. Foucault's point applies to style as well as content; he stands athwart both politics and the discourse game of polemic, no matter what the topic. In one sense, his argument returns to a traditional relation between intellectual and political work: because problematization considers the framing of politics rather than issues already framed as politics, it has the reflexive structure that has traditionally been the role of theory or philosophy. But the path back to a new politics is one on which the intellectual is no privileged guide.

Interestingly, Foucault's arguments for a practice of problematization over polemic turn out to be ethical rather than political. He does not say that problematization is more radical or more effective. He says it is morally essential, as well as harder and more fun ("a game that is at once pleasant and difficult"). He sees it as a resource of humor and equanimity. If this is one of the reasons why he sometimes avoided polemic, he was wise. But one doesn't always have that luxury. Eribon, an unusually sympathetic interpreter, writes that Foucault's remarks stem in part from the habitually aristocratic manner of prominent French intellectuals. Problematization's relation to polemic, and to politics, in his case partly expresses prestige and security. It seems to require something like the university system to mediate both the social space of its "domain" and the reflexive relation of thought to politics. Foucault's remarks go far to reimagining the relation between professional intellectuals and politics. Yet he had little to say about mediations and publics. Fame had made that question moot for him.

Foucault's relation to the public/private distinction still awaits systematic treatment as far as I can tell. With *Madness and Civilization* and *Discipline and Punish*, he had already begun developing an account of power designed to show the inadequacy of liberal norms. This project, continued in *The History of Sexuality*, is the most thorough assault yet mounted against the idea of private life as a realm of freedom distinct from state power. Foucault did not pretend, of course, that the distinction between public and private was without consequence in modern society; but he showed that neither public/private nor state/civil society corresponded to a difference between power and freedom, authority and liberty. *Discipline and Punish* and *The History of Sexuality* especially demonstrate that new ways of imagining publicity (regulatory or therapeutic) also fashioned a new kind of private person in the image of its regulatory model. In the domains of reason, justice, and personal life, Foucault's three major treatises show that the modern order requires relations of power that saturate civil society and the most intimate dimensions of personhood. The very private life thought to be the locus of freedom and rights was instead the laboratory of a regulatory order, one that could by no means be equated with the state or even with a class that ruled indirectly through the state (as in Marxism). What would it mean to challenge this framework of governance? Foucault relocated the possible frontiers of politics so radically that nothing is in principle off-limits. As his late studies of "governmentality" were designed to show, the result was a rethinking of "politics," and with it all the implications of public and private.[23]

The project Foucault calls problematization does remain oriented to a public; Foucault speaks not of questioning in the abstract of theory but of "the development of a domain of acts, practices, and thoughts that seem to me to pose problems for politics." In this sense, it is consistent with Foucault's project of displacing the self-understanding of philosophy outward to the world, a project he identified with Adorno and the Frankfurt School and against which he thought Habermas was fighting a reaction. Problematization, in order to be the development of a domain of acts and practices, must have a public scene, not just a reflexive relation to one. This public scene, however, must also have a different temporality from the public of polemic, because it is defined by its ability to "pose problems for politics" and is therefore not to be subordinated to the urgencies and action schemes of the political system.

Foucault seems to be on the verge of describing intellectual work as a kind of counterpublic. He does not do so, of course, because he sets aside all questions of circulation and medium. It might be that the idealization of dialogue prevented him from seeing how little that genre corresponded to his own practice. Or it might be that he wanted to stand outside the language game of the public sphere conceived as circulation. In any case, he imagines thought as more than fungible argument. He describes it as oriented to strangeness, risk, and world making in a scene of concretely mediated but open-ended exchange. This is a useful picture of how intellectual work could be important, one that does not reduce importance to numerical extensiveness and contemporaneity. Because it identifies a multi-leveled temporality that is often forgotten in the romance of the public intellectual, it may be a way of recovering the orientation to futurity in academic work. This is not to say that the address of journalistic style or even polemic might not also be necessary to the risk of public intellectual work. The publics in which problematizing work circulates cannot remain forever functionally segregated from all other publics if they are to transform politics. Certainly a public practice oriented to redefining public practice is a paradoxical task, not finally dissimilar to the problem of Orwell's diarist. It is a way of imaging a speech for which there is yet no scene, and a scene for which there is no speech.

CHAPTER FOUR

The Mass Public and the Mass Subject*

The Egocrat coincides with himself, as society is
supposed to coincide with itself. An impossible
swallowing up of the body in the head begins to take
place, as does an impossible swallowing up of the head
in the body. The attraction of the whole is no longer
dissociated from the attraction of the parts
— Claude Lefort, "The Image of the Body
and Totalitarianism."[1]

During these assassination fantasies Tallis became
increasingly obsessed with the pudenda of the
Presidential contender mediated to him by a thousand
television screens. The motion picture studies of
Ronald Reagan created a scenario of the conceptual
orgasm, a unique ontology of violence and disaster.
— J.G. Ballard, "Why I Want to Fuck
Ronald Reagan"[2]

*Originally published in *Habermas and the Public Sphere*, ed Craig Calhoun
(Cambridge, MA: MIT Press, 1991).

As the subjects of publicity — its hearers, speakers, viewers, and doers — we have a different relation to ourselves, a different affect, from that which we have in other contexts. No matter what particularities of culture, race, gender, or class we bring to bear on public discourse, the moment of apprehending something as public is one in which we imagine, if imperfectly, indifference to those particularities, to ourselves. We adopt the attitude of the public subject, marking to ourselves its nonidentity with ourselves. There are any number of ways to describe this moment of public subjectivity: as a universalizing transcendence, as ideological repression, as utopian wish, as schizocapitalist vertigo, or simply as a routine difference of register. No matter what its character for the individual subjects who come to public discourse, however, the rhetorical contexts of publicity in the modern Western nations must always mediate a self-relation different from that of personal life. This becomes a point of more than usual importance, I will suggest, in a period such as our own when so much political conflict revolves around identity and status categories.

Western political thought has not ignored the tendency of publicity to alter or refract the individual's character and status. It has been obsessed with that tendency. But it has frequently thought of publicity as distorting, corrupting, or, to use the more current version, alienating individuals. The republican notion of virtue, for example, was designed exactly to avoid any rupture of self-difference between ordinary life and publicity. The republican was to be the same as citizen and as man. He was to maintain continuity of value, judgment, and reputation from a domestic economy to affairs of a public nature. And lesser subjects — noncitizens such as women, children, and the poor — were equally to maintain continuity across both realms, as nonactors. From republicanism to populism, from Rousseau to Reagan, self-unity has been held to be a public value, and publicity has not been thought of as requiring individuals to have discontinuous perceptions of themselves. (Hegel, it is true, considered the state a higher-order subjectivity unattainable in civil society. But because he considered the difference both normative and unbridgeable within the frame of the individual, a historical and political analysis of discontinuous self-relations did not follow.)

One reason why virtue was spoken about with such ardor in the seventeenth and eighteenth centuries was that the discursive conventions of the public sphere had already made virtuous self-unity archaic. In the bourgeois public sphere, talk of a citizen's virtue was already partly wishful. Once a public discourse had become specialized in the Western model, the subjective attitude adopted in public discourse became an inescapable but always unrecognized political force, governing what is publicly sayable — inescapable because only when images or texts can be understood as meaningful to a public rather than simply to oneself, or to specific others, can they be called public; unrecognized because this strategy of impersonal reference, in which one might say, "The text addresses me" and "It addresses no one in particular," is a ground condition of intelligibility for public language. The "public" in this sense has no empirical existence and cannot be objectified. When we understand images and texts as public, we do not gesture to a statistically measurable series of others. We make a necessarily imaginary reference to the public as opposed to other individuals. Public opinion, for example, is understood as belonging to a public rather than to scattered individuals. (Opinion polls in this sense are a performative genre. They do not measure something that already exists as public opinion, but when they are reported as such, they are public opinion.) So also it is only meaningful to speak of public discourse where it is understood as the discourse of a public rather than as an expansive dialogue among separate persons.

The public sphere therefore presents problems of rhetorical analysis. Because the moment of special imaginary reference is always necessary, the publicity of the public sphere never reduces to information, discussion, will formation, or any of the other scenarios by which the public sphere represents itself. The mediating rhetorical dimension of a public context must be built into each individual's relation to it as a meaningful reference point against which something could be grasped as information, discussion, will formation. To ask about the relation between democracy and the rhetorical forms of publicity, we would have to consider how the public dimension of discourse can come about differently in different contexts of mediation, from official to mass-cultural or subcultural. There is not simply *a* public discourse and a *we* who apprehend it. Strategies of public reference have different meanings for the individuals who suddenly find themselves incorporating the public subject, and the rhetorics that mediate publicity have undergone some important changes.

Utopias of Self-Abstraction

In the eighteenth century, as I have argued elsewhere, the imaginary reference point of the public was constructed through an understanding of print.[3] At least in the British American colonies, a style of thinking about print appeared in the culture of republicanism according to which it was possible to consume printed goods with an awareness that the same printed goods were being consumed by an indefinite number of others. This awareness came to be built into the meaning of the printed object, to the point that we now consider it simply definitional to speak of printing as "publication." In print, understood this way, one surrendered one's utterance to an audience that was by definition indefinite. Earlier writers might have responded with some anxiety to such mediation or might simply have thought of the speaker-audience relation in different terms. In the eighteenth century, the consciousness of an abstract audience became a badge of distinction, a way of claiming a public disposition.

The transformation, I might emphasize, was a cultural rather than a technological one; it came about not just with more use of print but also with the extension of the language of republicanism to print contexts as a structuring metalanguage. It was in the culture of republicanism, with its categories of disinterested virtue and supervision, that a rhetoric of print consumption became authoritative, a way of understanding the publicness of publication. Here, for example, is how the *Spectator* in 1712 described the advantage of being realized in the medium of print:

> It is much more difficult to converse with the World in a real than a personated Character. That might pass for Humour, in the *Spectator*, which would took like Arrogance in a Writer who sets his Name to his Work. The Fictitious Person might contemn those who disapproved him, and extoll his own Performances, without giving Offence. He might assume a Mock-Authority; without being looked upon as vain and conceited. The Praises or Censures of himself fall only upon the Creature of his Imagination, and if any one finds fault with him, the Author may reply with the Philosopher of old, *Thou dost but beat the Case of* Anaxarchus.[4]

The Spectator's attitude of conversing with the world is public and disinterested. It elaborates republican assumptions about the citizen's exercise of virtue. But it could not come about without a value placed on the anonymity here associated with print. The Spectator's point about himself is that he is different from the person of Richard Steele. Just as the Spectator here secures a certain liberty in not calling himself Richard Steele, it would take a certain liberty for us to call the author of this passage Richard Steele — all the more so since the pronoun reference begins to slip around the third sentence ("those who disapproved *him*"). The ambiguous relation between Spectator and writer, Steele says, liberates him. The Spectator is a prosthetic person for Steele, to borrow a term from Lauren Berlant — prosthetic in the sense that it does not reduce to or express the given body.[5] By making him no longer self-identical, it allows him the negativity of debate — not a pure negativity, not simply reason or criticism, but an identification with a disembodied public subject that he can imagine as parallel to his private person.

In a sense, however, that public subject does have a body, because the public, prosthetic body takes abuse for the private person. The last line of the passage refers to the fact that Anaxarchus was pummeled to death with iron pestles after offending a despotic ruler. In the ventriloquistic act of taking up his speech, therefore, Steele both imagines an intimate violation of his person and provides himself with a kind of prophylaxis against violation (to borrow another term from Berlant). Anaxarchus was not so lucky. Despite what Steele says, the privilege he obtains over his body in this way does not in fact reduce to the simple body/soul distinction that Anaxarchus's speech invokes. It allows him to think of his public discourse as a routine form of self-abstraction quite unlike the ascetic self-integration of Anaxarchus. When Steele impersonates the philosopher and has the Spectator (or someone) say, "*Thou dost but beat the Case of* Anaxarchus," he appropriates an intimate subjective benefit of publicity's self-abstraction.

Through the conventions that allowed such writing to perform the disincorporation of its authors and its readers, public discourse turned persons into a public. At points in *The Structural Transformation of the Public Sphere*, Jürgen Habermas makes a similar point. One of the great virtues of that book is the care it takes to describe the cultural-technical context in which the public of the bourgeois public sphere was constituted: "In the *Tatler*, the *Spectator*, and the *Guardian* the public held up a mirror to itself.... The public that read and debated this sort of thing read and debated about itself."[6] It is worth remembering also that *persons* read and debated this sort of thing, but in reading and debating it as a public, they adopted a very special rhetoric about their own personhood. Where earlier writers had typically seen the context of print as a means of personal extension — they understood themselves in print essentially to be speaking in their own persons — people began to see it as an authoritative mediation. That is clearly the case with the Steele passage, and pseudonymous serial essays like the *Spectator* did a great deal toward normalizing a public print discourse.

In the bourgeois public sphere, which was brought into being by publication in this sense, a principle of negativity was axiomatic: the validity of what you say in public bears a negative relation to your person. What you say will carry force not because of who you are but despite who you are. Implicit in this principle is a utopian universality that would allow people to transcend the given realities of their bodies and their status. But the rhetorical strategy of personal abstraction is both the utopian moment of the public sphere and a major source of domination, for the ability to abstract oneself in public discussion has always been an unequally available resource. Individuals have to have specific rhetorics of disincorporation; they are not simply rendered bodiless by exercising reason. And it is only possible to operate a discourse based on the claim to self-abstracting disinterestedness in a culture where such unmarked self-abstraction is a differential resource. The subject who could master this rhetoric in the bourgeois public sphere was implicitly, even explicitly, white, male, literate, and propertied. These traits could go unmarked, even grammatically, while other features of bodies could only be acknowledged in discourse as the humiliating positivity of the particular.

The bourgeois public sphere claimed to have no relation to body image at all. Public issues were depersonalized so that, in theory, any person would have the ability to offer an opinion about them and submit that opinion to the impersonal test of public debate without personal hazard. Yet the bourgeois public sphere continued to rely on features of certain bodies. Access to the public came in the whiteness and maleness that were then denied as forms of positivity, since the white male *qua* public person was only abstract rather than white and male. The contradiction is that even while particular bodies and dispositions enabled the liberating abstraction of public discourse, those bodies also summarized the constraints of positivity, the mere case of Anaxarchus, from which self-abstraction can be liberating.

It is very far from being clear that these asymmetries of embodiment were merely contingent encumbrances to the public sphere, residual forms of illiberal "discrimination." The difference between self-abstraction and a body's positivity is more than a difference in what has officially been made available to men and to women, for example. It is a difference in the cultural/symbolic definitions of masculinity and femininity.[7] Self-abstraction from male bodies confirms masculinity. Self-abstraction from female bodies denies femininity. The bourgeois public sphere is a frame of reference in which it is supposed that all particularities have the same status as mere particularity. But the ability to establish that frame of reference is a feature of some particularities. Neither in gender nor in race nor in class nor in sexualities is it possible to treat different particulars as having merely paratactic, or serial, difference. Differences in such realms already come coded as the difference between the unmarked and the marked, the universalizable and the particular. Their internal logic is such that the two sides of any of these differences cannot be treated as symmetrical — as they are, for example, in the rhetoric of liberal toleration or "debate" — without simply resecuring an asymmetrical privilege. The bourgeois public sphere has been structured from the outset by a logic of abstraction that provides a privilege for unmarked identities: the male, the white, the middle class, the normal.

That is what Pier Paolo Pasolini meant when he wrote, just before his murder, that "tolerance is always and purely nominal":

> In fact they tell the "tolerated" person to do what he wishes, that he has every right to follow his own nature, that the fact that he belongs to a minority does not in the least mean inferiority, etc. But his "difference" — or better, his "crime of being different" — remains the same both with regard to those who have decided to tolerate him and those who have decided to condemn him. No majority will ever be able to banish from its consciousness the feeling of the "difference" of minorities. I shall always be eternally, inevitably conscious of this.[8]

Doubtless it is better to be tolerated than to be killed, as Pasolini was. But it would be better still to make reference to one's marked particularities without being specified thereby as less than public. As the bourgeois public sphere paraded the spectacle of its disincorporation, it brought into being this minoritizing logic of domination. Publicness is always able to encode itself through the themes of universality, openness, meritocracy, and access, all of which derhetoricize its self-understanding, guaranteeing at every step that difference will be enunciated as mere positivity, an ineluctable limit imposed by the particularities of the body, a positivity that cannot translate or neutralize itself prosthetically without ceasing to exist. This minoritizing logic, intrinsic to the

167

deployment of negativity in the bourgeois public sphere, presents the subjects of bodily difference with the paradox of a utopian promise that cannot be cashed in for them. The very mechanism designed to end domination is a form of domination.

The appeal of mass subjectivity, I will suggest, arises largely from the contradiction in this dialectic of embodiment and negativity in the public sphere. Public discourse from the beginning offered a utopian self-abstraction, but in ways that left a residue of unrecuperated particularity, both for its privileged subjects and for those it minoritized. Its privileged subjects, abstracted from the very body features that gave them the privilege of that abstraction, found themselves in a relation of bad faith with their own positivity. To acknowledge their positivity would be to surrender their privilege, as, for example, to acknowledge the objectivity of the male body would be to feminize it. Meanwhile, minoritized subjects had few strategies open to them, but one was to carry their unrecuperated positivity into consumption. Even from the early eighteenth century, before the triumph of a liberal metalanguage for consumption, commodities were being used, especially by women, as a kind of access to publicness that would nevertheless link up with the specificity of difference.[9]

Consumption offered a counterutopia precisely in a balance between a collectivity of mass desires and an unminoritized rhetoric of difference in the field of choices among infinite goods. A great deal of noise in modern society comes from the inability to translate these utopian promises into a public sphere where collectivity has no link to the body and its desires, where difference is described not as the paratactic seriality of illimitable choice but as the given constraints of preconscious nature. Where consumer capitalism makes available an endlessly differentiable subject, the subject of the public sphere proper cannot be differentiated. It can represent difference as other, but as an available form of subjectivity it remains unmarked. The constitutional public sphere, therefore, cannot fully recuperate its residues. It can only display them. In this important sense, the "We" in "We the People" is the mass equivalent of the Spectator's prosthetic generality, a flexible instrument of interpellation but one that exiles its own positivity.

From the eighteenth century we in the modern West have inherited an understanding of printing as publication, but we now understand a vast range of everyday life as having the reference of publicity. The medium of print is now only a small part of our relation to what we understand as the public, and the fictitious abstraction of the Spectator would seem conspicuously out of place in the modern discourse of public icons. So although the bourgeois public sphere continues to secure a minoritizing liberal logic of self-abstraction, its rhetoric is increasingly complicated by other forms of publicity. At present, the mass-cultural public sphere continually offers its subject an array of body images. In earlier varieties of the public sphere, it was important that images of the body not figure centrally in public discourse. The anonymity of the discourse was a way of certifying the citizen's disinterested concern for the public good. But now public body images are everywhere on display, in virtually all media contexts. Where printed public discourse formerly relied on a rhetoric of abstract disembodiment, visual media, including print, now display bodies for a range of purposes: admiration, identification, appropriation, scandal, and so on. To be public in the West means to have an iconicity, and this is true equally of Muammar Qaddafi and of Karen Carpenter.

The visibility of public figures for the subject of mass culture occurs in a context in which publicity is generally mediated by the discourse of consumption. It is difficult to realize how much we observe public images with the eye of the consumer. Nearly all of our pleasures come to us coded in some degree by the publicity of mass media. We have brand names all over us. Even the most refined or the most perverse among us could point to his or her desires or identifications and see that in most cases they were public desires, even mass-public desires, from the moment that they were his or her desires. This is true not only in the case of salable commodities — our refrigerators, sneakers, lunch — but also in other areas where we make symbolic identifications in a field of choice: the way we bear our bodies, the sports we follow, or our erotic objects. In such areas, our desires have become recognizable through their display in the media, and in the moment of wanting them, we imagine a collective consumer witnessing our wants and choices.

The public discourse of the mass media has increasingly come to rely on the intimacy of this collective witnessing in its rhetoric of publicity, iconic and consumerist alike. It is a significant part of the ground of public discourse, the subjective apprehension of what is public. In everyday life, for one thing, we have access to the realm of political systems in the same way we have access to the circulation of commodities. Not only are we confronted by slogans that continually make this connection for us ("America wears Hanes," "The heartbeat of America"); more important, the contexts of commodities and politics share the same media and, at least in part, the same metalanguage for constructing our notion of what a public or a people is. When the citizen (or noncitizen — for contemporary publicity, the difference hardly matters) goes down to the 7-Eleven to buy a Budweiser and a *Barbie Magazine* and scans from the news headlines to the tabloid stories about the Rob Lowe sex scandal, several kinds of publicity are involved at once. Nevertheless, it is possible to speak of all these sites of publicity as parts of a public sphere, insofar as each is capable of illuminating the others in a common discourse of the subject's relation to the nation and its markets.

In each of these mediating contexts of publicity, we become the mass-public subject but in a new way unanticipated within the classical bourgeois public sphere. Moreover, if mass-public subjectivity has a kind of singularity, an undifferentiated extension to indefinite numbers of individuals, those individuals who make up the "we" of the mass-public subject might have very different relations to it. It is at the very moment of recognizing ourselves as the mass subject, for example, that we also recognize ourselves as minority subjects. As participants in the mass subject, we are the "we" that can describe our particular affiliations of class, gender, sexual orientation, race, or subculture only as "they." This self-alienation is common to all of the contexts of publicity, but it can be variously interpreted within each. The political meaning of the public subject's self-alienation is one of the most important sites of struggle in contemporary culture.

The Mirror of Popularity

In an essay called "The Image of the Body and Totalitarianism," Claude Lefort speculates that public figures have recently begun to play a new role. He imagines essentially a three-stage history of the body of publicity. Drawing on the work of Ernst Kantorowicz, he sketches first a representative public sphere in which the person of the prince stands as the head of the corporate body, summing up in his person the principles of legitimacy, though still drawing that legitimacy from a higher power. Classical bourgeois democracy, by contrast, abstracted the public, corporate body in a way that could be literalized in the decapitation of a ruler. "The democratic revolution, for so long subterranean, burst out when the body of the king was destroyed, when the body politic was decapitated and when, at the same time, the corporeality of the social was dissolved," Lefort writes. "There then occurred what I would call a 'disincorporation' of individuals."[10]

171

According to Lefort, the new trend, however, is again toward the display of the public official's person. The state now relies on its double in "the image of the people, which . . . remains indeterminate, but which nevertheless is susceptible of being determined, of being actualized on the level of phantasy as an image of the People-as-One." Public figures increasingly take on the function of concretizing that phantasmic body image, or, in other words, of actualizing the otherwise indeterminate image of the people. They embody what Lefort calls the Egocrat, whose self-identical representativeness is perverse and unstable in a way that contrasts with the representative person of the feudal public sphere: "The prince condensed in his person the principle of power . . . but he was supposed to obey a superior power. . . . That does not seem to be the position of the Egocrat or of his substitutes, the bureaucratic leaders. The Egocrat coincides with himself, as society is supposed to coincide with itself. An impossible swallowing up of the body in the head begins to take place, as does an impossible swallowing up of the head in the body."[11] Lefort sees the sources of this development in democracy, but he associates the trend with totalitarianism, presumably in the iconographies of Stalin and Mao. But then, Lefort wrote this essay in 1979; since that time, it has become increasingly clear that such phantasmic public embodiments have come to be the norm in Western democratic bureaucracies.

Habermas has an interestingly similar narrative. He, too, describes a first stage of a representative public sphere in which public persons derived their power in part from being on display. The idealizing language of nobility did not abstract away from the body: "Characteristically, in none of [the aristocracy's] virtues did the physical aspect entirely lose its significance, for virtue must be embodied, it had to be capable of public representation."[12] For Habermas, as for Lefort, this ceased to be the case with the bourgeois public sphere, in which the public was generalized away from physical, theatrical representation. It was relocated instead to the mostly written contexts of rational debate. And Habermas, again like Lefort, speaks of a more recent return to the display of public representatives, a return that he calls "refeudalizing": "The public sphere becomes the court before [which] public prestige can be displayed — rather than in which public critical debate is carried on."[13]

Why should modern regimes so require a return to the image of the leader in the peculiar form that Lefort calls the Egocrat? We can see both how powerful and how complicated this appeal in mass publicity can be by taking the example of Ronald Reagan's popularity. Reagan is probably the best example because, more than any other, his figure blurs the boundary between the iconicities of the political public and the commodity public. George Bush, Michael Dukakis, and the others were less adept at translating their persons from the interior of the political system to the surface of the brand-name commodity. The Reagan-style conjunction of these two kinds of appeal is the ideal-typical moment of national publicity against which they are measured. So, regardless of whatever skills they have within the political system, Bush and others like him have not been able to bring to their superbureaucratic persons the full extended reference of publicity. Reagan, by contrast, was the champion spokesmodel for America, just as he had earlier been a spokesmodel for Westinghouse and for Hollywood. It's easy to understand why the left clings to its amnesia about the pleasures of publicity when confronted with a problem like the popularity of a Ronald Reagan. But we do not have a clear understanding of the nature of the public with which Reagan was popular, nor do we have a clear understanding of the attraction of such a public figure.

A 1989 report in the *Nation* has it that Reagan was not a popular president at all. Gallup opinion polls, over the duration of his two terms, rated him far less favorably than Franklin D. Roosevelt, John F. Kennedy, or Dwight D. Eisenhower. He was not appreciably more popular than Gerald Ford or Jimmy Carter. For the left-liberal readership of the *Nation*, this surprising statistic spells relief. It encourages us to believe that the public might not be so blind, after all. Indeed, in the story that presents the statistics, Thomas Ferguson claims exactly this sort of populist vindication. For him, the point of the story is simply that journalists who genuflect before Reagan's popularity are mistaken and irresponsible. The people, he implies, know better, and politics would be more reasonable if the media better represented the public. Not without sentimentality, the *Nation* regards the poll as the public's authentic expression and the media picture as its distortion.[14]

But even if the figures represent an authentic public, it's far from clear how to take reassurance from such a poll. What could it mean to say that Reagan's popularity was simply illusory? For Congress discovered that it was not. And so did the media, since editors quickly learned that the journalistic sport of catching Reagan in his errors could make their audiences bristle with hostility. Reagan in one sense may have had no real popularity, as polls record it. But in another sense, he had a substantial and positive popularity, which he and others could deploy both within the political system and within the wider sphere of publicity. So if we characterize the poll as the authentic opinion of the public, while viewing the media reports of Reagan's popularity as a distortion, then both the genesis and the force of that distortion become inexplicable. It would be clearly inadequate to say, in what amounts to a revival of old talk about the conspiracy of the bosses, that the media were simply "managed" or "manipulated," despite the Republicans' impressive forensics of spin control.[15]

The *Nation*, then, gives a much too easy answer to the question of Reagan's attraction when it claims that there simply never was any. If that answer seems mistaken, the poll shows that it would be equally mistaken to see the public as successfully recruited into an uncritical identification with Reagan and an uncritical acclamation of Reaganism. It might otherwise have been comforting to believe, by means of such explanations, that Reagan really was popular, that the people were suckered. Then, at least, we could tell ourselves that we knew something about "the people." In fact, we have no way of talking abut the public without theorizing the contexts and strategies in which the public could be represented. If we believe in the continued existence of a rational-critical public, as the *Nation* does, then it is difficult to account for the counter-democratic tendencies of the public sphere as anything other than the cowardice or bad faith of some journalists. On the other hand, if we believe that the public sphere of the mass media has replaced a rational and critical public with one that is consumerist and acclamatory, then we might expect it to show more consumer satisfaction, more acclaim.

"Reagan" as an image owes its peculiar character in large part to the appeal of the other media construction that is jointly offered with it: "the public." In publicity, we are given a stake in the imaginary of a mass public in a way that dictates a certain appeal not so much for Ronald Reagan in particular as for the kind of public figure of which he is exemplary. Different figures may articulate that appeal differently, and with important consequences, but there is a logic of appeal to which Reagan and Jesse Jackson equally submit. Publicity puts us in a relation to these figures that is also a relation to an unrealizable public subject, whose omnipotence and subjectivity can then be figured both on and against the images of such men. A public, after all, cannot have a discrete, positive existence; something becomes a public only through its availability for subjective identification. "Reagan" bears in its being the marks of its mediation to a public, and "the public" equally bears in its being the marks of its mediation for identification. Indeed, the most telling thing of all about the article in the *Nation* is Ferguson's remark that the myth of Reagan's popularity is itself "ever-popular." The problem is not Reagan's popularity but the popularity of his popularity. "Reagan," we might even say, is a relay for a kind of metapopularity. The major task of Western leaders has become producing popularity, which is not the same as being popular.

What makes figures of publicity attractive to people? I do not mean this to be a condescending question. This question does not ask simply how people are seduced or manipulated. It asks what kinds of identifications are required or allowed in the discourse of publicity. The rhetorical conditions under which the popular can be performed are of consequence not only for policy outcomes but, more important, for who we are.

Self-Abstraction and the Mass Subject

Part of the bad faith of the *res publica* of letters was that it required a denial of the bodies that gave access to it. The public sphere is still enough oriented to its liberal logic that its citizens long to abstract themselves into a privileged public disembodiment. And when that fails, they can turn to another kind of longing, which, as Berlant shows, is not so much to cancel out their bodies as to trade them in for a better model. The mass public sphere tries to minimize the difference between the two, surrounding the citizen with trademarks through which she can trade marks, offering both positivity and self-abstraction. This has meant, furthermore, that the mass public sphere has had to develop genres of collective identification that will articulate both sides of this dialectic.

Insofar as the two sides are contradictory, however, mass identification tends to be characterized by what I earlier called noise, which typically appears as an erotic-aggressive disturbance. Here it might be worth thinking about a genre in which the display of bodies is also a kind of disembodiment: the discourse of disasters. At least since the great Chicago fire, mass disaster has had a special relationship to the mass media. Mass injury can always command a headline; it gets classed as immediate-reward news. But whatever kind of reward makes disaster rewarding, it evidently has to do with injury to a mass body — an already abstracted body assembled by the simultaneity of the disaster somewhere other than here. When massive numbers of separate injuries occur, they fail to command the same fascination. This discrepancy in how seriously we take different organizations of injury is a source of never-ending frustration for airline executives. They never tire of pointing out that although the fatality rate for automobiles is astronomically higher than for airplanes, there is no public panic of supervision about automobiles. In the airline executives' interested exasperation, that seems merely to prove the irrationality of journalists and congressmen. But I think this fondness of the mass media for a very special kind of injury makes rigorous sense. Disaster is popular because it is a way of making mass subjectivity available, and it tells us something about the desirability of that mass subject.

John Waters tells us in *Shock Value* that one of his hobbies in youth was collecting disaster coverage. His all-time favorite photograph, he claims, is a famous shot of the stadium collapsing at the Indianapolis 500, a photograph he proudly reproduces. But despite his pride in the aura of perversion that surrounds this disclosure, he is at some pains to point out that his pleasure is a normal feature of the discourse. "It makes the newspapers worth the quarter," he writes, and "perks up the local news shows." What could be the dynamic of this link between injury and the pleasures of mass publicity? Waters stages the intimacy of the link in the following story about his childhood, in what I think of as a brilliant corruption of Freud's *fort/da* game:

177

Even as a toddler, violence intrigued me.... While other kids were out playing cowboys and Indians, I was lost in fantasies of crunching metal and people screaming for help. I would sweet-talk unsuspecting relatives into buying me toy cars — any kind, as long as they were new and shiny.... I would take two cars and pretend they were driving on a secluded country road until one would swerve and crash into the other. I would become quite excited and start smashing the car with a hammer, all the while shouting, "Oh, my God, there's been a terrible accident!"[16]

Exactly what kind of pleasure is this? It isn't just the infantile recuperation of power that the *fort/da* game usually represents. The boy Waters, in other words, is not just playing out identification and revenge in the rhythm of treasuring and destroying the cars.

Nor is Waters simply indulging the infantile transitivism of which Jacques Lacan writes: "The child who strikes another says that he has been struck; the child who sees another fall, cries."[17] In fact, Waters's pleasure in the scene seems to have little to do with the cars at all. Rather, it comes about largely through his identification with publicity. Not only does Waters have access to auto disaster in the first place through the public discourse of news; he dramatizes that discourse as part of the event. Whose voice does he take up in exclaiming, "Oh, my God, there's been a terrible accident!"? And just as important, to whom is he speaking? He turns himself into a relay of spectators, none of whom is injured so much as horrified by the witnessing of injury. His ventriloquized announcer and his invisible audience allow him to internalize an absent witness. He has been careful to imagine the cars as being on "a secluded country road" so that his imaginary audience can be anywhere else. It is, in effect, the mass subject of news.

In this sense, the story shows us how deeply publicity has

come to inform our subjectivity. But it also reveals, through Waters's camp humor, that the mass subject's absent witnessing is a barely concealed transitivism. The disaster audience finds its body with a revenge. Its surface is all sympathy: there's been a terrible accident. The sympathetic quality of its identification, however, is only half the story since, as Waters knows, inflicting and witnessing mass injury are two sides of the same dynamic in disaster discourse. Being of necessity anywhere else, the mass subject cannot have a body except the body it witnesses. But in order to become a mass subject, it has left that body behind, abstracted away from it, canceled it as mere positivity. It returns in the spectacle of big-time injury. The transitive pleasure of witnessing/injuring makes available our translation into the disembodied publicity of the mass subject. By injuring a mass body — preferably a really massive body, somewhere — we constitute ourselves as a noncorporeal mass witness. (I do not, however, mean to minimize Waters's delirious perverseness in spelling out this link between violence and spectatorship in mass subjectivity. The perverse acknowledgment of his pleasure, in fact, helps him to violate in return the minoritizing disembodiment of the mass subject. It therefore allows Waters a counterpublic embodied knowledge in the mode of camp.) The same logic informs an astonishing number of mass publicity's genres, from the prophylaxes of horror, assassination, and terrorism, to the organized prosthesis of sports. (But, as Waters writes, "Violence in sports always seemed so pointless, because everyone was prepared, so what fun could it possibly be?"[18]) The mass media are dominated by genres that construct the mass subject's impossible relation to a body.

In the genres of mass-imaginary transitivism, we might say, a public is thinking about itself and its media. This is true even in the most vulgar of the discourses of mass publicity, the tabloid pastime of star puncturing. In the figures of Elvis, Liz, Michael,

Oprah, Geraldo, Brando, and the like, we witness and transact the bloating, slimming, wounding, and general humiliation of the public body. The bodies of these public figures are prostheses for our own mutant desirability. That is not to say that a mass imaginary identification is deployed with uniform or equal effect in each of these cases. A significant subgenre of tabloid publicity, for instance, is devoted not to perforating the iconic bodies of its male stars but to denying them any private power behind their iconic bodies. Johnny Carson, Clint Eastwood, Rob Lowe, and others like them are subjected to humiliating forms of display not for gaining weight or having cosmetic surgery but for failing to exercise full control over their lives. By chronicling their endless romantic/matrimonial disasters, publicity keeps them available for our appropriation of their iconic status by reminding us that they do not possess the phallic power of their images — we do.

In this respect, we would have to say that Reagan stands in partial contrast to these other male icons of publicity. He does not require a discourse of star puncturing because he seems to make no personal claim on the phallic power of his own image. His body, impossible to embarrass, has no private subject behind it. The gestures stay the same, undisturbed by reflection or management. Reagan never gives a sense of modulation between a public and a private self, and he therefore remains immune to humiliation. That is why it was so easy for news reports to pry into his colon without indiscretion. His witless self-continuity is the modern equivalent of virtue. He is the perfect example of what Lefort calls the Egocrat: he coincides with himself and therefore concretizes a fantasy-image of the unitary people. He is popularity with a hairdo, an image of popularity's popularity.

The presentation of Reagan's body was an important part of his performance of popularity. J.G. Ballard understood that as early as 1968 in a story titled "Why I Want to Fuck Ronald Reagan." In that story, every subject of publicity is said to share the secret but powerful fantasy of violating Reagan's anus. In sharing that fantasy, Ballard suggests, we demonstrate the same thing that we demonstrate as consumers of the Kennedy assassination: the erotics of a mass imaginary. Like Waters's perverse transitivism, Ballard's generalized sadistic star cult theorizes the public sphere and ironizes it at the same time. His characters, especially in *Crash*, are obsessed with a violent desire for the icons of publicity. But theirs is not a private pathology. Their longing to dismember and be dismembered with Ronald Reagan or Elizabeth Taylor is understood as a more reflective version of these public icons' normal appeal. In the modern nations of the West, individuals encounter in publicity the erotics of a powerful identification not just with public icons but also with their popularity.

It's important to stress, given the outcome of such a metapopularity in the realm of policy, that the utopian moments in consumer publicity have an unstable political valence. Responding to an immanent contradiction in the bourgeois public sphere, mass publicity promises a reconciliation between embodiment and self-abstraction. That can be a powerful appeal, especially to those minoritized by the public sphere's rhetoric of normative disembodiment. Mass subjectivity, however, can result just as easily in new forms of tyranny of the majority as it can in the claims of rival collectivities. Perhaps the clearest example now is the discourse on AIDS. As Simon Watney and others have shown, one of the most hateful features of AIDS discourse has been its construction of a "general public."[19] A spokesman for the White House, asked why Reagan had not even mentioned the word "AIDS" or its problems until late in 1985, explained, "It hadn't spread into the general population yet."[20] In pursuit of a public demanded by good professional journalism, the mass media have pursued the same logic, interpellating their public as unitary and as heterosexual.

181

Moreover, they have deployed the transitivism of mass identification in order to exile the positivity of the body to a zone of infection; the unitary public is uninfected but threatened. In this context, it is heartbreakingly accurate to speak of the prophylaxis held out by mass publicity to those who will identify with its immunized body.

Hateful though it is to those exiled into positivity by such a discourse, in a sense everyone's relation to the public body must have more or less the same logic. No one really inhabits the general public. This is true not only because it is by definition general but also because everyone brings to such a category the particularities from which she has to abstract herself in consuming this discourse. Of course, some particularities, such as whiteness and maleness, are already oriented to that procedure of abstraction. (They can scarcely even be imagined as particularities; think, for example, of the asymmetry between the semantics of "feminism" and "masculinism.") But the given of the body is nevertheless a site of countermemory, all the more so since statistically everyone will be mapped into some minority or other, a form of positivity minoritized precisely in the abstracting discourse with which everyone also identifies.

So in this sense, the gap that gay people register within the discourse of the general public might well be an aggravated form, though a lethally aggravated form, of the normal relation to the general public. I'm suggesting, in other words, that a fundamental feature of the contemporary public sphere is this double movement of identification and alienation: on one hand, the prophylaxis of general publicity; on the other hand, the always inadequate particularity of individual bodies, experienced both as an invisible desire within a visible body and, in consequence, as a kind of closeted vulnerability. The centrality of this contradiction in the legitimate textuality of the video-capitalist state, I think, is the reason why the discourse of the public sphere is so entirely given over to a violently desirous speculation on bodies. What I have tried to emphasize is that the effect of disturbance in mass publicity is not a corruption introduced into the public sphere by its colonization through mass media. It is the legacy of the bourgeois public sphere's founding logic, the contradictions of which become visible whenever the public sphere can no longer turn a blind eye to its privileged bodies.

For the same reasons, the public sphere is also not simply corrupted by its articulation with consumption. If anything, consumption sustains a counterpublicity that cuts against the self-contradictions of the bourgeois public sphere. One final example can show how. In the 1980s, graffiti writing took a new form. Always a kind of counterpublicity, it became the medium of an urban and mostly black male subculture. The major cities each devoted millions of dollars per year to obliterate it, and to criminalize it as a medium, while the art world moved to canonize it out of its counterpublic setting. In an article from 1987, Susan Stewart argues that the core of the graffiti writers' subculture lay in the way it took up the utopian promise of consumer publicity, and particularly of the brand name. These graffiti do not say "U.S. out of North America," or "Patriarch go home," or "Power to the queer nation"; they are personal signatures legible only to the intimately initiated. Reproduced as quickly and as widely as possible (unlike their canonized art equivalents), they are trademarks that can be spread across a nearly anonymous landscape. The thrill of brand-name dissemination, however, is linked to a very private sphere of knowledge, since the signature has been trademarked into illegibility. Stewart concludes:

> Graffiti may be a petty crime but its threat to value is an inventive one, for it forms a critique of the status of all artistic artifacts, indeed

a critique of all privatized consumption, and it carries out that threat in full view, in repetition, so that the public has nowhere to look, no place to locate an averted glance. And that critique is paradoxically mounted from a relentless individualism, an individualism which, with its perfected monogram, arose out of the paradox of all commodity relations in their attempt to create a mass individual; an ideal consumer; a necessarily fading star. The independence of the graffiti writer has been shaped by a freedom both promised and denied by those relations — a freedom of choice which is a freedom among delimited and clearly unattainable goods. While that paradise of consumption promised the transference of uniqueness from the artifact to the subject, graffiti underlines again and again an imaginary uniqueness of the subject and a dissolution of artifactual status *per se.*[21]

The graffiti of this subculture, in effect, parody the mass media; by appearing everywhere, they aspire to the placeless publicity of mass print or televisualization. They thus abstract away from the given body, which in the logic of graffiti is difficult to criminalize or minoritize because it is impossible to locate. ("Nowhere to look, no place to locate an averted glance" exactly describes the abstraction of televisualized space.) Unlike the self-abstraction of normal publicity, however, graffiti retain their link to a body in an almost parodic devotion to the sentimentality of the signature. As Stewart points out, they claim an imaginary uniqueness promised in commodities but canceled in the public sphere proper. Whenever mass publicity puts its bodies on display, it reactivates this same promise. And although emancipation is not around the corner, its possibility is visible everywhere.

Obviously, the discursive genres of mass publicity vary widely. I group them together to show how they become interconnected as expressing a subjectivity that each genre helps to construct. In

such contexts, the content and the media of mass publicity mutually determine each other. Mass media thematize certain materials — a jet crash, Michael Jackson's latest surgery, or a football
game — to find a way of constructing their audiences as mass audiences. These contents then function culturally as metalanguages,
giving meaning to the medium. In consuming the thematic materials of mass-media discourse, persons construct themselves as its
mass subject. Thus the same reciprocity that allowed the *Spectator*
and its print medium to be mutually clarifying can be seen in the
current mass media. But precisely because the meaning of the
mass media depends so much on their articulation with a specific
metalanguage, we cannot speak simply of one kind of mass subjectivity or one politics of mass publicity. Stewart makes roughly
the same observation when she remarks that the intrication of
graffiti, as a local practice, with the systemic themes of access —
"access to discourse, access to goods, access to the reception of
information" — poses a methodological problem, "calling into
question the relations between a micro- and a macro-analysis:
the insinuating and pervasive forms of the mass culture are here
known only through localizations and adaptations."[22]

Nevertheless, some things are clear. In a discourse of publicity
structured by deep contradictions between self-abstraction and
self-realization, contradictions that have only been forced to the
fore in televisual consumer culture, there has been a massive shift
toward the politics of identity. The major political movements of
the last half century have been oriented toward status categories.
Unlike almost all previous social movements — Chartism, temperance, or the French Revolution — they have been centrally about
the personal identity formation of minoritized subjects. These
movements all presuppose the bourgeois public sphere as background. Their rallying cries of difference take for granted the official rhetoric of self-abstraction. It would be naive and sentimental

to suppose that identities or mere assertions of status will precip-
itate from this crisis as its solution, since the public discourse
makes identity an ongoing problem. An assertion of the full equality of minoritized statuses would require abandoning the structure of self-abstraction in publicity. That outcome seems unlikely
in the near future. In the meantime, the contradictions of status
and publicity are played out at both ends of the public discourse.
We, as the subjects of mass publicity, ever more find a political
stake in the difficult-to-recognize politics of our identity, and the
egocrats who fill the screens of national fantasy must summon all
their skin and hair to keep that politics from getting personal.

CHAPTER FIVE

Sex in Public*

By Lauren Berlant and Michael Warner

There Is Nothing More Public Than Privacy
An essay titled "Sex in Public" teases with the obscurity of its
object and the twisted aim of its narrative. In this essay, we talk
not about the sex people already have clarity about, or identities
and acts,[1] or a wildness in need of derepression;[2] rather, we talk
about sex as it is mediated by publics. Some of these publics have
an obvious relation to sex: pornographic cinema, phone sex,
"adult" markets for print, lap dancing. Others are organized
around sex but not necessarily sex *acts* in the usual sense: queer
zones and other worlds estranged from heterosexual culture, but
also more tacit scenes of sexuality like official national culture,
which depends on a notion of privacy to cloak its sexualization of
national membership.

The aim of this essay is to describe what we want to promote
as the radical aspirations of queer culture building: not just a safe
zone for queer sex, but the changed possibilities of identity, intelligibility, publics, culture, and sex that appear when the heterosexual couple is no longer the referent or privileged example of
sexual culture. Queer social practices like sex and theory try to

*Originally published in *Critical Inquiry* 24.2 (Winter 1998).

unsettle the garbled but powerful norms supporting that privilege — including the project of normalization that has made hetero-sexuality hegemonic — as well as those material practices that, though not explicitly sexual, are implicated in the hierarchies of property and propriety that we will describe as heteronormative.[3] We open with two scenes of sex in public.

Scene One

In 1993, *Time* magazine published a special issue about immigration called "The New Face of America."[4] The cover girl of this issue was morphed via computer from head shots representing a range of U.S. immigrant groups: an amalgam of "Middle Eastern," "Italian," "African," "Vietnamese," "Anglo-Saxon," "Chinese," and "Hispanic" faces. The new face of America is supposed to represent what the modal citizen will look like when, in the year 2004, there will no longer be a white statistical majority in the United States. Naked, smiling, and just off-white, *Time*'s divine Frankenstein aims to organize hegemonic optimism about citizenship and the national future. *Time*'s theory is that by the twenty-first century interracial reproductive sex will have taken place in the United States on such a mass scale that racial difference itself will be finally replaced by a kind of family feeling based on blood relations. In the twenty-first century, *Time* imagines, hundreds of millions of hybrid faces will erase American racism altogether: the nation will become a happy racial monoculture made up of "one mixed blood."[5]

The publication of this special issue caused a brief flurry of interest but had no important effects; its very banality calls us to understand the technologies that produce its ordinariness. The fantasy banalized by the image is one that reverberates in the law and the most intimate crevices of everyday life. Its explicit aim is to help its public process the threat to "normal" or "core" national culture currently phrased as "the problem of immigra-tion."[6] But this crisis image of immigrants is also a *racial mirage* generated by a white-dominated society, supplying a concrete phobia to organize its public so that a more substantial discussion of exploitation in the United States can be avoided and then re-maindered to the part of collective memory sanctified not by nos-talgia but by mass aversion. Let's call this the amnesia archive. The motto above the door is: "Memory is the amnesia you like."

But more than exploitation and racism are forgotten in this whirl of projection and suppression. Central to the transfiguration of the immigrant as a nostalgic image to shore up core national cul-ture and allay white fears of minoritization is something that can-not speak its name, though its signature is everywhere: national heterosexuality. National heterosexuality is the mechanism by which a core national culture can be imagined as a sanitized space of sentimental feeling and immaculate behavior, a space of pure citizenship. A familial model of society displaces recognition of structural racism and other systemic inequalities. This is not entirely new: the family form has functioned as a mediator and metaphor of national existence in the United States since the eigh-teenth century.[7] We are arguing that its contemporary deploy-ment increasingly supports the governmentality of the welfare state by separating the aspirations of national belonging from the critical culture of the public sphere and from political citizenship.[8] Immigration crises have also previously produced feminine icons that function as prostheses for the state — most famously, the Statue of Liberty, which symbolized seamless immigrant assimila-tion to the metaculture of the United States. In *Time*'s face, it is not symbolic femininity but practical heterosexuality that guarantees the monocultural nation.

The nostalgic family-values covenant of contemporary Ameri-can politics stipulates a privatization of citizenship and sex in a number of ways. In law and political ideology, for example, the fetus and the child have been spectacularly elevated to the place of sanctified nationality. The state now sponsors stings and laws to purify the Internet on behalf of children. New welfare and tax "reforms" passed under the cooperation between the Contract with America and Clintonian familialism seek to increase the legal and economic privileges of married couples and parents. Vouchers and privatization rezone education as the domain of parents rather than of citizens. Meanwhile, senators such as Ted Kennedy and Jesse Helms support amendments that refuse federal funds to organizations that "promote, disseminate, or produce materials that are obscene or that depict or describe, in a patently offensive way, sexual or excretory activities or organs, including but not limited to obscene depictions of sadomasochism, homo-eroticism, the sexual exploitation of children, or any individuals engaged in sexual intercourse."[9] These developments, though distinct, are linked in the way they organize a hegemonic national public around sex. But because this sex public officially claims to act only in order to protect the zone of heterosexual privacy, the institutions of economic privilege and social reproduction informing its practices and organizing its ideal world are protected by the spectacular demonization of any represented sex.

Scene Two

In October 1995, the New York City Council passed a new zoning law by a forty-one-to-nine vote. The Zoning Text Amendment covers adult book and video stores, eating and drinking establishments, theaters, and other businesses. It allows these businesses only in certain nonresidential zoning areas, most of which turn out to be on the waterfront. Within the new reserved districts, adult businesses are disallowed within five hundred feet of another adult establishment or within five hundred feet of a house of worship, school, or day-care center. They are limited to one per lot and limited in size to ten thousand square feet. Signs are limited in size, placement, and illumination. All other adult businesses are required to close within a year. Of the estimated 177 adult businesses in the city, all but 28 may have to close under this law. Enforcement of the bill is entrusted to building inspectors.

The court challenge to the bill was brought by a coalition that also fought it in the political process: anticensorship groups such as the New York Civil Liberties Union, Feminists for Free Expression, People for the American Way, and the National Coalition Against Censorship, as well as gay and lesbian organizations such as the Lambda Legal Defense and Education Fund, the Empire State Pride Agenda, and the AIDS Prevention Action League. (An appeal was still pending as of July 1997.) These latter groups joined the anticensorship groups for a simple reason: the impact of rezoning on businesses catering to queers, especially to gay men, will be devastating. All five of the adult businesses on Christopher Street will be shut down, along with the principal venues where men meet men for sex. None of these businesses has been a target of local complaints. Gay men have come to take for granted the availability of explicit sexual materials, theaters, and clubs. That is how they have learned to find each other, to map a commonly accessible world, to construct the architecture of queer space in a homophobic environment, and, for the last fifteen years, to cultivate a collective ethos of safer sex. All of that is about to change. Now gay men who want sexual materials, or who want to meet men for sex, will have two choices: they can cathect the privatized virtual public of phone sex and the Internet; or they can travel to small, inaccessible, little-trafficked, badly lit areas, remote from public transportation and from any residences, mostly on the waterfront, where heterosexual porn users will also be relocated and where risk of violence will consequently be higher.[10] In either case, the result will be a sense of isolation and diminished expectations for queer life, as well as an attenuated capacity for political community. The nascent lesbian sexual culture, including the Clit Club and the only video-rental club catering to lesbians, will also disappear. The impact of the sexual purification of New York will fall unequally on those who already have the fewest publicly accessible resources.

Normativity and Sexual Culture

Heterosexuality is not a thing. We speak of heterosexual culture rather than heterosexuality because that culture never has more than a provisional unity.[11] It is neither a single Symbolic nor a single ideology nor a unified set of shared beliefs.[12] The conflicts between these strands are seldom more than dimly perceived in practice, where the givenness of male-female sexual relations is part of the ordinary rightness of the world, its fragility masked in shows of solemn rectitude. Such conflicts have also gone unrecognized in theory, partly because of the metacultural work of the very category of heterosexuality, which consolidates as *a sexuality* widely differing practices, norms, and institutions, and partly because the sciences of social knowledge are themselves so deeply anchored in the process of normalization to which Foucault attributes so much of modern sexuality.[13] Thus when we say that the contemporary United States is saturated by the project of constructing national heterosexuality, we do not mean that national heterosexuality is anything like a simple monoculture. Hegemonies are nothing if not elastic alliances, involving dispersed and contradictory strategies for self-maintenance and reproduction.

Heterosexual culture achieves much of its metacultural intelligibility through the ideologies and institutions of intimacy. We want to argue here that although the intimate relations of private personhood appear to be the realm of sexuality itself, allowing "sex in public" to appear like matter out of place, intimacy is itself publicly mediated, in several senses. First, its conventional spaces presuppose a structural differentiation of "personal life" from work, politics, and the public sphere.[14] Second, the normativity of heterosexual culture links intimacy only to the institutions of personal life, making them the privileged institutions of social reproduction, the accumulation and transfer of capital, and self-development. Third, by making sex seem irrelevant or merely personal, heteronormative conventions of intimacy block the building of nonnormative or explicit public sexual cultures. Finally, those conventions conjure a mirage: a home base of pre-political humanity from which citizens are thought to come into political discourse and to which they are expected to return in the (always imaginary) future after political conflict. Intimate life is the endlessly cited *elsewhere* of political public discourse, a promised haven that distracts citizens from the unequal conditions of their political and economic lives, consoles them for the damaged humanity of mass society, and shames them for any divergence between their lives and the intimate sphere that is alleged to be simple personhood.

Ideologies and institutions of intimacy are increasingly offered as a vision of the good life for the destabilized and struggling citizenry of the United States, the only (fantasy) zone in which a future might be thought and willed, the only (imaginary) place where good citizens might be produced away from the confusing and unsettling distractions and contradictions of capitalism and politics. Indeed, one of the unforeseen paradoxes of national-capitalist privatization has been that citizens have been led through heterosexual culture to identify both themselves *and their politics* with privacy. In the official public, this involves making sex private; reintensifying *blood* as a psychic base for identification; replacing state mandates for social justice with a privatized ethics of responsibility, charity, atonement, and "values"; and enforcing boundaries between moral persons and economic ones.[15]

A complex cluster of sexual practices gets confused, in heterosexual culture, with the love plot of intimacy and familialism that signifies belonging to society in a deep and normal way. Community is imagined through scenes of intimacy, coupling, and kinship.[16] And a historical relation to futurity is restricted to generational narrative and reproduction. A whole field of social relations becomes intelligible as heterosexuality, and this privatized sexual culture bestows on its sexual practices a tacit sense of rightness and normalcy. This sense of rightness — embedded in things and not just in sex — is what we call heteronormativity. Heteronormativity is more than ideology, or prejudice, or phobia against gays and lesbians; it is produced in almost every aspect of the forms and arrangements of social life: nationality, the state, and the law; commerce; medicine; education; plus the conventions and affects of narrativity, romance, and other protected spaces of culture. It is hard to see these fields as heteronormative because the sexual culture straight people inhabit is so diffuse, a mix of languages they are just developing with notions of sexuality so ancient that their material conditions feel hardwired into personhood.

But intimacy has not always had the meaning it has for contemporary heteronormative culture. Along with Foucault and other historians, the classicist David Halperin, for example, has shown that in ancient Athens, sex was a transitive act rather than a fundamental dimension of personhood or an expression of intimacy. The verb for having sex appears on a late antique list of things that are not done in regard to or through others: "namely, speaking, singing, dancing, fist-fighting, competing, hanging oneself, dying, being crucified, diving, finding a treasure, having sex, vomiting, moving one's bowels, sleeping, laughing, crying, talking to the gods, and the like."[17] Halperin points out that the inclusion of fucking on this list shows that sex is not here "knit up in a web of mutuality." In contrast, modern heterosexuality is supposed to refer to relations of intimacy and identification with other persons, and sex acts are supposed to be the most intimate communication of them all.[18] The sex act protected in the zone of privacy is the affectional nimbus that heterosexual culture protects and from which it abstracts its model of ethics; but this utopia of social belonging is also supported and extended by acts less commonly recognized as part of sexual culture: paying taxes, being disgusted, philandering, bequeathing, celebrating a holiday, investing for the future, teaching, disposing a corpse, carrying wallet photos, buying economy size, being nepotistic, running for president, divorcing, or owning anything "His" and "Hers."

The elaboration of this list is a project for further study. Meanwhile, to make it, and to laugh at it, is not immediately to label any practice as oppressive, uncool, or definitive. We are describing a constellation of practices that everywhere disperses heterosexual privilege as a tacit but central organizing index of social membership. Exposing it inevitably produces what we have elsewhere called a wrenching sense of recontextualization as its subjects, even its gay and lesbian subjects, begin to piece together how it is that social and economic discourses, institutions, and practices that don't feel especially sexual or familial collaborate to produce as a social norm and ideal an extremely narrow context for living.[19] Heterosexual culture cannot recognize, validate, sustain, incorporate, or remember much of what people know and experience about the cruelty of normal culture even to the people who identify with it.

But that cruelty does not go unregistered. Intimacy, for example, has a whole public environment of therapeutic genres dedicated to witnessing the constant failure of heterosexual ideologies and institutions. Every day in many countries now, people's

failure to sustain or be sustained by institutions of privacy is testi-
fied to on talk shows, in scandal journalism, even in the ordinary
course of mainstream journalism addressed to middlebrow culture. We can learn a lot from these stories of love plots that have
gone astray: about the ways quotidian violence is linked to complex pressures from money, racism, histories of sexual violence,
cross-generational tensions. We can learn a lot from listening to
the increasing demands on love to deliver the good life it promises.
And we can learn a lot from the extremely punitive responses that
tend to emerge when people seem not to suffer enough for their
transgressions and failures.

Maybe we would learn too much. Recently the proliferation
of evidence for heterosexuality's failings has produced a backlash
against talk-show therapy. It has even brought William Bennett to
the podium; but rather than confessing his transgressions or making a complaint about someone else's, he calls for boycotts and
suppression of heterosexual therapy culture altogether. Recognition of heterosexuality's daily failures agitates him as much as
queerness. "We've forgotten that civilization depends on keeping
some of this stuff under wraps," he said. "This is a tropism toward
the toilet."[20]

But does civilization need to cover its ass? Or does heterosexual
culture actually secure itself through banalizing intimacy? Does
belief that normal life is actually possible *require* amnesia and the
ludicrous stereotyping of a bottom-feeding culture apparently
inadequate to intimacy? On these shows, no one ever blames the
ideology and institutions of heterosexuality. Every day, even the
talk-show hosts are newly astonished to find that people who are
committed to hetero intimacy are nevertheless unhappy. After all is
said and done, the prospects and promises of heterosexual culture
still represent the optimism for optimism, a hope to which people
apparently have already pledged their consent — at least in public.

Biddy Martin has written that some queer social theorists have produced a reductive and pseudo-radical antinormativity by actively repudiating the institutions of heterosexuality that have come to oversaturate the social imaginary. She shows that the kinds of arguments that crop up in the writings of people like Andrew Sullivan are not just right-wing fantasies. "In some queer work," she writes, "the very fact of attachment has been cast as only punitive and constraining because already socially constructed.... Radical anti-normativity throws out a lot of babies with a lot of bathwater.... An enormous fear of ordinariness or normalcy results in superficial accounts of the complex imbrication of sexuality with other aspects of social and psychic life, and in far too little attention to the dilemmas of the average people that we also are."[21]

We think our friend Biddy might be referring to us, although in this segment she cites no one in particular. We would like to clarify the argument. To be against heteronormativity is not to be against norms. To be against the processes of normalization is not to be afraid of ordinariness. Nor is it to advocate the "life without limit" she sees as produced by bad Foucauldians. Nor is it to decide that sentimental identifications with family and children are waste or garbage, or make people into waste or garbage. Nor is it to say that any sex called "lovemaking" isn't lovemaking; whatever the ideological or historical burdens of sexuality have been, they have not excluded, and indeed may have entailed, the ability of sex to count as intimacy and care. What we have been arguing here is that the space of sexual culture has become obnoxiously cramped from doing the work of maintaining a normal metaculture. When Martin calls us to recognize ourselves as "average people," to relax from an artificially stimulated "fear of ... normalcy," the image of average personhood appears to be simply descriptive. But its averageness is also normative, in exactly the sense that Foucault meant by "normalization": not the imposition

197

of an alien will, but a distribution around a statistically imagined norm. This deceptive appeal of the average remains heteronormative, measuring deviance from the mass. It can also be consoling, an expression of a utopian desire for unconflicted personhood. But this desire cannot be satisfied in the current conditions of privacy. People feel that the price they must pay for social membership and a relation to the future is identification with the heterosexual life narrative; that they are individually responsible for the rages, instabilities, ambivalences, and failures they experience in their intimate lives, while the fractures of the contemporary United States shame and sabotage them everywhere. Heterosexuality involves so many practices that are not sex that a world in which this hegemonic cluster would not be dominant is, at this point, unimaginable. We are trying to bring that world into being.

Queer Counterpublics

By queer culture we mean a world-making project, where world, like public, differs from community or group because it necessarily includes more people than can be identified, more spaces than can be mapped beyond a few reference points, modes of feeling that can be learned rather than experienced as birthright. The queer world is a space of entrances, exits, unsystematized lines of acquaintance, projected horizons, typifying examples, alternate routes, blockages, incommensurate geographies.[22] World making, as much in the mode of dirty talk as of print-mediated representation, is dispersed through incommensurate registers, by definition *unrealizable* as community or identity. Every cultural form, be it a novel or an after-hours club or an academic lecture, indexes a virtual social world in ways that range from a repertoire of styles and speech genres to referential metaculture. A novel like *Dancer from the Dance* relies much more heavily on referential metaculture than does an after-hours club that survives on word of mouth and may be a major scene because it is only barely coherent *as* a scene. Yet for all their differences, both allow for the concretization of a queer counterpublic. We are trying to promote this world-making project, and a first step in doing so is to recognize that queer culture constitutes itself in many ways other than through the official publics of opinion culture and the state or through the privatized forms normally associated with sexuality.

Queer and other insurgents have long striven, often dangerously or scandalously, to cultivate what good folks used to call criminal intimacies. We have developed relations and narratives that are only recognized as intimate in queer culture: girlfriends, gal pals, fuckbuddies, tricks. Queer culture has learned not only how to sexualize these and other relations but also how to use them as a context for witnessing intense and personal affect while elaborating a public world of belonging and transformation. Making a queer world has required the development of kinds of intimacy that bear no necessary relation to domestic space, to kinship, to the couple form, to property, or to the nation. These intimacies *do* bear a necessary relation to a counterpublic — an indefinitely accessible world conscious of its subordinate relation. They are typical both of the inventiveness of queer world making and of the queer world's fragility.

Nonstandard intimacies would seem less criminal and less fleeting if, as used to be the case, normal intimacies included everything from consorts to courtiers, friends, amours, associates, and co-conspirators.[23] Along with the sex it legitimates, intimacy has been privatized; the discourse contexts that narrate true personhood have been segregated from those that represent citizens, workers, or professionals.

This transformation in the cultural forms of intimacy is related both to the history of the modern public sphere and to the modern discourse of sexuality as a fundamental human capacity. In *The*

Structural Transformation of the Public Sphere, Habermas shows that the institutions and forms of domestic intimacy made private people private, members of the public sphere of private society rather than the market or the state. Intimacy grounded abstract, disembodied citizens in a sense of universal humanity. In *The History of Sexuality*, Foucault describes the personalization of sex from the other direction: confessional and expert discourses of civil society continually posit an inner personal essence, equating this true personhood with sex, and surrounding that sex with dramas of secrecy and disclosure. There is an instructive convergence here in two thinkers who otherwise seem to be describing different planets.[24] Habermas overlooks the administrative and normalizing dimensions of privatized sex in sciences of social knowledge because he is interested in the norm of a critical relation between state and civil society. Foucault overlooks the critical culture that might enable transformation of sex and other private relations because he wants to show that modern epistemologies of sexual personhood, far from bringing sexual publics into being, are techniques of isolation; they identify persons as normal or perverse for the purpose of medicalizing or otherwise administering them as individuals. Yet both Habermas and Foucault point to the way a hegemonic public has founded itself by a privatization of sex and the sexualization of private personhood. Both identify the conditions in which sexuality seems a property of subjectivity rather than a publicly or counterpublicly accessible culture.

Like most ideologies, normal intimacy may never have been an accurate description of how people actually live. It was from the beginning mediated not only by a structural separation of economic and domestic space but also by opinion culture, correspondence, novels, and romances; Rousseau's *Confessions* is typical both of the ideology and of its reliance on mediation by print and by new, hybrid forms of life narrative. Habermas notes, "Subjectivity, as the innermost core of the private, was always oriented to an audience," adding that the structure of this intimacy includes a fundamentally contradictory relation to the economy:

> To the autonomy of property owners in the market corresponded a self-presentation of human beings in the family. The latter's intimacy, apparently set free from the constraint of society, was the seal on the truth of a private autonomy exercised in competition. Thus it was a private autonomy denying its economic origins ... that provided the bourgeois family with its consciousness of itself.[25]

This structural relation is no less normative for being imperfect in practice. Its force is to prevent the recognition, memory, elaboration, or institutionalization of all the nonstandard intimacies that people have in everyday life. Affective life slops over onto work and political life; people have key self-constitutive relations with strangers and acquaintances; and they have eroticism, if not sex, outside the couple form. These border intimacies give people tremendous pleasure. But when that pleasure is called sexuality, the spillage of eroticism into everyday social life seems transgressive in a way that provokes normal aversion, a hygienic recoil even as contemporary consumer and media cultures increasingly trope toiletward, splattering the matter of intimate life at the highest levels of national culture.

In gay male culture, the principal scenes of criminal intimacy have been tearooms, streets, sex clubs, and parks — a tropism toward the public toilet.[26] Promiscuity is so heavily stigmatized as nonintimate that it is often called anonymous, whether names are used or not. One of the most commonly forgotten lessons of AIDS is that this promiscuous intimacy turned out to be a lifesaving public resource. Unbidden by experts, gay people invented safer sex; and as Douglas Crimp wrote in 1987:

We were able to invent safe sex because we have always known that sex is not, in an epidemic or not, limited to penetrative sex. Our promiscuity taught us many things, not only about the pleasures of sex, but about the great multiplicity of those pleasures. It is that psychic preparation, that experimentation, that conscious work on our own sexualities that has allowed many of us to change our sexual behaviors — something that brutal "behavioral therapies" tried unsuccessfully for over a century to force us to do — very quickly and very dramatically.... All those who contend that gay male promiscuity is merely sexual *compulsion* resulting from fear of intimacy are now faced with very strong evidence against their prejudices.... Gay male promiscuity should be seen instead as a positive model of how sexual pleasures might be pursued by and granted to everyone if those pleasures were not confined within the narrow limits of institutionalized sexuality.[27]

AIDS is a special case, and this model of sexual culture has been typically male. But sexual practice is only one kind of counterintimacy. More important is the critical practical knowledge that allows such relations to count as intimate, to be not empty release or transgression but a common language of self-cultivation, shared knowledge, and the exchange of inwardness.

Queer culture has found it necessary to develop this knowledge in mobile sites of drag, youth culture, music, dance, parades, flaunting, and cruising — sites whose mobility makes them possible but also renders them hard to recognize as world making because they are so fragile and ephemeral. They are paradigmatically trivialized as "lifestyle." But to understand them only as self-expression or as a demand for recognition would be to misrecognize the fundamentally unequal material conditions whereby the institutions of social reproduction are coupled to the forms of hetero culture.[28] Contexts of queer world making depend on parasitic and fugitive elaboration through gossip, dance clubs, softball leagues, and the phone-sex ads that increasingly are the commercial support for print-mediated left culture in general.[29] Queer is difficult to entextualize *as* culture.

This is particularly true of intimate culture. Heteronormative forms of intimacy are supported, as we have argued, not only referentially, in overt discourse such as love plots and sentimentality, but materially, in marriage and family law, in the architecture of the domestic, in the zoning of work and politics. Queer culture, by contrast, has almost no institutional matrix for its counterintimacies. In the absence of marriage and the rituals that organize life around matrimony, improvisation is always necessary for the speech act of pledging, or the narrative practice of dating, or for such apparently noneconomic economics as joint checking. The heteronormativity in such practices may seem weak and indirect. After all, same-sex couples have sometimes been able to invent versions of such practices. But they have done so only by betrothing the couple form and its language of personal significance, leaving untransformed the material and ideological conditions that divide intimacy from history, politics, and publics. The queer project we imagine is not just to destigmatize those average intimacies, not just to give access to the sentimentality of the couple for persons of the same sex, and definitely not to certify as properly private the personal lives of gays and lesbians.[30] Rather, it is to support forms of affective, erotic, and personal living that are public in the sense of accessible, available to memory, and sustained through collective activity.

Because the heteronormative culture of intimacy leaves queer culture especially dependent on ephemeral elaborations in urban space and print culture, queer publics are also peculiarly vulnerable to initiatives such as Mayor Rudolph Giuliani's zoning law. The law aims to restrict any counterpublic sexual culture by regulating its economic conditions; its effects will reach far beyond the adult businesses it explicitly controls. The gay bars on Christopher Street draw customers from people who come there because of its sex trade. The street is cruisier because of the sex shops. The boutiques that sell freedom rings and Don't Panic T-shirts do more business for the same reasons. Not all of the thousands who migrate or make pilgrimages to Christopher Street use the porn shops, but all benefit from the fact that some do. After a certain point, a quantitative change is a qualitative change. A critical mass develops. The street becomes queer. It develops a dense, publicly accessible sexual culture. It therefore becomes a base for nonporn businesses, like the Oscar Wilde Bookshop. And it becomes a political base from which to pressure politicians with a gay voting bloc.

No group is more dependent on this kind of pattern in urban space than queers. If we could not concentrate a publicly accessible culture somewhere, we would always be outnumbered and overwhelmed. And because what brings us together is sexual culture, there are very few places in the world that have assembled much of a queer population without a base in sex commerce; and even those that do exist, such as the lesbian culture in Northampton, Massachusetts, are stronger because of their ties to places like the West Village, Dupont Circle, West Hollywood, and the Castro. Respectable gays like to think that they owe nothing to the sexual subculture they think of as sleazy. But their success, their way of living, their political rights, and their very identities would never have been possible but for the existence of the public sexual culture they now despise. Extinguish it, and almost all *out* gay or queer culture will wither on the vine. No one knows this connection better than the right. Conservatives would not so flagrantly contradict their stated belief in a market free from government interference if they did not see this kind of hyperregulation as an important victory.

The point here is not that queer politics needs more free-market ideology but that heteronormative forms, so central to the accumulation and reproduction of capital, also depend on heavy interventions in the regulation of capital. One of the most disturbing fantasies in the zoning scheme, for example, is the idea that an urban locale is a community of shared interest based on residence and property. The ideology of the neighborhood is politically unchallengeable in the current debate, which is dominated by a fantasy that sexual subjects only reside, that the space relevant to sexual politics is the neighborhood. But a district like Christopher Street is not just a neighborhood affair. The local character of the neighborhood depends on the daily presence of thousands of nonresidents. Those who actually live in the West Village should not forget their debt to these mostly queer pilgrims. And we should not make the mistake of confusing the class of citizens with the class of property owners. Many of those who hang out on Christopher Street — typically young, queer, and African-American — couldn't possibly afford to live there. Urban space is always a host space. The right to the city extends to those who use the city.[31] It is not limited to property owners. It is not because of a fluke in the politics of zoning that urban space is so deeply misrecognized; normal sexuality requires such misrecognitions, including their economic and legal enforcement, in order to sustain its illusion of humanity.

Tweaking and Thwacking

Queer social theory is committed to sexuality as an inescapable category of analysis, agitation, and refunctioning: like class relations, which in this moment are mainly visible in the polarized embodiments of identity forms, heteronormativity is a fundamental motor of social organization in the United States, a founding condition of unequal and exploitative relations throughout even straight society. Any social theory that miscomprehends this participates in their reproduction.

The project of thinking about sex in public does not only engage sex when it is disavowed or suppressed. Even if sex practice is not the object domain of queer studies, sex is everywhere present. But where is the tweaking, thwacking, thumping, sliming, and rubbing you might have expected — or dreaded — in an essay on sex? We close with two scenes that might have happened on the same day in our wanderings around the city. One afternoon, we were riding with a young straight couple we know in their station wagon. Gingerly, after much circumlocution, they brought the conversation around to vibrators. These are people whose reproductivity governs their lives, their aspirations, their relations to money and entailment, mediating their relations to everyone and everything else. But the woman in this couple had recently read an article in a women's magazine about sex toys and other forms of nonreproductive eroticism. She and her husband did some mail-order shopping and became increasingly involved in what from most points of view would count as queer sex practices: their bodies have become disorganized and exciting to them. They said to us: you're the only people we can talk to about this; to all of our straight friends, this would make us perverts. In order not to feel like perverts, they had to make *us* into a kind of sex public.

Later, the question of aversion and perversion came up again. This time, we were in a bar that on most nights is a garden-variety leather bar but that on Wednesday nights hosts a sex-performance event called "Pork." Shows typically include spanking, flagellation, shaving, branding, laceration, bondage, humiliation, wrestling — you know, the usual: amateur, everyday practitioners strutting for everyone else's gratification, not unlike an academic conference. This night, word was circulating that the performance was to be erotic vomiting. This sounded like an appetite spoiler, and the thought of leaving early occurred to us but was overcome by a simple curiosity: What would the foreplay be like? Let's stay until it gets messy. Then we can leave.

A boy, twentyish, very skateboard, comes on the low stage at one end of the bar, wearing Lycra shorts and a dog collar. He sits loosely in a restraining chair. His partner, the vomiting top, comes out and tilts the bottom's head up to the ceiling, stretching out his throat. Behind them is an array of foods. The top begins pouring milk down the boy's throat, then food, then more milk. It spills over, down his chest and onto the floor. A dynamic is established between them in which they carefully keep at the threshold of gagging. The bottom struggles to keep taking in more than he really can. The top is careful to give him just enough to stretch his capacities. From time to time, a baby bottle is offered as a respite, but soon the rhythm intensifies. The boy's stomach is beginning to rise and pulse, almost convulsively.

It is at this point that we realize we cannot leave, cannot even look away. No one can. The crowd is transfixed by the scene of intimacy and display, control and abandon, ferocity and abjection. People are moaning softly with admiration, then whistling, stomping, screaming encouragements. They have pressed forward in a compact and intimate group. Finally, as the top inserts two, then three fingers in the bottom's throat, insistently offering his own stomach for the repeated climaxes, we realize that we have never seen such a display of trust and violation. We are breathless. But, good academics that we are, we also have some questions to ask. Word has gone around that the boy is straight. We want to know: What does that mean in this context? How did you discover that this is what you want to do? How did you find a male top to do it with? How did you come to do it in a leather bar? Where else do you do this? How do you feel about your new partners, this audience?

207

We did not get to ask these questions, but we have others that we can pose now about these scenes where sex appears more sublime than narration itself, neither redemptive nor transgressive, moral nor immoral, hetero nor homo, or sutured to any axis of social legitimation. We have been arguing that sex opens a wedge to the transformation of those social norms that require only its static intelligibility or its *deadness* as a source of meaning.[32] In these cases, though, paths through publicity led to the production of nonheteronormative bodily contexts. They intended nonheteronormative worlds because they refused to pretend that privacy was their ground; because they were forms of sociability that delinked money and family from the scene of the good life; because they made sex the consequence of public mediations and collective self-activity in a way that made for unpredicted pleasures; because, in turn, they attempted to make a context of support for their practices; because their pleasures were not purchased by a redemptive pastoralism of sex or by mandatory amnesia about failure, shame, and aversion.[33]

We are used to thinking about sexuality as a form of intimacy and subjectivity, and we have just demonstrated how limited that representation is. But the heteronormativity of U.S. culture is not something that can easily be rezoned or disavowed by individual acts of will, by a subversiveness imagined only as personal rather than as the basis of public formation, or even by the lyric moments that interrupt the hostile cultural narrative that we have been staging here. Remembering the utopian wish behind normal intimate life, we also want to remember that we aren't married to it.

CHAPTER SIX

Something Queer

About the Nation-State*

Because the term has been understood to promise so much, it's embarrassing that both the word "queer" and the concept of queerness turn out to be thoroughly embedded in modern Anglo-American culture. Having energized a subcultural style, a political movement, and a wave of rethinking among intellectuals, queerness has come to stand for a far-reaching change in sexual politics. Under its banner, some have gone so far as to herald a general subversion of identity. Others have linked queer politics to a globalizing culture of postmodernism. In my view, these readings of queerness have vaulted over the conditions in which queer politics has made sense. The term does not translate very far with any ease, and its potential for transformation seems mostly specific to a cultural context that has not been brought into focus in the theory of queerness. Even in cultures with well-organized gay movements and a taste for Americanisms, there has been little attempt to import the politics with which the label has been associated here. In the New World Order, we should be more than usually cautious about global utopianisms that require American slang.

*Originally published in *After Political Correctness*, ed. Christopher Newfield (Boulder, CO: Westview Press, 1995).

The historical moment of queer political culture, so understanding itself, is remarkably recent. As a politically usable term,
"queer" dates not even from the Reagan years but from the Bush-
Thatcher-Mulroney era. Both the political language of queerness
and its subcultural style — and these two have become very closely
associated — made their first appearance in the context of AIDS
organizing, as is well known.[1] First in ACT UP, then in OutRage and
Queer Nation, queer rhetoric came into competition with les-
bian/gay liberation rhetoric primarily in relation to the state. All of
these groups were explicitly organized around a language of "direct
action," meaning non-state-mediated action. ACT UP's self-defini-
tion reads: "A diverse, nonpartisan group united in anger and committed to direct action to end the AIDS crisis." Direct action here
means (nonviolent) enterprises that have urban space and public-
sphere mass media as their main contexts — not state agencies or
political parties or even service organizations. Equally important is
a concept of activism as an informal mode of representation. In
some ways, this set of groups — and more generally the practices
associated with them — have carried implicitly an enormous faith in
the public sphere. They have believed that political struggles were
to be carried out neither through the normal state apparatus nor
through revolutionary combat but through the non-state media in
which public opinion is invested with the ability to dissolve power.

Queer activism has never seemed traditional, however, because it scorns the traditional debate styles that form the self-
understanding of the public sphere: patient, polite, rational-critical
discussion. The officials, civil servants, and pundits who cling to
that self-understanding have been consistently viewed by queer
activists as mystifying their own exercise of power and as practicing a kind of media management that conflicts with their own
claims about open debate. Queer politics, by contrast, has evolved
around a frankly skeptical and often instrumental relation to the

public sphere: its experiments in public art were from the beginning accompanied by sound-bite management, expert public relations, and what is called social marketing.[2]

At the same time, queer politics has essentially abandoned the traditional conception of civil disobedience, which values the expression of individual integrity as a moral act, regardless of its effect. For many in queer politics, this conception seems as naive as the ideology of open public discussion, and for the same reasons. Civil disobedience and direct action count as strategic obstruction — not acts of personal morality, but something to be managed through a media strategy. Public opinion, though virtually the sole medium in which politics was carried out by these groups, has been viewed as a toxic cloud of irrationality, to be steered out to sea by any means at hand.

Queer politics has been innovative because of the degree to which it cultivates self-consciousness about public-sphere-mediated society and because of the degree to which that self-consciousness has been incorporated into the self-understanding of a metropolitan sexual subculture. These are no mean feats. Nevertheless, they point out how much the entire range of queer politics has continued to be guided by the institutions of the civil-society public-sphere type, even though queer rhetoric has been in many ways critical of the liberal faith that legitimates those institutions.

Now the commitment to a non-state public-sphere context has turned out to be determining. Some of the most serious crises in the history of ACT UP had to do with the question of lobbying and other kinds of coordination between ACT UP members and representatives of state agencies such as the U.S. Centers for Disease Control. The government seemed at times to be listening to ACT UP in productive ways; but many were upset, as one member put it, to see some activists demonstrating in the streets against Dr. Anthony Fauci by day and then calling him Tony at a cocktail party in the evening. What became visible in these crises was a split between the style of action specific to ACT UP and queer culture, on one hand, and a style of activism involving routine interaction with the state, on the other. Negotiation with state agencies, as a normal kind of activism, is typically organized by ideas of minority politics, community representation, and state coordination of special interests. Those who do it typically describe themselves as lesbian and gay rather than queer — even though many such activists call themselves queer in other contexts.

This alignment between two different identitarian rhetorics and two different contexts of state-related politics seems to me to have remained fairly consistent since the emergence of AIDS activism. In contemporary Anglo-American lesbian and gay politics, an impressive list of contested issues bear directly on the state — from AIDS policy and health care to military-personnel policy, domestic-partnership legislation, public-school curricula, NEA and NEH funding, immigration policy, and so on. But most of the imaginative energies of queer culture have come to be focused on a rigorously anti-assimilationist rhetoric invoked only in non-state public-sphere contexts such as Modern Language Association panels. When we hold endorsement sessions for local politicians or draft antidiscrimination laws, we invoke a more traditional rhetoric of minority identity. There is no Queer Men's Health Crisis, for example, and for good reason. The differences between these political strategies are not simply strategic, because each posture toward the state and toward the public sphere has strong links with a different rhetoric of identity and sexuality. (That's also the reason style and sexual subculture have been able to carry over much of the energy of queer politics, even though ACT UP and Queer Nation and OutRage have all been perceived lately as having lost momentum.)

Queer theory has for the most part occupied itself with only half of this history, describing the difference between the two rhetorics of identity and sexuality, queer and gay/lesbian.[3] It is becoming increasingly clear, however, that these rhetorics belong not to different epochs, or to different populations, but to different contexts. Queer activists are also lesbians and gays in other contexts — as, for example, where leverage can be gained through bourgeois propriety, or through minority-rights discourse, or through more gender-marked language (it probably won't replace lesbian feminism). Some people are in some contexts meaningfully motivated by queer self-characterizations; others are not. This distinction is not the same as that between those who are straight and those who are gay and lesbian. No one adheres to queer self-characterizations all the time. Even when some of us do so, it may be to exploit rhetorics in ways that have relatively little to do with our characters, identities, selves, or psyches. Rhetoric of queerness neither saturates identity nor supplants it. Queer politics, in short, has not just replaced older modes of lesbian and gay politics; it has come to exist alongside those older modes, opening up new possibilities and problems whose relation to more familiar problems is not always clear.

The Anglo-American world sports a heavily identitarian culture. As a result, it supercharges any form of sexuality by tying it to the individual's expressive capacities. Consumer culture, to begin with, accustoms us to link up choice, affect, display, and identity. American religion has also created such a culture of sincerity that even ironic parodies of identity are ultimately read as sincere gestures of self-expression. In this context, queerness reads as a public affirmation of the expressive/affective complexities that underwrite personal singularity.[4] The culture of identitarianism has also a state-related institutional dimension. Canada, Britain, and especially the United States have a very pronounced civil-society tradition for opposing voluntary association to the state. (This may be another reason why queer politics works in Anglo-American nations but has not much caught on in countries with stronger conceptions of socialist democracy.) The vast infrastructure of voluntarist culture — from churches to twelve-step programs — interprets itself through an identitarian discourse to which queer is rapidly becoming assimilated.

The state also contributes more directly to the intelligibility of queerness. The modern state claims to be the agency of our wills and the site of our reason; that's why it works so well with a culture of voluntarism. The feudal and monarchical states, by contrast, did not do so; they were able to support themselves by representing their own alienness, their imposition from above, as essential to their legitimacy. Constitutionalism and representational government have both undermined that element in the self-representation of the state; the state began to represent itself as an expression or outcome of its subjects' own actions, wills, interests, debates, opinions, needs, and so on. But of course it could never sustain that fiction in the everyday lives of people for whom the state is an irrational limit or, worse, the arm of hostile interests. To some extent, that is true for everybody. The state, in short, creates noise. It does so even in totalitarian systems, but the noise is more audible wherever a civil-society tradition has invested non-state association with normative significance. And nowhere has that tradition been more pronounced than in the United States over the last two centuries. As Tocqueville put it, "In no country in the world has the principle of association been more successfully used or applied to a greater multitude of objects than in America. The citizen of the United States is taught from infancy to rely upon his own exertions in order to resist the evils and the difficulties of life; he looks upon the social authority with an eye of mistrust and anxiety." In this context of normatively sustained anxiety about an overarching social authority, queerness can resonate as a general condition of political life because of the implausibility in the modern state's representational claims.

In this culture, suspicion toward the state's representational claims is not only widespread but imperative. And the imperative gives a political self-understanding to the infrastructure of voluntarist culture. When Tocqueville writes of the "principle of association," he has in mind especially the mass movements of bourgeois propriety, such as temperance, but it is important to remember that temperance and other forms of early-nineteenth-century voluntary association were the predecessors of modern identitarian movements. They articulated a space of non-state association, investing it with supreme legitimacy. They articulated a general and public form of association based in elective affinities. They elaborated a language of the volitional individual and the public relevance of her affective/appetitive nature. And the experience of movements such as temperance could entail a rich phenomenology of negativity — with respect to the state, with respect to public sociality, and with respect to one's own body and self-characterization — even though all of these were denied at the thematic level of control, consensus, integration, and discipline.

For few groups of Anglo-American citizens did the state seem more clearly a vehicle of hostile interests and irrationality than for gay men and lesbians at the historical moment that gave rise to queer rhetoric. National governments, dominated in Anglo-American societies by conservative reaction, were more than usually opaque to rational-critical institutions. Moreover, the state institutions most needed in the AIDS crisis — the complex web of agencies relating to health care — were being systematically inhibited by George Bush, Margaret Thatcher, and Brian Mulroney in the name of "the private sector." Seldom has the needs discourse of the welfare state been so dramatically unresponsive, so unexpressive of democratic culture, so visibly encrusted with positivity.

215

But queer politics did not arise simply in response to those conservative policies in the executive branch. The utopian appeal of queer politics from the beginning far exceeded its ability to overcome a blockage in national administrative policy. Moreover, the period of Bushite reaction was itself in some ways only a part of long-standing crises in the welfare state's peculiar blend of regulatory administration and democratic legitimation.

These contemporary crises, which I take to be the local incitement to queer politics, have been brewing for almost exactly the same period as the homosexual and gay rights movements have been on the scene. Their nature was succinctly summarized by Habermas in a 1984 address to the Spanish Parliament:

> In short, a contradiction between its goal and its method is inherent in the welfare state project as such. Its goal is the establishment of forms of life that are structured in an egalitarian way and that at the same time open up arenas for individual self-realization and spontaneity. But evidently this goal cannot be reached via the direct route of putting political programs into legal and administrative form. Generating forms of life exceeds the capacities of the medium of power.[5]

The more the welfare state tries to democratize by administrative methods, the more it sinks into this problem:

> Social welfare programs need a great deal of power to achieve the force of law financed by public budgets — and thus to be implemented within the lifeworld of their beneficiaries. Thus an ever denser net of legal norms, of governmental and para-governmental bureaucracies is spread over the daily life of its potential and actual clients.[6]

216

Habermas sketches this crisis, largely following Claus Offe, in order to explain the exhaustion of utopian projects for refiguring relations among state, society, and labor. (One can also hear in the background, I think, his arguments for a lifeworld conceptualization of the democratic. The system — lifeworld distinction is not, I think, any more useful for queer theory than it is for feminist theory, but the sketch of the welfare state will look familiar to any queer.)

Now, in keeping with my hunch that two identitarian rhetorics — one gay and lesbian, one queer — tend to link up with two postures vis-à-vis the state, it is easy to see that queer politics takes the contradiction of the welfare state as its opportunity, its strategic environment. Queer activism, considered as politics, presupposes and exploits the impossibility of the welfare state's own project. The alienation of the administrative state has put more and more strain on the Hegelian understanding of the state as a supreme means of self-transcendence; and at the same time, an ideal of sexualized non-state association has developed as a perceptible limit on the state's representational abilities.

But does this have any consequences for the meaning of queerness in contexts less directly defined by activism, politics, and the public sphere? Certainly it is true that many different cultural pressures come to bear at once on the significance of something as complex as queer sexuality or queer self-understanding. But the most intimate forms of life in modern culture are mediated by public-sphere forms. I would suggest even that the state-society relation in voluntarist culture is definitive in, even necessary to, the opposition of queer and normal. In saying this, I follow, rather improbably, Hannah Arendt. Arendt describes the social as a specifically modern phenomenon: "The emergence of the social realm, which is neither private nor public, strictly speaking, is a relatively new phenomenon whose origin coincided with the emergence of the modern age and which found its political form in the nation-state."[7] She identifies society in this sense with "conformism, the assumption that men behave and do not act with respect to each other" — an assumption embedded in economics and other knowledges of the social that "could achieve a scientific character only when men had become social beings and unanimously followed certain patterns of behavior, so that those who did not keep the rules could be considered to be asocial or abnormal."[8]

The social realm, in short, is a cultural form, interwoven with the political form of the administrative state and with the normalizing assumptions of modern social knowledge. The nation-state is the political form of the social in that the social is what it both represents and administers, though in our own time this relation between the state form and the cultural form of the social has become noticeably strained. Can we not hear in the resonances of queer protest an objection to the normalization of behavior in this broad sense and thus to the cultural phenomenon of societalization? Queers, incessantly told to alter their "behavior," can be understood as protesting not just the normal behavior of the social but the *idea* of normal behavior.

Liberal society has entailed fundamental contradictions on the subject of the abnormal, on one hand producing the abnormal everywhere as the other to a liberal and system-oriented conception of the social, on the other hand valuing it as the ground of expressive individuality. Henry Thoreau, who chewed up political economy and spat it out precisely because it presupposed the regularization of persons in its conception of the social, best articulates the dilemma when he writes, with substantial irony:

> I seek rather, I may say, even an excuse for conforming to the laws of the land. I am but too ready to conform to them. Indeed I have reason to suspect myself on this head; and each year, as the tax-gatherer

218

comes round, I find myself disposed to review the acts and position of the general and state governments, and the spirit of the people, to discover a pretext for conformity. I believe that the State will soon be able to take all my work of this sort out of my hands, and then I shall be no better a patriot than my fellow-countrymen.[9]

Here Thoreau gives expression to that "mistrust and anxiety" toward the state that struck Tocqueville as so American. "The State never intentionally confronts a man's sense, intellectual or moral, but only his body, his senses. It is not armed with superior wit or honesty, but with superior physical strength."[10]

It is equally a mistrust and anxiety toward a social field of majoritarianism. We might expect its result to be the modern, post-traditional individual, and often enough in Thoreau that is just what happens. The perception of the state's positivity yields a new affirmation of the civil-society principle of voluntary association, for which he was our first and greatest spokesmodel: "Know all men by these presents, that I, Henry Thoreau, do not wish to be regarded as a member of any incorporated society which I have not joined."[11] Queer theory is commonly understood as a fundamental critique of liberal individualism, where the latter is understood as a belief in voluntarism and the ego-integrated self. But I distrust this metanarrative of queer theory. Queer politics continues regularly to invoke norms of liberal modernity such as self-determination and self-representation; it continues to invoke a civil-society politics against the state; and, most significant to my mind, it continues to value sexuality by linking it to the expressive capacities of individuals. David Halperin and others have taught us that this expressive notion of sexuality is distinctively modern, but although queer theory expresses skepticism about other elements of the modern sexual ideology, it relies absolutely on norms of expressive individualism and an understanding of sexuality in terms of those norms.

Again Thoreau is one of the first and clearest exponents of those norms, in their queer extremity. He frequently writes from a sense that the alignment of the state and the social monopolizes the conditions of intelligibility. At such moments, Thoreau regards the experience of queerness — meaning not only strangeness but also the nonnormal and the imperfectly intelligible — as a necessary subjective dimension. "We need to witness our own limits transgressed," he writes toward the end of *Walden*. "We are cheered when we observe the vulture feeding on the carrion which disgusts and disheartens us and deriving health and strength from the repast."[12] Such a remark may seem to conflict with the austerely integrated ego of Thoreau's liberal political theory; but in fact there has always been a close and necessary relation between the cultural form of voluntary association and the cultural norms of expressive individualism, a dialectic between the two implied views of individuals — volitional and appetitive, self-determining and self-transgressing. Thus in the same year that he wrote "Civil Disobedience," making himself the theorist of "direct action," he also wrote, in "Ktaadn": "I stand in awe of my body, this matter to which I am bound has become so strange to me." Thoreau's anxiety and mistrust toward social authority, including the state and the social itself, are always especially strong at such moments, or whenever the context allows any reference to sexuality. When he is struggling to keep his body or his eroticism representable, he is least willing to imagine rapprochement with the terms of representation established in the state-society relation.

Something very like this tension seems to me to govern the self-understanding of queer subculture in its relation to the public sphere. Indeed, I find it hard to imagine how the notion of queerness could have much mobilizing appeal outside this context of societalized society, an administrative state, and public-sphere forms. Queerness might be opposed to any number of things — righteousness or purity or the habitual, for example — but only when it is opposed to normal society and the representative state does it acquire the sense of transformative significance that it now displays. (Even those with little manifest interest in politics, such as Dennis Cooper, tend to infuse queerness with this sense of transformative and significant rejection. In Cooper as much as in the most ardent demonstrator, queerness implies that the realm of the normal, the social, and its representation by the state has become inaccessible, lacquered over.)

Queer politics, in short, isn't always or only about sexuality. More generally, one might even want to say that sexuality isn't always or only about sexuality, that it is not an autonomous dimension of experience. The demands and strategies of queer politics are burdened by — which also means motivated or energized by — less articulate but still powerful demands that have to do with the organization of social and public life. In a similar way, feminist and racial movements, along with the lesbian and gay movement, are frequently animated by displaced frustrations with atomizing conditions of market-mediated life, frustrations that find expression in the otherwise misleading and damaging ideal of "community."

But this leads me to my final point, that we are beginning to witness an aporia between queer politics, on one hand, and lesbian and gay politics, on the other. Queer politics is anti-assimilationist, non-individualist, and mobilizes non-communitarian practices of public-sphere media against both the welfare state and the normalizing ideal of the social. Lesbian and gay politics relies on a framework of individual identity, community representation, needs and rights discourses, and state provision. Queer politics has developed little in the way of an agenda for the state.

In my view, this is a reason not for abandoning queer rhetoric but for making articulate some of its driving aspirations. From the beginning of queer politics, queer issues were linked to political struggles not centrally identified with sexuality or with the AIDS issues of queers. "Health care is a right" became one of the slogans of ACT UP. That slogan has now entered, however fitfully, the agenda of the national state. It was a deft piece of translation, even though the specifically queer resonances of protest disappeared in that translation. Perhaps one way to reanimate the promise of queer politics would be to ask how more of the specifically queer dimensions of queer political energies and strategies could be made representable.

The potential is vast, partly because any number of factors make for a pool of queer sentiment in persons otherwise distant or phobic about queerness. Anxiety and mistrust toward the state, and toward public-sphere mass majoritarianism, for example, are hardly confined to metropolitan sexual culture; but their expression has so far been much more coherent and sustained in neoconservatism than in queer rhetoric. Talk-show spectacle and mass-disaster fetishism both point to the resonance of a sense of embodied queerness in almost everybody, even while those same genres contradictorily presume the normal sociality of the audience. Queer sentiment can be largely independent of queer sexual practice and therefore an opportunity for translation work.

Beyond that, however, I would hope that queer politics can put forward in a sustained way what I am arguing has been one of its central energies all along: the positivity of the state and the normal society for which it stands. There is no utopian program on the horizon, but queer politics names this environment as a problem. The instruments available for naming it as a problem are themselves public-sphere forms that are oriented to the civil-society tradition. It is therefore difficult to name that tradition as a problem in public-sphere media; the temptation is always to imagine a policy redress in the area of the state or an expression of popular will to reform it, and that is to lapse back into the social imaginary against which queerness defines itself. A great deal of effort will therefore be required to keep this central issue of queer politics from being trumped, in the hierarchy of discourses, by the political end of the public sphere.

The turn back to a state-oriented politics in the American gay movement, always a danger in the public-sphere discourse environment, represents a real loss of insight and action in dominant circles of lesbian and gay organizing. In the 1993 march on Washington, for example, organizers pushed the gays-in-the-military issue, rather than AIDS, into the spotlight. In a culture of patriotism where dying for one's country is thought to be virtuous, this shift of emphasis did not simply enlarge the queer agenda. With its vision of patriotic death, its vision of national loyalties trumping all other partisan ties, the military issue almost seems designed to produce amnesia about AIDS. What besides patriotism could smother the antinational sensibilities of queers who have seen so many die for no country? What could more affirm the state's expression of the nation? What could more weaken the culture of resistance to a state that has added AIDS inaction to its earlier history of heteronormative policing? During the march on Washington, some people were heard chanting, "We're here, we're queer, we want to serve our country." It's possible to oppose the ban on gays in the military and still believe that this sentiment costs too much.

CHAPTER SEVEN

A Soliloquy "Lately Spoken

at the African Theatre":

Race and the Public Sphere in New York City, 1821*

By Michael Warner

with Natasha Hurley, Luis Iglesias, Sonia Di Loreto,

Jeffrey Scraba, and Sandra Young

In 1821, a small theater opened in New York City, billing itself
as the American Theatre, but known to most New Yorkers only
as the African Theatre. After playing with frequent interruptions,
it apparently closed in 1824. Although it was the first African-
American theater, and although William Brown, its impresario, is
known to have authored at least one play, very little is known about
the theater, about Brown, or about his lost play. Even Brown's first
name was disputed until recent archival discoveries by George
Thompson. In the absence of texts, the African Theatre has
remained an obscure trace, a scholarly footnote to American literary history.[1]

*This essay began as a project in the Advanced Research Methods course in the
English department at Rutgers University. The authors thank the other members of the class for their contribution to the initial discussions. The authors re-
searched and discussed the material jointly; Michael Warner then wrote the text
of the article. Originally published in *American Literature* 73.1 (March 2001).

On December 4, 1821, however — when the theater was wide-ly known in New York City and when controversy swirled around it in the newspapers — a new literary periodical called *St. Tam-many's Magazine* published a text titled "Soliloquy of a Maroon Chief in Jamaica."[2] The magazine, now extremely rare, has been unnoticed by scholars.[3] According to its editor's headnote, the monologue was "*Lately spoken at the African Theatre.*" Could this text be the earliest surviving work of African-American theater?

The possibility would be enough to give the monologue tre-mendous importance to scholars. But the text has more than anti-quarian interest. Whatever its origin, and whether or not it was in fact delivered onstage, the monologue is an extraordinary reflec-tion on racial conflict and on the very idea of race. It may be described as one of the most radical statements on the topic by any American before the Civil War. It explicitly engages the lan-guage of scientific racism, which was only then emerging. It chal-lenges all the current grounds for claims of white superiority, whether based in racial nature or in arts of civilization. At more than one point, it challenges the very coherence of racial general-ization — both the false label "black" and the equally false one "white" — and offers especially pointed scorn for the emergent rhetoric of whiteness. It suggests violent resistance, providing its speaker a notable opportunity for sword rattling. And it does all this, as we shall see, in a highly charged political context in which whiteness was for the first time being advanced as a condition for suffrage and other political rights in New York. If it is true that the monologue was "lately spoken at the African Theatre" in the fall of 1821, then its timing and its delivery could hardly have been more dramatic.

The text of the "Soliloquy" follows. The remainder of this essay will introduce the context of the "Soliloquy" for readers rather than provide an extensive interpretation. It will turn out,

however, that some of the mysteries surrounding its publication
raise difficult interpretive questions.

Soliloquy of a Maroon Chief in Jamaica
(Lately spoken at the African Theatre.)

Are we the links 'twixt men and monkeys then?
Or are we all baboons? or not all men?
O lily-tinctured liars! o'er whom terror
Hangs her white flag! why need I prove your error?
Cold is your blood as snow that paints your skin;
And impotent Albinos are your kin.
Your hue is of the pallid cocoa-nut;
Ye fear the stains of parent Earth's own smut;
Ye shun the fiery god who gilds our hides,
And fills with generous fire life's ruddy tides;
In graceful curls who crisps our stubborn hair,
The matted helm which 'gainst our foes we wear;
Whose warmth prolific fills all heaven and earth,
Whose lawful child is nature's every birth.
We, in the image of primeval man,
Are what our fathers were when life began:
From virgin earth's red breast red Adam rose;
And we are red, — not black, like bats and crows;
Black is the absence of all colours — say,
Look at my face — is it not ruddy bay?
Who ever saw a black man, — if not him —
The devil — of whom the whiteman's terrors dream?
Ye are the whitewashed race! art's feeble sons —
Almighty nature all your line disowns!
She in her generous hive the comb had dyed,
But your bleached skins have all her care belied;

227

And when your chalky sires had lost her hue,
They lost her vigour and her sweetness too!
Say ye the impetuous fire that fills our veins
Has baked our skulls, and dried up all our brains?
What is the end of all your boasted lore?
What can those *nine* gods teach, whom ye adore?
Can ye commune with spirits? heave one breath
Beyond the appointed moment due to death?
Can ye improve on nature? make pain less?
Or give new poignancy to happiness?
Can learning, priestcraft, medicine, wit or wealth,
Whet appetite, or give immortal health?
Man, in himself content, alone is blest,
Smoke, shadows, bubbles, wind, is all the rest!
Art can but teach new wants — their aim unknown
Had left us less to seek, and less to moan,
With ignorance and peace of mind our own.
All hail ye palmy shades where burns the flame
Of love, love only worthy of the name!
All hail ye burning wastes where tigers range,
Exult in liberty, and ask no change!
But come, ye whites, browns, yellows, iron grey,
All call yourselves cream-white, and so ye may,
Brag of the symbol of your own disgrace,
And wear your mealy infamy in your face!
Come on! and let us reason. We are men,
As I said first, and as I say agen,
Men like yourselves. I'll prove it by my word,
And ye, just Gods! avouch it by my sword!
Strait as yourselves, erect we gaze on heaven;
To us articulate language has been given;
Our hands are fairly cast in nature's mould;

Smooth as your own, our glistening skin behold;
We laugh; we weep; all properties can show;
Perspicuous eyelashes we wear below;
We feel when tickled; and our hearts incline
To the left side — at least it's so with mine;
They palpitate; and prominent are our knees;
We blush; turn pale; our noses bleed; we sneeze;
Our features are as pliant as your own; —
And if our lips are thicker, be it known,
That nature, anxious for her children's bliss,
Vouchsafed them for a more capacious kiss.
If our heel's long, and our feet splay are found
We take the firmer grip of parent ground;
Large are our bladders — copious are our brains;
And we can dream — O yes! — of Afric's plains!
Love's genial warmth we feel at every season;
From these reflections you perceive we've reason;
And if to feel, till feeling is no more,
A wrong, and wear it in the vital core, —
If this be godlike, even in chains, and rods,
And slavery, we assimilate the gods!

"Lately spoken at the African Theatre" is, it must be said, an ambiguous assertion. It does not tell us who wrote the mono-logue, or when, or whether it is part of a larger work. It does not tell us whether the author was white or black — a question that for modern readers often makes a difference. Can we believe that the text in fact derives from the theater? Or was it, rather, the work of an anonymous contributor to the magazine? These seemingly elementary questions will require a good deal of explanation. There is evidence on both sides, all of it somewhat inconclusive. We may presume that the claim is accurate in some degree simply because the text was published at a time when at least some of the magazine's readers would have been able to confirm or contradict it. Yet there were also reasons why other literary New Yorkers might have ventriloquized such a speech, or at least adapted it for publication.

To anticipate the discussion a bit, the most likely way to reconcile the evidence is to imagine that the text does in fact represent a speech given at the theater but perhaps reconstructed or embroidered by another hand. The most probable authors behind the "Soliloquy" at the theater are James Hewlett, principal actor of the African Theatre, and William Brown, its impresario. Both are known to have composed texts of this kind, and some indications of style and content point especially strongly to Hewlett. But authorship in this case is not likely to have been a simple matter, and before looking at the evidence for Hewlett's involvement, we should first consider the presentation of the text.

"Soliloquy of a Maroon Chief in Jamaica" appeared in *St. Tammany's Magazine* as the third in a series called "Negro Melodies." Of the three texts, only the "Soliloquy" purports to come from the theater. The first two, "Song of an Obeah Priestess" and "Setting Obi," are radically different works: they share neither its overt reference to a dramatic situation, nor its pentameter couplets, nor its general style.[4] "Song of an Obeah Priestess" especially presents itself more as a literary exercise than as a dramatic performance. It sports footnotes to Herodotus, Thomas Moore, and Ovid; floridly Latinate diction even by the standards of 1821 ("bids the refluent wave return"); a vaunting of African exotica; and a generally anthropological cast. It has clearly been either written or adapted for magazine publication. Both of the first two poems may be the work of a poet unconnected to the theatre, using the cultural interest in Obeah as a literary pretext. Such a poet might have been aware of the notoriety of the African

Theatre and the fortuitous circumstance of its having recently mounted a production of *Obi*, taking advantage of the opportunity in order to perform a rather virtuosic set of verse fantasias on African themes.

The leading candidate would have to be Robert C. Sands. Now largely forgotten, Sands was a rising young author in 1821, having just published, with his friend James Eastburn, a six-canto poem on King Philip's War called *Yamoyden*. According to his friend Gulian C. Verplanck, Sands edited *St. Tammany's Magazine*.[5] And Sands's surviving work shows a consistent interest both in practices of magic — a theme of *Yamoyden*, for example — and in quasi-ethnographic knowledge. (He later wrote an article for the *Knickerbocker Magazine* titled "Esquimaux Literature.") He also demonstrates familiarity with the authors footnoted in "Song of an Obeah Priestess" and a strong interest in theater, particularly Greek tragedy and Shakespeare.[6] It is quite possible that he wrote the first two of the "Negro Melodies," attended the African Theatre, and transcribed or reconstructed the "Soliloquy" for his magazine.

The "Negro Melodies" texts, it should be noted, differ sharply from the emergent local-dialect literature on African-Americans. It was not uncommon for local authors to write in blackface; newspapers and magazines in New York City made African-American characters a kind of stock-in-trade.[7] But "Song of an Obeah Priestess" makes its African voodoo priestess a channel for power, erudition, and eloquence. The "Negro Melodies" texts have much more in common with a transatlantic literary tradition, particularly marked in Anglophone West Indian writing, in which poetry was a vehicle for anthropological knowledge about exotic locales. That literature also had a strong natural-rights tradition in keeping with themes of the "Soliloquy." From *Othello* to *Oroonoko* to the more recent literature of British and American antislavery, including some earlier versions of *Obi*, white authors commonly ventriloquized political eloquence through black speakers.[8]

But this style was by no means confined to white writers. Lofty eloquence of this sort was also favored by African-American poets. From Phillis Wheatley half a century earlier, to George Moses Horton in the following decade, African-Americans wrote quite deliberately in the most erudite style available to them (though seldom with the kind of ethnographic glosses found in "Song of an Obeah Priestess"). They did so partly to show that they could and to claim the cultural capital of the formal style. But they also did so because they had not yet formed the very special cultural context in which a distinctive idiom would be intelligible or valuable. Although recent scholarship has focused on evidence of deliberate cultivation of an ethnically marked style, we should not assume that early-nineteenth-century African-American authors themselves felt the self-evident need to write in a distinctive African-American "voice." Such an aesthetic might well presuppose the ethnicizing context of the modern nation-state, and to demand it as a criterion of authenticity or value in an early-nineteenth-century text might be an anachronistic projection of modern criticism.[9]

The "Soliloquy" asks us to imagine its speaker as "a Maroon Chief in Jamaica." (Maroons, or *cimarróns*, were descended from escaped slaves; in Jamaica as in Brazil, groups of Maroons had established independent enclaves that held out against white armies for generations, beginning in the sixteenth century.[10]) To theater audiences in 1821, this would probably have suggested the character "Three-Finger'd Jack," a Jamaican bandit of 1780 who appears in a popular melodrama of English origin called *Obi; or, Three-Finger'd Jack*. This association of the "Maroon Chief" with *Obi* makes the attribution to the African Theatre more plausible, because two surviving handbills from the theatre advertise productions of *Obi; or, Three-Finger'd Jack*. One dates from 1824, the other probably from 1823. Since the theater is known to have had this production in its repertory, then, it is not hard to imagine that the play — or part of it — was staged there in the fall of 1821 or that this fact would have been known to readers of *St. Tammany's*. The African Theatre was already notorious in the city, to such a degree that the magazine may have assumed its readers would connect "Song of an Obeah Priestess" and "Setting Obi" to the African Theatre, before the December 4 issue made the link explicit between the theater and the "Soliloquy."

All three "Negro Melodies" draw on sources that include a number of Anglo-American texts. *Obi; or, The History of Three-Fingered Jack* was an epistolary novel by William Earle published in London around 1800.[11] A play, *Life and Exploits of Mansong*, by William Burdett, is contemporary with it, also treating of "Three-Finger'd Jack, the Terror of Jamaica." A separate two-act pantomime version by (John?) Fawcett was produced in July 1800 as *Obi; or, Three Finger'd Jack*. An undated melodrama of the same title was performed at Drury Lane and published in London with an attribution to William Murray. The Fawcett version was staged in New York in 1801 by William Dunlap and published in Philadelphia in the second decade of the nineteenth century. Earle's novel was reprinted by Isaiah Thomas in Worcester, Massachusetts, in 1804. The character and the play, in other words, would have been familiar among white audiences and readers — so much so that it is not hard to imagine Sands or another author in the *St. Tammany's* circle using the play as a pretext for these three "Negro Melodies."

Of course, these Anglo-American texts might themselves have had numerous intertexts in West Indian, Anglo-African, or African-American narrative or performance. The exchanges seem to have been complex. If the "Soliloquy" derives from the African Theatre as the magazine claims, it is likely to have been interpolated into a production framework that in other contexts was written by and for whites, giving us several layers of authorship. All the surviving texts of *Obi* are rather sketchy, in a way that suggests they were routinely completed by the performers.[12] We know also that the African Theatre was in the habit of giving loose adaptations of popular plays — though when they produced Shakespeare, their specialty, they evidently adhered more closely to the familiar texts. In the case of the play *Tom and Jerry* — at one point staged by the African Theatre as part of the same program as *Obi,* probably in 1823 — scenes were shuffled and reinvented.[13] So although the performers of the African Theatre came to *Obi* after that text had already been formed through several adaptations, they would certainly have filled out the drama with new material.

Indeed, it is clear from the handbill that the African Theatre's version of *Obi*, at least in this later staging, bears little resemblance to any of the previous versions. The handbill reduces the dozen characters of Fawcett's melodrama to a mere three players, as a pantomime afterpiece. It also lists the role of Obi as played by "Mr. Bates." But in the earlier versions, Obi is not a male character, let alone the African name of Jack. A character does appear named the Obi Woman — that is, an Obeah priestess — but the handbill lists neither a priestess nor Jack. Is this an erratum on the handbill or a sign that the theater's version collapsed the priestess and Jack into a single character? Whatever the explanation, the production was evidently a very liberal adaptation. It may not have been based on any written text at all. It is also possible that the theater had earlier staged a fuller version in the fall of 1821, perhaps as the unnamed play advertised on October 27. Bates is not known to have been with the theater before 1823. If there was a production in 1821 it may have starred James Hewlett, who played Richard III then, or Charles Taft, who played Othello.[14] Yet another possibility is that the theater performed not the whole play in 1821 but only a few brief set pieces — not an uncommon practice, to judge from their surviving playbills.

The very looseness of the attribution in *St. Tammany's* — "Lately spoken at the African Theatre" — may reflect the promiscuous circulation of *Obi* texts: from the historical bandit named Three-Fingered Jack who flourished in Jamaica in 1780, to the epistolary novel, to the different melodramas in London and their printed versions, to the Anglo-American adaptations, to the printed American editions of both the novel and one of the plays, to the African Theatre's own truncated adaptation, to the version *St. Tammany's* attributed to that theater.

The magazine names neither the play nor the author. The omission was not unusual. Neither the name of the play nor the author seems to have been of much concern to its readers. Each successive version of the *Obi* text, in fact, displays a nearly total indifference to previous versions. The novel takes the historical Jack as pretext, nothing more. The plays radically but silently revise the novel and each other. The known productions depart sharply from the printed texts. And the magazine, while presuming some familiarity with the plot and context of *Obi*, shows no concern with fixing the version or its authorship. Under these circumstances, much as we might like to know who wrote the "Soliloquy," it is not surprising that it should prove difficult to determine the identity or the race of the author. Its publication illustrates what Meredith McGill calls the "culture of reprinting" in antebellum America; and as we shall see, this unauthored and promiscuous recycling may be a crucial feature of its politics in 1821.[15]

By attributing this soliloquy to the African Theatre, *St. Tammany's Magazine* asks us to imagine the lines uttered by a black actor on the small stage at Mercer and Bleecker Streets in New York — then the northern reach of the city, unpaved and unilluminated — facing the partly white crowd that the theater had begun to attract. (One not very friendly report tells us that breezes came in freely through the gaps in the boards of the walls; another, that the balcony was so close to the ceiling that spectators had to take off their hats to sit there.)[16] Even in the mouth of a stage character, the monologue must have unnerved the white members of the audience, and probably the readers of *St. Tammany's* as well. Previous dramatizations of Three-Fingered Jack give him speeches of defiance and passion for liberty; but they do not go as far as this soliloquy in its view of race. For example, in the 1800 novel *Obi; or, The History of Three-Fingered Jack*, Jack is asked by a white judge what could have motivated him to foment a rebellion:

> "What?" retorted Jack with the words of his heart in his eyes, "do you ask a slave what can urge him on to assume his native liberty? do you ask a man heart-broken, galled by repeated insults, whose back is daily gored by the lacerated whip, do you ask that man what can urge him to revenge? Think you we do not mingle with our groans curses on your race? or think you our hearts are callous to all feeling? Mistaken man, we feel as ye do. Think you we are dogs? Again mistaken; in the eyes of the great Creator, we are as ye are."[17]

This speech, though it names an antagonism between races, says nothing else about race; it draws on a universalist humanism and on the republican language of liberty and slavery — rhetorics common to the English antislavery movement and, of course, especially dear on the American side of the Atlantic. Englishmen could see themselves in this rhetoric.[18]

Because Three-Fingered Jack was known for such defiance, it is easy to see how the *Obi* text could lend itself to the purposes of the African Theatre. The new element added in the "Soliloquy" is its critique of the construction of whiteness. Many white New Yorkers seem to have gone to the African Theatre as a lark; they had read in their newspapers of the cultural pretensions of black actors and black theatergoers and wanted to see for themselves the absurdity of Africans playing Shakespeare.[19] Instead, if we are to believe *St. Tammany's*, they found themselves denounced, together with the notions of race and color. When the Maroon chief says "Ye are the whitewashed race!" should we not imagine the actor addressing his audience?

> But come, ye whites, browns, yellows, iron grey,
> All call yourselves cream-white, and so ye may,
> Brag of the symbol of your own disgrace,
> And wear your mealy infamy in your face!

It is not hard to imagine an actor at the African Theatre directing these lines to white theatergoers; a little more than a month before the magazine appeared, on October 27, the *National Advocate* announced that the "gentlemen of colour" had "graciously made a partition at the back of their house, for the accommodation of the whites." In this context, the speech addresses not only the characters to whom it is delivered within the play but, at different moments, distinct parts of the audience. A published account of the theater by one New Yorker who visited it in 1822 mentions the partition but also records that the "orchestra" consisted of two white musicians and a black one and that the crowd as a whole was a "*variegated* audience! for it was composed of white, black, copper-colored and light brown."[20] The author of this rather nasty pamphlet strikes a note of genteel amusement at the whole scene, and historians have taken this to be the white attitude in general. But the same author suggests that the variegated audience responded to the performance with a rowdy mix of catcalls, applause, laughter, vegetable flinging, cheering, and stomping.[21]

To read the "Soliloquy" in this light is to be struck by the self-reference of the speaker. His arguments are laced with performative illustrations. When he says

We are men,
As I said first, and as I say agen,
Men like yourselves. I'll prove it by my word,
And ye, just Gods! avouch it by my sword!

his word is there for us to hear and his sword for us to see. When he says "To us articulate language has been given," the claim is self-evidential. When he rebuts racist anatomies, he points to parts of his body. Most dramatically of all, when he argues that Africans are not, as common vocabulary would have it, black, he is able to say "Look at my face — is it not ruddy bay?" In the systematic exploitation of these indexical moments, the "Soliloquy" reaches out to the Mercer Street site.

It may also have grounded itself in the person of James Hewlett. William Brown may have had a hand in the composition of the speech, as we know he wrote "a new play" for the troupe the following January — also on the theme of West Indian insurrection.[22] And Charles Taft or another actor may have delivered the speech. But Hewlett is more likely. He was the principal star of the theater. He had high ambitions as an actor and as a Shakespearean, traveling to England some years later in hopes of making his name on the London stage. He was also a mulatto whose description fits the role. (Taft is described in one account as being "black as the ace of spades."[23]) And, most intriguing, we have a slightly later text signed by Hewlett in which the stylistic and thematic similarities to the "Soliloquy" are striking.

The occasion was a parody of Hewlett by the popular English actor Charles Mathews. Mathews specialized in one-man shows in which he personated a wide range of characters. On his American tour, he had visited the African Theatre and befriended Hewlett. Hewlett even took to offering one of Mathews's signature sketches onstage.[24] But Mathews was practicing his black dialect, and upon his return to England he made Hewlett's rendition of Hamlet's soliloquy the subject of a new sketch, in dialect, very much at the expense of Hewlett and his cultural pretensions.[25] In response, Hewlett wrote an open letter, published in the *National Advocate* in 1824:

> You have, I perceive by the programme of your performance, ridiculed our *African Theatre in Mercer-street,* and burlesqued me with the rest of the negroe actors, as you are pleased to call us — mimicked our styles — imitated our dialects — laughed at our anomalies — and lampooned, O shame, even our complexions. Was this well for a brother actor? ... Why these reflections on our color, my dear Matthews, so unworthy your genius and humanity, your justice and generosity? Our immortal bard says, (and he is *our* bard, as well as yours, for we are all descendants of the Plantaganets, the white and red rose;) our bard Shakspeare makes sweet Desdemona say,
>
> "I saw Othello's *visage* in his *mind.*"
>
> Now, when you were ridiculing the "chief black tragedian," and burlesquing the "real negro melody," was it my "mind," or my "visage," which should have made an impression upon you? Again, my dear Matthews, our favorite bard makes Othello, certainly an interesting character, speak thus:
>
> "*Haply,* for I am black."
>
> That is as much as to say, 'tis happy that I am black. Here then we see a General proud of his complexion. In our free and happy country, custom and a meridian sun hath made some distinctions and

239

classifications in the order of society relative to complexions, "'tis true, 'tis a pity, and pity 'tis, 'tis true;" but in England, where these anomalous distinctions are unknown, nay, where international marriages and blending of colors are sometimes seen, what warrant can you have for lampooning our complexion?[26]

In this letter, which Hewlett signs "Chief performer at the African Theatre," both syntax and diction resemble the "Soliloquy," duly allowing for the differences of genre. Even more interesting is the continuity of theme. Like the Maroon chief, Hewlett here both nominalizes and exploits racial categories, reducing them to shades of "complexion" while also embracing them as sources of pride. He also pluralizes classifications of race to a potentially infinite number of discriminations. Like the Maroon chief, he faults his white audience for failures of self-knowledge and goodwill. Like the Maroon chief, he points to achievements of mind as a common ground of humanity. And finally, he singles out Shakespearean soliloquy as the highest example of that common humanity. If the evidence may not support a conclusive attribution of the "Soliloquy" to Hewlett, it is at least safe to say that the author of Hewlett's letter and the speaker of the "Soliloquy" seem to be pointing in the same direction.

It may be mistaken to suppose that an important question of authenticity hangs in the balance, given how little such matters affected the circulation of the printed text in 1821. The striking fact about the speech is not just the role of any author known or hypothetical but the mingling of voices in the text as it comes to us. The "Maroon Chief in Jamaica" is a familiar figure used by all parties — blacks and whites, novelists and playwrights, English and Americans — to address white audiences. He is a type recognizable from Anglo-American fiction and drama, reaching back at least to *Oroonoko*. The mingling of voices and genres may indeed be the condition that allowed such extraordinary rhetoric to be heard at all. To understand this, we will need to reconstruct the circumstances under which the published text appeared and in which the theatrical performance is likely to have taken place.

What gives most point to the speech is that the nature of race had been a topic of heated debate that fall because of the New York state constitutional convention in Albany. There it had been proposed to add the word "white" for the first time to the qualifications for suffrage, thus disenfranchising the small but significant number of African-Americans who had voted in New York since the Revolution. Whether New Yorkers read the text in *St. Tammany's Magazine* or heard it at the African Theatre, they would have immediately understood that it referred both to the controversy over the legitimacy of an African theater and to the new racialization of citizenship. As we shall see, the "Soliloquy" refers directly to debates from the convention. This intertextual connection argues strongly against a source outside New York, and because the theater itself became central to the franchise dispute, it argues for the plausible attribution of the speech — at least in part — to Hewlett and/or Brown.[27]

The theatre, apparently, first came to the attention of white New Yorkers in August of that year, when it was not yet a theatre but merely an ice-cream garden of the Vauxhall style. On August 3, the principal New York City newspaper, the *National Advocate*, ran the following item:

Africans. — People of colour generally are very imitative, quick in their conceptions and rapid in execution; but it is in the lighter pursuits requiring no intensity of thought or depth of reflection. It may be questioned whether they could succeed in the abstruse sciences, though they have, nevertheless, some fancy and humour, and the domestics of respectable families are complete *fac similes* of the different branches of it, not only in dress but in habits and manners.

Among the number of ice cream gardens in this city, there were none in which the sable race could find admission and refreshment. Their modicum of pleasure was taken on Sunday evening, when the black dandys and dandizettes, after attending meeting, occupied the side walks in Broadway, and slowly lounged toward their different homes. As their number increased, and their consequence strengthened; partly from high wages, high living, and the elective franchise; it was considered necessary to have a place of amusement for them exclusively. — Accordingly, a garden has been opened somewhere back of the hospital called *African Grove*.

The *Advocate* continues with a description of the African Grove, located on Thomas Street. It is a stereotyped parody of black styles of dress, dialect, and cultural pretensions, concluding:

Thus they run the rounds of fashion; ape their masters and mistresses in every thing; talk of projected matches; reherse the news of the kitchen, and the follies of the day; and bating the "tincture of their skins," are as well qualified to move in the *haut ton*, as many of the white dandies and butterflies, who flutter in the sun shine. They fear no Missouri plot; care for no political rights; happy in being permitted to dress fashionable, walk the streets, visit African Grove, and talk scandal.[28]

This article launched the chain of events and debates in which the "Soliloquy of a Maroon Chief in Jamaica" is the culmination.

Following complaints by neighbors, the police closed down the African Grove sometime in the next month, along with a number of other pleasure-related establishments on the same street, including a brothel.[29] One scholar, Samuel Hay, has published a dramatic interpretation of this closure. He sees the *National Advo-*

cate as gunning for the African Theatre because it perceived in it a rival playhouse.[30] The *National Advocate*, as it happens, was edited by the playwright Mordecai Noah, who also served as sheriff of New York.[31] Hay has gone so far as to depict Noah as carrying on a personal vendetta against the African Theatre, masterminding its destruction in his triple capacity as rival, editor, and sheriff. More recently George Thompson has modified some key details of Hay's narrative on the basis of new research. Certainly, Noah began mocking the African Grove and its cultural aspirations *before* it became a theatre, when its entertainments consisted of a "big drum and clarionet." Only in September, after the police closure, did the garden's owner, William Brown, reopen it in order to stage *Richard III* in its upstairs rooms. The *Advocate*'s coverage from that point remains mildly parodic but suggests no competition for audience, funds, or glory. Noah could not have been much threatened by the African Theatre, which in its uptown location seems never to have been a very successful affair. Indeed, Brown's theater staged at least one of Noah's plays in November. There is no evidence that the sheriff's office closed the theater. In January 1822, the *National Advocate* reported that the police had closed a performance of *Richard III* by the African troupe; but that was not in their own theater on Mercer Street but downtown, in a hotel next door to the Park Theater. Since no arrests appear in the court records, the *Advocate*'s account may be somewhat inflated; and Brown himself attributed the police harassment on this occasion not to Noah but to Stephen Price, manager of the Park. Brown must not have blamed Noah, because he staged another play by Noah, *The Fortress of Sorrento*, a week later. In any event, the troupe was performing again on Mercer Street the following week. And later in 1822, when the theater was the target of a riot, the police arrested the rioters and protected the theater.[32]

If the *National Advocate* was singling out the African Grove

and the African Theatre in the fall of 1821, then, its motive probably had little to do with Noah's jealousies as playwright or with
his power as sheriff. As Hay rightly points out, it had one clear
rationale, besides the ordinary anxieties about race and cultural
authority: the statewide constitutional convention, about to open
in Albany, was due to consider the extension of the franchise. The
Advocate had already begun building the issue in July, more than
two weeks before the item on the African Grove, when it offered
a brief comment on the franchise (with a reference to Addison's
Cato that was to become a refrain in public discussions throughout the fall):

> If the question of admitting the blacks to vote is agitated in the Con-
> vention, it must be done on grounds of *expediency* alone because no
> one will deny their natural rights, or will believe that the mere "tinc-
> ture of the skin" is to destroy claims which are unalienable. Let it
> then be discussed on the ground of expediency alone, and confine all
> arguments to that point.[33]

It is in this context that the *Advocate* noticed the African Grove
in August, stressing that an ice-cream garden for blacks became
necessary: "As their number increased, and their consequence
strengthened; partly from high wages, high living, *and the elective
franchise.*" As it depicts a threat of cultural aspiration on the part of
these freedmen, it assures its readers that the blacks "fear no Missouri plot; care for no political rights." Mordecai Noah's August 3
article, in other words, laid the groundwork for disenfranchise-
ment. It tried to build popular support for white suffrage by suggesting a specter of creeping black power, while also painting a
picture of happy darkies who do not care about political rights.

The number of slaves in New York had dropped precipitously
in the decades before the theater's founding. As the 1827 deadline

for emancipation in New York State drew nearer, more and more owners manumitted slaves, fewer bought them, and many of the growing free population moved to the city. In 1820, only 518 slaves remained in New York City. The free black population in Manhattan, according to the 1820 census, numbered 10,368, in a city of 123,706; because of property qualifications, however, fewer than 200 typically voted in any given election. When Noah's editorials fret about the proportionate power of the black population in New York, therefore, the worry has more to do with their freedom and enfranchisement — especially if property qualifications were removed, as Noah was urging for white voters — than with their numbers.[34]

How could such a small bloc of votes be regarded as a threat? The reason is that blacks, who typically sided with the Federalists, had been widely seen as the swing vote in more than one of New York's famously contested elections.[35] Washington Irving wrote a letter in 1807 about being a Federalist poll worker in one such election:

> We have toiled through the purgatory of an Election and "may the day stand for aye accursed on the Kalender," for never were poor devils more intollerably beaten & discomfitted than my forlorn bretheren the federalists. What makes me the more outrageous is that I got fairly drawn into the vortex and before the third day was expired I was as deep in mud & politics as ever a moderate gentleman would wish to be — and I drank beer with the multitude, and I talked handbill fashion with the demagogues, and I shook hands with the mob — whom my heart abhorreth.... I shall not be able to bear the smell of small beer or tobacco for a month to come, and a negro is an abomination unto me. Not that I have any disrespect for Negroes — on the contrary I hold them in particular estimation, for by some unaccountable freak they have all turned out for the federalists to a

man! poor devils! I almost pitied them — for we had them up in an enormous drove in the middle of the day waiting round the poll for a chance to vote. The Sun came out intollerably warm — and being packed together like sheep in a pen, they absolutely fermented, and a cloud of vapour arose like frank incense to the skies — had Jupiter (who was a good federalist still) been there, he would have declared it was a sweet smelling savour. Truly this serving ones country is a nauseous piece of business — and if patriotism is such a dirty virtue — prythee no more of it — I was almost the whole time at the seventh ward — as you know — that the most fertile ward in mob-riot & incident — and I do assure you the scene was exquisitely ludicrous — Such haranguing & puffing & strutting among all the little great men of the day — Such shoals of unfledged heroes from the lower wards, who had broke away from their mamas and run to electioneer with a slice of bread & butter in their hands. Every carriage that drove up disgorged a whole nursery of these pigmy wonders.[36]

This letter, incidentally, represents Irving's fullest account of his turn from politics to belles lettres. Mordecai Noah was drawing on this background when he began writing about the African Grove.

The state constitutional convention opened on August 28, 1821. Two weeks later, on September 12, a petition was presented to the convention by "the coloured people of the city of New-York," pleading for protection against legislative interference with their rights and especially with the right of suffrage.[37] The petition was tabled. Immediately afterward the suffrage committee presented its draft for the franchise qualifications, inserting for the first time the word "white." The result was a protracted debate, with complex political maneuvering. The arguments were still raging in Albany when Brown opened his first performance, a production of *Richard III*. On September 21, the *Advocate* noted this development in language that strongly links it to the franchise debate:

> *African Amusements.* — We noticed, some time ago, the opening of a tea garden and evening serenades for the amusement of our black gentry; it appears that some of the neighbors, not relishing the jocund nightly sarabands of these sable fashionables, actually complained to the Police, and the avenues of African Grove were closed by authority; and thus were many of our ebony friends excluded from a participation in those innocent recreations to which they are entitled, by virtue of the great charter that declares "all men are equal." These imitative inmates of the kitchens and pantries, not relishing the strong arm of the law thus rudely exercised, were determined to have some kind of amusement; and after several nightly caucusses, they resolved to get up a *play*, and the upper apartments of the neglected African Grove were pitched upon for the purpose.[38]

The *Advocate*'s account continues with a satiric description of the production, rendering the speech of the actors in dialect ("Gib me noder horse"), with numerous malapropisms. But the paper's language here, with its reference to the Declaration of Independence, its language of entitlement, its images of "caucusses" and resolutions, suggests that the franchise issue motivates not only the paper's interest in the theater but also the African-Americans' interest in the theater. The account seems to imply that the troupe chose to mount a play at least in part as a political demonstration of rights. (The *Advocate*'s use of this caucusing vocabulary may, of course, also be satiric, but we shall see further evidence that it reflects the attitude of William Brown.) Since the number of African-Americans who met the property qualifications for suffrage was not large, and since the African Grove seems to have catered to those with some income and social aspiration, some of those who produced and attended the play are also likely to have been those who petitioned the convention a week earlier. The *Advocate*'s language dramatizes that connection.

Meanwhile, at Albany things were not going to the *Advocate*'s satisfaction. Led by strong opposition from Peter Jay and others, and following extensive debate, the convention on a vote of sixty-three to fifty-nine agreed to eliminate the word "white" from the draft of the suffrage clause. The *Advocate* responded on September 25:

> Blacks. — Our colored population increases daily; the south sends us an annual number of the emancipated; their votes in time will become formidible; they even now have great influence or weight in the charter election for the first and second wards, and, if they are organized and led by designing persons, they will give us great trouble. It is inexpedient to allow them a vote, for it is not necessary for their comfort, security and happiness. The people generally condemn the vote given in their favor; it creates great sensation in this city.

Perhaps fearing that the satire of the African Theatre had not been sufficiently pointed in its link to the franchise issue, Noah's *National Advocate* also ran another item in the same issue:

> African Amusements. — The following is a copy of a printed play bill of gentlemen of *colour*. — They now assemble in groups; and since they have crept in favour with the convention, they are determined to have balls and quadrille parties, establish a forum, solicit a seat in the assembly or in the common council, which, if refused, let them look to the elections. They can out vote the whites, as they say. One black gentleman most respectfully insinuated, that he thought "as how he mout be put on the grand jury!"
>
> Mr. Brown, respectfully informs his Friends of Colour in this

248

city, that on Monday Evening, Sept. 24, 1821, at half past seven o'clock, an Opera will take place, corner of Mercer and Bleeker-streets.

The rest of the playbill is then given, showing that the "Opera" in question is in fact another staging of *Richard III*, this time at the new space at the north end of the city.

Evidently, Mordecai Noah, himself both playwright and politician, saw more in the African Theatre than an easy way to inflame white fears. Inflame them he certainly does in this article, with its specter of a black man sitting on a grand jury in judgment on a white defendant. But his concern seems equally to be the potential for a theatrical public to become a political public or for "balls and quadrille parties" to become "a forum": "They now assemble in groups." On September 29, the *Advocate* again returned to the subject, perhaps in response to a letter of protest:

> The black letter is received. We have no disposition to make merry of our fellow citizens of colour, who, if the vote in Convention is not changed, will be too important to trifle with. They will choose the College of Cardinals, and other important officers. Our criticism on their play was not satire; it actually took place.[39]

Brown's company continued to stage *Richard III* in October. On October 4, a new subcommittee report was returned to the Albany convention with a compromise suffrage clause. It allowed some men of color to retain the franchise, but with a high property requirement ($250) — at the same time eliminating property restrictions for white men. This new clause was adopted by the convention on October 6 and endorsed by the *Advocate* on October 8. Thereafter the *Advocate* drops its abusive commentary on Brown's stage. Its only other item on the African Theatre in 1821 is the October 27 announcement, friendly in tone, of "another play," with the new partitioned seating. It was only after this point, with the theater well established as a controversy in the public eye, that the first two "Negro Melodies" appeared in the issue of *St. Tammany's Magazine* dated November 27, 1821.

The very need for partitioned seating, ironically, suggests that Noah's strategy of creating "great sensation in this city" over the theater had partly backfired. The publicity had the unintended effect of drawing white audiences there. We know from later published accounts that some of these white audience members went in order to amuse themselves at the expense of the actors and that audiences could be unruly to the point of riot. (In August 1822, on the night following the publication of a long satiric account of the theater in the *Commercial Advertiser*, a riot nearly destroyed it.)

But we also know that Brown could be defiant and that he had some white support. Evidence of his defiance comes from January 1822, when the police closed down his newest staging of *Richard III* — this time not in his own theater but downtown, in Hampton's Hotel, next door to the elegant Park Theater, which was owned by John Jacob Astor and John Beekman. A week afterward, on January 16, the following account ran in the *Commercial Advertiser*:

> African Theatre. — We published a few days since, a pleasant account from the Advocate, of the breaking up of the theatrical establishment of the colored heroes of the sock and buskin, adjoining the New Park theatre. It seems, however, from the following extract from a play bill posted through the city a few days subsequent to the merry farce of "*Turn Out*," that they are not so easily to be driven from the field in which Shakespeare, Garrick, Cooke, and our right worthy and jolly Sheriff [Mordecai Noah] have reaped such harvests of glory. The following is the extract: "Mr. Brown, the Manager of the Minor Theatre, respectfully informs the public, that in consequence of the

breaking up of his theatrical establishment, there will be no performance this week. Mr. B. believes it is through the influence of
his *brother Managers* of the Park Theatre, that the police interfered.
There is no doubt *that in fear of his opposition*, they took measures to
quell his rivalry. And in consequence of these jealousies, Mr. Brown
has been obliged to remove his theatrical corps to the old place, corner of Bleecker and Mercer-streets, where every means will be taken
to ensure the public patronage. For the benefit of Mr. Brown, will
next be presented the drama of the '*Fortress of Sorrento*,' from the
fruitful pen of Mr. Noah; after which an entire new play, written by
Mr. Brown (the sable manager,) called *Shotaway; or, the insurrection
of the Caribs, of St. Domingo.* King Shotaway, Devillee." Thus it seems
that these descendents of Africa, are determined to carry into full
practice the doctrine of *liberty and equality*, physically by acting
plays, and mentally by writing them. We are glad to find also, that
they are so patriotic as to give a preference to the productions of our
own country. Not, however, that they are insensible to the beauties
of Shakespeare, for they sometimes select for representation some of
the most popular and interesting of his productions. But with a laudable spirit of independence, and a taste that cannot be too highly
commended, they wander through the gardens of imagination in
both hemispheres, and cull the choicest flowers, no matter whether
they bud upon the banks of the Avon, or bloom upon those of the
majestic Hudson.[40]

When this article appeared, "Soliloquy of a Maroon Chief in
Jamaica" had been in print for a month. But it indicates that the
defiant posture of that soliloquy was fully in character for Brown
— in his refusal to let the theater die; in his willingness to confront
white opponents such as the powerful managers of the Park Theater; in his decision that doing so required a practical rebuttal of
racial superiority through the writing of plays; in his choice of

another West Indian rebel as his hero. The language of the *Commercial Advertiser* also suggests that despite the satiric commentary of the white press, the African Theatre had considerable white support for its "laudable spirit of independence," not just in choosing American plays but in its full understanding of "the doctrine of *liberty and equality*."

Further evidence of that white support is found in *St. Tammany's Magazine* itself, not least in the very fact of its having published the "Soliloquy." Despite its name, the magazine seems to have had nothing to do with Tammany Hall. The first issue is dated November 9, 1821 — the day before the closing of the Albany convention. "From the title of this work," the opening issue announced, "the ingenious might suspect that it was intended to be devoted to political purposes. This is not the fact." The magazine instead invokes the broadest aegis of "the great St. Tammany, whose life, martyrdom, canonization, and miracles, [it] intends to record hereafter, as time and place may serve."[41] The publisher of the magazine was Cornelius Van Winkle, who over the previous year had brought out Washington Irving's *Sketch Book*, the most famous character of which is named after him.[42] Van Winkle was a young printer, still establishing himself in the competitive New York market and apparently striving to do so by carving out for himself the high end of the trade. In addition to printing Irving's book, he had published most of the English Romantics, many editions of Sir Walter Scott, and a number of learned works. His model seems to have been the house of Murray in London, and *St. Tammany's Magazine* evidently represents his attempt to consolidate his position as the chief literary publisher in New York.

Van Winkle and Sands ran a number of items bearing on African-Americans and their rights. In the November 17 issue, for example, they included "Anecdote of Ichabod," a lengthy account of an African-American hero of the Revolutionary War. The fifth issue, the one following the "Soliloquy," also ran a puzzling but extremely interesting text titled "Journal of a Tour Through the Eastern States. By an English Woman." This text, in fact, describes a visit to the African Theatre, the earliest such account apart from Noah's satiric one:

> The people of colour in this city, have arrived at a high degree of refinement. They give balls and routs of uncommon splendor, which I am told are managed with the greatest decorum. I visited their theatre in the upper part of the city, which is fitted up with much taste. The performers were all dressed in the most appropriate costume; and Othello was enacted by a real blackamoor, with great effect. A melodrama, by Major Noah, the Shakspeare and Sheriff of the City, closed the performance. This last piece seemed to give general satisfaction, and on the falling of the curtain, the author was called for amid loud and reiterated plaudits. He accordingly made his appearance; telling the audience, that as he had only come to keep the peace, they must excuse him from making a speech on the occasion.
>
> Some of the black citizens, I am told, are immensely rich. In general, their dresses equal those of the whites in taste and magnificence. It is a pleasing sight, on a Sunday afternoon, to see them returning from church with their families; their countenances exhibiting genuine devotion, and their whole deportment great modesty and propriety. Honesty is a general characteristic among them: and though some delicate stomachs may object to their peculiar odour, I know no class of society more estimable for their worth, or more agreeable in their manners.[43]

It is difficult to assess the reliability of this report, because the "Journal" is at least partly meant to parody Frances Wright, whose *Views of Society and Manners in America* had just been published and had struck many American readers as overly sanguine about the literacy, patriotism, and unified sentiments of Americans.[44] The Englishwoman of *St. Tammany's* speaks in her first letter of her "proposed work on the Rights of Women," a subject already taken up by Wright. Her visit to the African Theatre would echo Fanny Wright's dramatic interests as well; Wright even staged a play in New York in 1819.

The "Journal" is probably not entirely parody. *St. Tammany's Magazine* later published a letter of Wright's and apparently remained sympathetic to her. And although some passages show evidence of a parodic intention, others do not. Van Winkle or Sands signals caution to the reader from the outset, affixing an editorial note at the beginning: "In the following letters, forming part of the voluminous unpublished correspondence of the fair authoress, we believe her credulity has been in one or two instances imposed upon by designing persons." Even where the "Journal" does seem designed as a parody, it is an extremely mild one, and the Englishwoman's letters in tone and content are generally consistent with the regular features of the magazine.

Perhaps the strongest note of satire is the following passage, in which she again mentions the capacities of African-Americans. It is this passage, if nothing else, that the editorial headnote is meant to flag for the reader's caution. She has just been engaged in a discussion of politics with an unusually philosophical seaman:

> As he was endeavouring to prove the fallacy of a doubtful theory of Montesquieu, I was surprised by the apparition of the black cook, who, suddenly emerging from the forecastle, mid volumes of smoke, displayed the upperhalf of his person, and quoted the Federalist, to disprove the assertions of the seaman.
>
> Having finished our discussion, I retired to the cabin. Seated by the table, I found the mulatto steward, reading Adam Smith on politi-

cal economy. One of the passengers was perusing Thucydides in the original; another was writing, he told me, on perpetual motion, and showed me the model of a machine, which, he said, had been going for a fortnight, and would never stop till it was worn out by the friction.

"Happy country!" exclaimed I, as I retired to my birth; "where every man is a politician, and a philosopher! where taxes are unknown! where worth and talent are the only passports to wealth and distinction; where faction and tyranny are alike strangers, and the rights of man are perfectly defined and vindicated!" I fell asleep; and dreamed that the whole world was revolutionized; and that women were declared capable of exercising the right of suffrage, and of holding any office, ministerial or judicial.[45]

It is easy enough to see this account as a joke, amply warranting the cautionary note. It refers fairly directly to two of Wright's letters on New York.[46] But the narrator herself recognizes the exaggerated optimism. And the Englishwoman's picture of Americans casually debating Montesquieu and quoting the *Federalist* looks less implausible when we remember that she claims to have been in New York sometime between September and the end of November 1821 — in the very period, in other words, when popular discussion was most animated by issues of political and constitutional theory, when New York City's black population was most concerned about the preservation of its rights, when the extension of suffrage was everywhere debated, and when the African Theatre was the touchstone for so many of these issues.[47]

In the passage about the African Theatre, more important, nothing is quite implausible. Even Mordecai Noah, in his satiric accounts, had stressed the genteel appearance, prosperity, and decorous manners of the city's African-Americans. He simply exaggerated these to imply class pretension, in that peculiarly jocular tone that makes it so difficult to gauge the evaluative attitude of so many texts from the literary culture of New York in the early national period. The "English Woman" pictures him in the theater, and he had, by his own account, visited the theater at least once in September. She represents the troupe as performing a Noah melodrama, and in fact we know that they did perform one in the fall of 1821, and a second one early in 1822.[48] If we are to imagine her as having seen a Noah melodrama at the African Theatre, moreover, the play she would have seen was *She Would Be a Soldier*. The *New-York Evening Post* reported on November 30 — two weeks before the "Journal" appeared — that the handbills for this production were "posted up on the corners of the streets."[49] *She Would Be a Soldier*, probably Noah's best-known play, deals with cross-dressing and female advancement in a way that must have resonated with Wright's interests. In these details, the account of the theater can be largely confirmed, despite the fun it has at Wright's expense.

Interestingly, on one further point the narrative seems to be borne out by other evidence. The "English Woman" claims to have seen Othello "enacted by a real blackamoor, with great effect." Previously it has been believed that the first black actor to play *Othello* was Ira Aldridge, who in his youth was associated with Brown and the African Theatre. But there has been no direct evidence that Brown's African Theatre itself staged *Othello* before 1822.[50] Thompson, however, located an account of a court case in New York City in November 1821 in which the defendant, Charles Beers — also known as Charles Taft — is linked to the theater. As the *New-York City-Hall Recorder* puts it in reporting the trial, "Several black gentlemen in this City, actuated, no doubt, with a laudable emulation, recently resolved to open a theatre: They organized a dramatic *corps*, at the head of which was the prisoner, who actually appeared on the stage, several times, and sustained the characters of Richard the third and Othello."[51]

Thompson discounts this claim, arguing that no other document reports a performance of Othello by Taft at the African Theatre. But at least one other document in his collection does connect Taft with Othello: it is a *National Advocate* story about Taft's arrest, on November 19.[52] The narrative in *St. Tammany's*, then, suggests either that such reports were widely circulated or that the author of the "Journal" had witnessed Charles Taft in the first performances of *Othello* by a black actor.

One final text from *St. Tammany's Magazine* deserves some attention. It is a speech on "Universal Suffrage" by Peter Livingston, which, according to an editorial headnote, was "intended to have been made" at the constitutional convention. The speech begins in a radical vein that resembles the Englishwoman's dream vision. Livingston entertains the idea of suffrage for women and the elimination of all property restrictions. But then he turns to African-Americans:

> Sir, I come next to an unfortunate subject; on which, however, I cannot avoid touching. I would shun a closer contact than is indispensably necessary. Sir, it is a gloomy, an unsavoury subject: I mean the negroes. Shall they be entitled to vote? Sir, it is a delicate matter to reconcile on this point our principles with our convenience. Universal equality among human beings, is very sublime in theory; but here it would not be very beautiful in practice. Let us get over it as easily as we can. Our fathers have imposed upon us a great burthen, in their Helots. They are welcome to go away, to enrich our sister states by the product of their industry; or to colonize the fertile deserts of Africa, and teach the natives the enlightened policy of this free country, the rights of man, and their natural equality. Sir, they may go to the devil if they please; any where, so we can be rid of them. If they will stay, we must use them with Christian benevolence: but we cannot let them vote. This is perfectly fair, and highly

257

honourable to our generosity. But we cannot let them vote. They have no right to ask it. Sir, they have never yet been able to prove that they have any souls; at any rate, that they are of the same species with ourselves. They have never got over the fact that their *rete mucosum* is black; that their wigs are woolly, their lips thick, their feet splay, and their perspiration by no means odoriferous.[53]

Van Winkle and Sands published this speech on November 17, a week after the convention officially closed and two weeks before they published the "Soliloquy." It shows how the emergent vocabulary of scientific racism, revolving around classification of species, circulated in discussions of the franchise.[54] Livingston's description of thick lips and splay feet, themselves conventional enough, seems to be echoed directly by the "Soliloquy":

> And if our lips are thicker, be it known,
> That nature, anxious for her children's bliss,
> Vouchsafed them for a more capacious kiss.
> If our heel's long, and our feet splay are found
> We take the firmer grip of parent ground.

This echo is so close that it might lead us to think that the author of the "Soliloquy" had before him a copy of Livingston's speech. But Livingston's language here is by no means unique, and the "Soliloquy" takes up other details of racial typing—notably large bladders and copious brains—that derive from other sources.

To read through the debates of the constitutional convention is to encounter enough racial stereotypes of this sort as to suggest that they were common in informal discussion. One delegate, arguing against Peter Jay's defense of African-American rights, raised the question of species. In response to Jay's claim that suffrage would "elevate" the black population, delegate Briggs retorted, "Would it elevate a monkey or a baboon to allow them to vote?"[55] Compare this remark with the opening of the "Soliloquy": "Are we the links 'twixt men and monkeys then? / Or are we all baboons? or not all men?" The "Soliloquy" seems to respond, point for point, to the arguments produced in the state convention. No doubt those arguments were much discussed both in the circle around William Brown's theater and in the circle around Cornelius Van Winkle's magazine.

Perhaps the most striking similarity is the echo of R. Clarke's speeches in the monologue's critique of whiteness. Clarke argued that classification by color was incoherent:

> By retaining the word "white," you impose a distinction impracticable in its operation. Among those who are by way of distinction called whites, and whose legitimate ancestors, as far as we can trace them, have never been slaves, there are many shades of difference in complexion. Then how will you discriminate? and at what point will you limit your distinction? Will you here descend to particulars, or leave that to the legislature? If you leave it to them, you will impose upon them a burden which neither you nor they can bear. You ought not to require of them impossibilities. Men descended from African ancestors, but who have been pretty well white-washed by their commingling with your white population, may escape your scrutiny; while others, whose blood is as pure from any African taint as any member of this Convention, may be called upon to prove his pedigree, or forfeit his right of suffrage, because he happens to have a swarthy complexion. Are you willing, by any act of this Convention, to expose any, even the meanest, of your white citizens, to such an insult? I hope not.[56]

Clarke's arguments here were echoed by the august chancellor James Kent, "the American Blackstone," who rose to point out,

"There was much difficulty in the practical operation of such a principle. What shall be the criterion in deciding upon the different shades of colour? The Hindoo and Chinese are called yellow — the Indian *red*! Shall these be excluded should they come to reside among us?"[57] The "Soliloquy" echoes these pragmatic constitutional questions in its nominalist approach to racial labels:

> And we are red, — not black, like bats and crows;
> Black is the absence of all colours — say,
> Look at my face — is it not ruddy bay?
> . . . .
> But come, ye whites, browns, yellows, iron grey,
> All call yourselves cream-white, and so ye may,
> Brag of the symbol of your own disgrace,
> And wear your mealy infamy in your face!

Now, it might be noted that the "Soliloquy" goes well beyond the arguments advanced by Clarke and Kent. In challenging the label "white," Clarke had not denied that African blood might be a "taint" or that its imputation would be an "insult" to a swarthy citizen. He had simply pointed to the pragmatic difficulties of racial labels, bringing to them some nominalist skepticism. The defense of the African-American franchise by Federalists such as Jay was also an interested one, since the black vote tended to be strongly Federalist. Yet the arguments of Clarke, Jay, and Kent remind us forcefully that the racialization of American politics was not yet in place. Perhaps the "Soliloquy" was able to launch its more thorough critique of whiteness because whiteness was, at the time, still being invented, in a way that left its contradictions visible. Ethnicizing ways of thinking still lacked consensual resonance in public discourse, at least in relation to the language of citizenship and rights.[58]

If the availability of this critique in public discourse does not help us resolve the authorship of the "Soliloquy" — since the circulation of these arguments would have put them at the disposal both of Brown's circle and of Sands's and Van Winkle's — it again dramatizes the way the "Soliloquy" represents not just a text with a single context but also a conjunction of several different publics. The resulting exchanges between these publics are often striking, so much so that the "Soliloquy" can only be understood in reference to all of them.

In part, this is because of the limitations of our evidence. The archival record from which the materials of this essay have been drawn does not give us an unfiltered view of how the suffrage discussion appeared to Brown, Hewlett, Taft, and the others who found "articulate language" through the space at Mercer and Bleecker. What we know of that space is what other publics record: the official publics of the courts and the convention, the private publics of the *National Advocate* and *St. Tammany's*. But the inter-reference of discourses and publics in these sources seems also to have been the general condition of publicness in New York City. In the African Theatre itself, audiences mingled to a degree, even after the partition was erected in late October to divide whites from blacks.

If we imagine the "Soliloquy" in that context, rather than simply on the page of *St. Tammany's*, what stands out is both the permeability of the speech to other contexts of public discourse and the distinguishing deictics by which the speech organizes the Mercer Street audience. Within the diegesis of the *Obi* play, of course, the "we" of the opening line refers to Jamaican Maroons, or more broadly to Africans. At Mercer Street, it also would have referred inevitably to the cast and a part of the audience. And where Three-Fingered Jack dramatically addresses a white Jamaican planter, we remember that no white actor is likely to have been onstage. The aggressive address of the "Soliloquy" — "Ye are the whitewashed race!" — indexes one side of the partition in the room. In doing so, it also responds implicitly to the newspapers and to its rival theaters (the allusions to Shylock's speech in *The Merchant of Venice*, for instance, may be an implicit reference to Mordecai Noah's Jewishness[59]). It responds more directly to the debates of the convention, as reported in the papers and as extended in informal discussions.

The "Soliloquy" might be seen as an early example of the phenomenon of counterpublicity.[60] Publics like the one that Brown and Hewlett brought into being through their theater are defined as counterpublics to the extent that participation in them is understood to involve antagonism to the dominant publics of the public-sphere system. In the "Soliloquy," as well as in the surviving documents of Brown and Hewlett, we can discern just this keen awareness of a broader public-sphere context, one that is hostile and irrational in what it takes for granted or in what passes as reasonable opinion. Even as it addresses the very local public of the theater, the "Soliloquy" also implies a reference to the public-sphere environment against which that public was antagonistically defined: the constitutional convention and dominant opinion.

It may be that the speech, initially presented in the theater, was inserted in the magazine, or reconstructed for it, by someone who moved between Brown's circles and Sands's and Van Winkle's. Given Van Winkle's demonstrable interest in the African issue, his publication of another account of the theater, and his ties to Federalist literary circles through the Irving family and others, such a connection is entirely plausible. By appearing in *St. Tammany's Magazine*, the speech was thus translated from the discrete public of the African Theatre to the same venue as both Livingston's speech and the works of writers with a broader literary appeal such as Washington Irving. The power of the speech depends on its ability to address all of these intertexts — not indiscriminately but by being multigeneric and flexible.

The Albany convention, Van Winkle's magazine, Noah's newspaper, Brown's theater, and now-untraceable informal discussions were all engaged in the fall of 1821 in a complex dance of triangulation and projection. Each represented a discrete vantage point from which a larger political world — ranging upward in scale from those physically present in the theater to an abstract audience of "humanity" — could be invoked. The stakes were nothing less than full membership in the publics that could be addressed from each of these vantage points. Each was discrete, marked by its own medium, its own public, its own mode of address, its own institutions, its own patterns of circulation. And some are less frank than others about the multiplicity of publics involved. Mordecai Noah, for example, often writes in the *National Advocate* as if the Africans of his account could not possibly be readers of his paper, as if "the people" and "the city" were utterly distinct from the public of the African Theatre — even while his own plays were performed there and he himself took a bow from the stage. At the same time, each of these vantage points within the unfolding events of the fall of 1821 was continually engaging the others. The topic of their common disputes, political membership, required that each of these points of address imagine or project others beyond it.

Coda

That process continued far beyond the civic publics of New York City. Very late in 1821, after the close of the state convention but at the height of the African Theatre's publicity, and well over a month after the "Soliloquy" appeared, New Yorkers responded with unexpected zeal to the publication of *The Spy*, a new novel by James Fenimore Cooper printed up in haste by Van Winkle's former partner, Charles Wiley. There, the debate over race and rights continues. The black servant Caesar, despite his comical obsequiousness to his masters, offers defiance whenever race is mentioned. ("No more negar than be yourself," he tells the title character near the beginning. "A black man so good as white."[61]) An extensive dialogue treats the contradiction between slavery and the Declaration of Independence[62]; another treats the question of the soul's race ("I have heard the good Mr. Whitfield say, that there was no distinction of colour in heaven"[63]).

If Cooper's novel seems to be responding directly to the controversy over the convention, it is not surprising. We know from Cooper's own account of the composition of the novel that he was still writing the second half virtually until the eve of the book's publication on December 22.[64] Cooper had expressed keen awareness of the debates; he had himself worked hard for the Federalists in Westchester County during the 1821 election; and he stayed in close contact with members of the Jay family.[65] It was Peter Jay, brother of Cooper's childhood friend William Jay, who had moved to have the word "white" deleted from the suffrage clause. (He had also been the leading force behind the 1817 law to abolish slavery in New York by 1827.) And according to Cooper's later account, it was Peter's father, the former governor and chief justice John Jay, who gave Cooper the anecdote that served as the germ of *The Spy*.

There are also suggestions in *The Spy* that Cooper's understanding of the race issue was shaped by the controversy over the African Theatre. Theatricality figures prominently among the novel's themes, beginning in the second paragraph, where we are told that the neutral ground between British and rebel forces was so anarchic as to force people to wear "masks, which even to this day have not been thrown aside."[66] Cooper carries the theatrical figure to such an extreme that almost every major character is at one point or another in disguise. The two great masters of role-playing and impersonation in the novel are the title character Harvey Birch and, absurdly enough, George Washington. Their secret rendezvous, a hut in the forest, turns out to be a regular prop room, lined with costumes.

The climax in this mounting tension of masquerade comes late in the novel and requires the loyalist captain Wharton to disguise himself as his black servant Caesar, and vice versa. The trick is managed by Birch, who applies a parchment mask and a wool wig to Wharton: "The mask was stuffed and shaped in such a manner as to preserve the peculiarities, as well as the colour, of the African visage; and the wig was so artfully formed of black and white wool, as to imitate the pepper-and-salt colour of Caesar's own head, and to exact plaudits from the black himself, who thought it an excellent counterfeit in every thing but quality." [67] Birch goes so far as to say that Wharton would "pass well at a Pinkster frolic."[68]

Interestingly, no attempt is made to produce a white mask for Caesar. That seems to be beyond even Birch's makeup artistry. Caesar is given the captain's powdered wig and uniform and instructed to keep his face to the wall. But unable to maintain even this minimal disguise, he "incautiously removed the wig a little from one of his ears, in order to hear the better, without in the least remembering that its colour might prove fatal to his disguise." [69] The black body gives itself away. This moment has been prepared throughout the novel by remarks on Caesar's color, his comic physiognomy, and his dialect speech. These asymmetries of marking allow the white captain to pass while the black servant cannot. For these reasons, despite the explicit speeches about slavery and race, the comedy of the novel fundamentally resembles Noah's and other parodies of the African Theatre in which black bodies and black dialect give away all attempts at cultural passing. To read the "Soliloquy" against this pattern in

The Spy is to be reminded of the speech's radical import in the fall of 1821.

Ironically, when the dramatic adaptation of Cooper's novel made its way to the stage in London in 1825, the role of Caesar was taken by one Mr. Buckstone, a white actor. But on the same program, making his first appearance in London, was Ira Aldridge, acting under the name Keene and listed on the playbill as the "Tragedian of Colour, from the African Theatre, New York." He was playing the role of Oroonoko, which demonstrates, the playbill tells us, "the Terrific Effect of an injured African's Vengeance."[70]

The line between defiant African-American theater and the emergent white performance of blackface, in short, seems to have been remarkably fine in the 1820s. Cooper's Caesar is not the first black character onstage, but the figure enjoyed a vogue with white audiences for the rest of the century. Popular songs from New York in black dialect exist from as early as 1815 and by the early 1830s had developed into the minstrelsy genre.[71] Just at the cusp of these developments, sometimes on the same stage and reported in the same papers, stands the African Theatre. The intermingling of these apparently antithetical ways of representing race seems to bear out the argument of W. T. Lhamon. In his book *Raising Cain*, Lhamon asserts that blackface minstrelsy was more than simply a vehicle for the racist construction of whiteness. Initially, he claims, it grew out of an interracial culture in which poor workers represented their own antagonism to genteel authority through an imaginative identification with the comic black figures of minstrel performance.

Lhamon never mentions the African Theatre or its public controversies, but his evidence of an interracial performance culture begins in the years around 1820, in neighborhoods of New York City very close to the site of the theater.[72] There was no black ghetto in 1821. Blacks and poor whites typically lived side by side.[73] When the evidence of the African Theatre is reexamined in this light, one thing that stands out sharply is the participation of a working-class white audience. As one 1833 illustration vividly pictures, white audiences who attended the minstrel performances of T.D. Rice in the 1830s were fond of getting up on the stage, sometimes crowding him so that he could hardly find room to do the "Jim Crow" dance that made him famous.[74] In an 1824 account of James Hewlett at the African Theatre, we are told that "white folks all got on the stage" and sang along with Hewlett's song. After a big sword fight between Hewlett and Bates, the anonymous author writes: "White folks had all the fun to 'emselves now. Some on 'em begin to dance, box, whistle, sing, and the dickens knows what all." At the end of the show, the same pattern is repeated: "When the play was over, and the audience and Hewlett had a right good jig together, we all started away in high spirits."[75]

It seems likely, given these accounts, that Rice's blackface performances in the following decade stem from and refashion the culture of the African Theatre. The succession, in fact, may have been direct. Rice would have been about thirteen in 1821, just beginning his apprenticeship to a wood-carver. According to one source, he was already "doing little Negro bits between the acts at the Columbia Street Theatre" in 1826.[76] It is not difficult to imagine him as part of that audience, two years earlier, crowding up to the stage to dance and sing along with James Hewlett, just as audiences would soon do with his own performances.

As with the mingled voices of the print media, these overlapping performance contexts could still be deeply antagonistic. When Charles Mathews performed a similar appropriation for a more genteel context, Hewlett wrote his eloquent letter of denunciation. But because blackface minstrelsy never had the genteel public sanction that Mathews enjoyed, such protest could not so easily be heard. And by the time Rice began his popular run on the stage with Jim Crow, the African Theatre had closed, Hewlett's career had been cast into shadow, and the "Soliloquy" had been forgotten.

CHAPTER EIGHT

Whitman Drunk*

> I am as independent as the United States of America.
>
> — Anonymous drunk of the 1840s,
>
> being escorted from a bar

In November 1842, New Yorkers would have been able to buy, for twelve and a half cents each, or for eight dollars per hundred, an object that would be hard to classify today. It was called *Franklin Evans; or, The Inebriate*. Now it is encountered as a book and is usually described as a novel. In 1842, it was a newspaper supplement — a special issue of the *New World*, unbound, printed on cheap paper, in newspaper columns. Any reader would have recognized it as a tract as well. The *New World*'s advertisements for it had begun, "Friends of Temperance, Ahoy!" The first sentence makes no bones about these extranovelistic features: "The story I am going to tell you, reader, will be somewhat aside from the ordinary track of the novelist."

Many who read *Franklin Evans* today, as a novel, find it unsatisfactory; one reason for this is that the work addressed publics that

---

*Originally published in *Breaking Bounds*, eds. Betsy Erkkila and Jay Grossman (New York: Oxford University Press, 1996).

were not simply novelistic publics. Newspaper subscribers and "Friends of Temperance" would have brought to the object the mass-mediated self-understanding of the temperance movement. And that was a public in a new way. Temperance publications like *Franklin Evans* brought together two tendencies of the early national period: an ever more aggressive press, which had become strongly entrepreneurial; and a tradition of association that by the time of Tocqueville's American tour had come to seem to be the defining feature of American culture. Temperance activism had been a prominent part of this early national pattern of association. In the ten or fifteen years before *Franklin Evans*, however, the press and voluntary association had transformed each other in the context of temperance. The early national entrepreneurial press became a mass medium, and the temperance reform societies that had been popping up in every American locale became a full-scale, mass-mediated social movement — that is, one that understood itself as such.

Temperance and the mass press planted each other on the national scene. The American Temperance Society from its beginnings in 1826 drew on a tradition of tract-distributing reform groups, especially the American Tract Society, and pushed the publishing trade to an unprecedented outreach. Temperance tracts — five million copies by 1851 — dominated the American Tract Society's output. And papers such as the Albany *Temperance Recorder* achieved mass circulation in exactly the same years that saw the first penny daily newspapers. Even before the arrival of the new steam presses — the first penny daily, the New York *Sun*, was printed on a flatbed handpress — tract writers and newspapermen were developing the basis of a mass public. Not only were temperance societies and newspapers expanding; they incorporated an awareness of non-state "society" in the culture of their membership and readership. As Charles Sellers tellingly notes:

270

Americans were first habituated to statistics by the Benevolent Empire's bourgeois passion for enumerating souls saved, money raised, Bibles circulated, tracts printed, missionary years expended. Endlessly temperance reformers calculated the dollar costs of alcohol, including crime, pauperism, and lost labor. The $94,425,000 total of one tally would "buy up all the houses, lands, and slaves in the United States every five years."[1]

This statistical consciousness, combined with a vast network of non-state association and an equally vast body of print, brought a mass public into awareness of itself and its distinctness from the national state. The Washington Temperance Society, founded in 1840, was especially emphatic about the social scale of the voluntary movement; and the Washingtonians quickly outstripped the more elite-based American Temperance Society.

In this essay, I will argue that the thematic language of temperance rhetoric had much to do with the emergence of the cultural form of the social movement, which from the 1830s to the present has been one of the givens of the political world. Temperance ideology shifted so radically in this process as to become virtually the opposite of temperance, as will become clear. I will also argue that both temperance rhetoric and the temperance movement were the context in which the tract's author, the newspaperman Walt Whitman, first articulated what would later become the major issues of his career. I will be especially interested in two residues from his temperance publishing: a dialectic or tension that would eventually become sexual expressivism; and the strange conception of a public that distinguishes his poetic writing and his publishing practice.

For all his trumpeting about the friends of temperance, Whitman, when he is talking about alcohol in *Franklin Evans*, often seems to be thinking about something else. Franklin Evans has his first encounter with musical drinking shops shortly after he arrives in New York from the country, when his new city-boy friend, Colby, says to him, "Let us go out and cruise a little, and see what there is going on."[2] "How delicious everything seemed!" Franklin exclaims:

> Those beautiful women — warbling melodies sweeter than ever I had heard before, and the effect of the liquor upon my brain, seemed to lave me in happiness, as it were, from head to foot!
>
> Oh, fatal pleasure! There and then was my first false step after coming in the borders of the city — and *so soon* after, too! . . .
>
> Colby saw at length that he had been too heedless with me. Used as he was to the dissipation of city life, he forgot that I was from the country, and never in my life before engaged in such a scene of *pleasure*.[3]

This passage tries simultaneously to articulate pleasure and to manage it. Self-mastery and self-abandonment struggle for supremacy in a way that is visibly absent from earlier writing on alcohol, such as Benjamin Franklin's or Washington Irving's. Fatal pleasure, but also *Oh*, fatal pleasure.[4] Thematically, the focus is on drink. But Whitman does not write, "Oh, fatal alcohol."

If alcohol does not seem quite to be the subject here, still it is no accident that Whitman's first extended treatment of a dialectic between self-mastery and self-abandonment should occur in the form of temperance fiction. The temperance movement *invented* addiction. Thomas De Quincey never uses the term (though current editions supply it in prefaces and notes), and only some decades after the concept was developed in temperance was it extended to drugs other than alcohol. Addiction had been a legal term, describing the performative act of bondage, before it was metaphorized to describe a person's self-relation. Someone who is addicted to, say, Sabbath breaking could be understood as having developed a habit, bound himself to a custom. In temperance rhetoric, the concept loses the sense of an active self-abnegation on the part of the will. Desire and will became distinct in a way that Jonathan Edwards had been able to dismiss: "A man never, in any instance, wills any thing contrary to his desires, or desires any thing contrary to his Will ... the thing which he wills, the very same he desires. ... It cannot truly be said ... that a drunkard, let his appetite be never so strong, cannot keep the cup from his mouth."[5]

Temperance reformers began imagining the reverse — that the drunkard *cannot* keep the cup from his mouth even if he wants to do so. At this point, they gave up on the traditional concept of temperance in favor of abstinence and the treatment of addiction as disease. In the culture of modernity, where people are held responsible for the disposition of their lives as an act of will, it became possible to imagine desire no longer as self but as the paradigm case of heteronomy. Controlling your body *had* made you temperate. Now it made you free. Where desire and will had been one for Edwards, temperance reformers — like liberal evangelicals — began radicalizing the concept of volition. The corollary was an expanded concept of desire as the limit on the will.

In *Franklin Evans,* Whitman is on the cutting edge of addiction theory when he writes:

> Reader! perhaps you despise me. Perhaps, if I were by you at this moment, I should behold the curled lip of scorn, and the look of deep contempt. Oh, pause stern reverencer of duty, and have pity for a fellow-creature's weakness! ... Thou sayest, perhaps — Begin a reformation, and custom will make it easy. But what if the beginning be dreadful? The first steps, not like climbing a mountain, but going through fire? What if the whole system must undergo a

change, violent as that which we conceive of the mutation of form in some insects? What if a process comparable to flaying alive, have to be endured? Is the weakness which sinks under such struggles, to be compared with the pertinacity which clings to vice, for itself and its gross appetites?[6]

What if it isn't vice at all, this, or at least not vice *for itself*? What if it's, well, what could it be called? Flaying, infrapersonal trouble, the shudders of a mutating bug. "Impotent attempts to make issue with what appears to be our destiny." Whitman or Evans pleads by this logic for humanity: "The drunkard, low as he is, is a *man*." He articulates an antinomy between will and desire, the moral solution to which is in fact a much more radical valuing of will: "The GLORIOUS TEMPERANCE PLEDGE."[7]

How does a picture of the body's own heteronomy (so to speak) produce the alien solution of the voluntary pledge? Eve Kosofsky Sedgwick has astutely observed this pattern in our own day, witnessed in a wild proliferation of addiction theories to the point that she speaks of epidemics of the will:

> So long as an entity known as "free will" has been hypostatized and charged with ethical value, for just so long has an equally hypostatized "compulsion" had to be available as a counter-structure always internal to it, always requiring to be ejected from it. The scouring descriptive work of addiction-attribution is propelled by the same imperative: its exacerbated perceptual acuteness in detecting the compulsion behind everyday voluntarity is driven, ever more blindly, by its own compulsion to isolate some new, receding but absolutized space of *pure* voluntarity.[8]

The glorious temperance pledge marks the receding horizon of that relatively absolute voluntarity. Whitman, pursuing the volun-

tarist utopia of pledging to an extreme, interpolates a dream
vision, a Jacobin fantasy about a stateless festival republic in which
every last peasant will have signed the temperance pledge, bringing all born persons into the Washingtonian associational network.
In Franklin's dream, he appears in the crowd during this big event:

> A venerable old man came forward upon the scaffold, and presented
> a document to the speaker. He received it with evident delight; and
> snatching a pen from a table, he wrote his name under it, and held it
> up to the view of the people.
>
> It were impossible to describe the thunder-peal of hurrahs that
> arose in the air, and sounded to the skies, as the Full Work was con-
> summated thus. They cried aloud —
>
> "Victory! Victory! The Last Slave of Appetite is free, and the
> people are regenerated!"[9]

If it weren't so queer, this passage would be a true nightmare of
democratic totalitarianism. It *is* rather queer, partly because the
ideal of political union, this delirious consummation, takes place
in the public witnessing of a man's relation to his own appetitive
body; partly because of the campy feudalism involved in calling John
Doe the Last Vassal; partly because of the odd mixture of humiliation and heroization involved in parading him about; partly because
of Franklin Evans's phantom self on the margin of the whole scene.

What interests me most here is the fantasy of stateless public
association, because I think this points to the institutional context
for addiction culture. Temperance was not just another discourse
but a rather special kind of social movement. The assumptions
of addiction discourse silently explicate the associational style
of temperance, which was of course a civil-society phenomenon, arguably the largest and most sustained social movement in
modernity. In the year of the novel's publication, 1842, hundreds

of American cities had held temperance festivals on Washington's birthday; but, as one temperance lecturer announced, "the festival at New York surpassed all others in its extent, beauty, and appropriateness."[10] There were even more festivals on July 4 of that year. There were also new temperance publications, including the *New York Washingtonian*, in which Whitman published a temperance story in March 1842 and in which he would publish the beginning of a second novel, *The Madman*, in 1843. Festivals and publications alike helped to mediate for temperance participants an understanding of the social movement as part of a repertoire of action. Their sense of membership and the very nature of their participation were mediated by the idea that temperance organizing was an action on the part of non-state society. *Franklin Evans* also helped to mediate that constitutive self-understanding.

Whitman in later life told Horace Traubel that *Franklin Evans* was essentially commissioned by two temperance activists, "Parke Godwin and another somebody" — probably, in fact, Park Benjamin and James Burns.[11] The idea of commissioning fiction as propaganda had been part of the public strategy of the temperance movement since 1836, when the second convention of the American Temperance Union, in Saratoga, formally voted to endorse fiction and other "products of the fancy" as public-sphere instruments.[12] Whitman echoed this notion of the instrumental role of fiction in the preface and conclusion of his novel:

> Issued in the cheap and popular form you see, and wafted by every mail to all parts of this vast republic; the facilities which its publisher possesses, giving him the power of diffusing it more widely than any other establishment in the United States; the mighty and deep public opinion,...its being written *for the mass*...all these will give "THE INEBRIATE," I feel confident, a more than ordinary share of patronage.[13]

Both the temperance movement in general and *Franklin Evans* in particular are therefore embedded in a context of non-state political association.

Just seven years before the publication of the novel, Tocqueville had given this social form the ideologization by which it has been known ever since: voluntary association.

> In no country in the world has the principle of association been more successfully used or applied to a greater multitude of objects than in America.... The citizen of the United States is taught from infancy to rely upon his own exertions in order to resist the evils and the difficulties of life; he looks upon the social authority with an eye of mistrust and anxiety, and he claims its assistance only when he is unable to do without it.... If some public pleasure is concerned, an association is formed to give more splendor and regularity to the entertainment. Societies are formed to resist evils that are exclusively of a moral nature, as to diminish the vice of intemperance.[14]

In Tocqueville's account, as in *Franklin Evans*, the imperative of will for the individual ("to resist the evils and the difficulties of life") translates directly into a form of association. Americans fill up their social space with a vast network of associations all formed occasionally, entered and left at will, existing only to make the exercise of will more powerful. Temperance was shaped organizationally by this ideologization, not only in being open-member associations like so many other moral reform groups but also in calling attention to voluntarism by the ritual of pledge signing. The thematic content of self-management and addiction in this context was able to provide an implicit metalanguage by which association might be perceived as valuable *because* voluntary. (Compare Thoreau's statement of only a few years later: "Know all men by these presents, that I, Henry Thoreau, do not wish to be regarded as a member of any incorporated society which I have not joined."[15])

Perhaps another way of showing how important these metasocial themes are in Whitman's treatment of alcohol is to show how unimportant alcohol itself is. Certain moralizing passages claim that all bad things in the story come from drink. But actually very little follows directly from alcohol in the plot. The "Oh, fatal pleasure" scene is perfectly typical: Franklin's dissipation comes as much from sopranos as from gin. Alcohol never plays more than an ancillary role in such gothic disasters as his marriage, on impulse, to a Creole slave who later turns into a homicidal madwoman. (It's a very male text.)

Indeed, so unimportant is alcohol to the plot that Whitman was able to republish the novel with a new title that made no reference to it — twice: first as *Franklin Evans; or, The Merchant's Clerk: A Tale of the Times* (advertised through the same *New World* in 1843); then again in 1846 in Whitman's own paper, the Brooklyn *Daily Eagle*, as *Fortunes of a Country Boy*. The latter version especially is no longer a temperance novel. The interpolated tales have been removed, but most of these had little to do with alcohol themselves, as, for example, in the tale of Wind-Foot (an exquisite Indian boy who does what Indians do best in white American literature: die in erotically thrilling ways). By means of such cuts and some discreet alterations — "dissipation" replaces "drunkenness" — *Fortunes of a Country Boy* becomes a novel about self-development and urban associational space. Addiction is replaced by a character flaw: "weakness of resolution, and liability to be led by others."[16] Franklin's final conversion to the total abstinence pledge is dropped, which means that his return from the dark night of his Southern sojourn is marked only by the sudden reappearance of Stephen Lee, who leaves him a large inheritance. "So, at an age which was hardly upon the middle verge of life, I found myself possessed of a comfortable property; and, as the term is 'unincumbered' person."[17] (When Evans asks the reason for this largesse, Lee says, "My own fancy."[18] At the beginning of the novel, he says, "I do not wish to conceal that I am somewhat interested in your case."[19])

What both versions share is an interest in the dilemmas of self-coherence. In the following passage from *Franklin Evans*, Whitman sounds almost like De Quincey:

> How refreshing it is to pause in the whirl and tempest of life, and cast back our minds over past years! I think there is even a kind of satisfaction in deliberately and calmly reviewing actions that we feel were foolish or evil. It pleases us to know that we have the learning of experience. The very contrast, perhaps, between what we are, and what we were, is gratifying....
>
> From no other view can I understand how it is, that I sometimes catch myself turning back in my reflection, to the very dreariest and most degraded incidents which I have related in the preceding pages, and thinking upon them without any of the bitterness and mortification which they might be supposed to arouse in my bosom. The formal narration of them, to be sure, is far from agreeable to me — but in my own self-communion upon the subject, I find a species of entertainment. I was always fond of day-dreams — an innocent pleasure, perhaps, if not allowed too much latitude.[20]

As a pretext for introducing the daydream about the Last Slave of Appetite, this transitional passage assumes a fair amount of latitude and stands out all the more for that reason as an index to the novel's characteristic obsessions. Franklin indicates the autobiographical act as a version of liberal individual morality, an act of taking responsibility for one's entire disposition. But he quickly begins instead to describe the perverse pleasures of self-discontinuity, even self-repudiation and self-abjection. The scenes he contemplates are dreary, even degrading; though he says he contemplates them without bitterness or mortification, he also tells us that the contemplation is pleasurable because he knows it *should* be bitter and mortifying.

The dialectic between these two moments — liberal self-integration and perverse self-contemplation — governs the entire narrative. *Franklin Evans* seems designed more than anything else to narrate its title character into as many disparate social spaces as possible and to compound his integration problems with the endless resurgence of appetite. From his first appearance en route from rural Long Island to Manhattan, Franklin is the subject of his elective associations, especially male (he will marry twice and take one mistress, with fatal consequences for all three women). He falls in with some fast boys who introduce him to male circles of urban appetitive decadence. He also meets Lee, the mysterious older widower who takes a special interest in him. His path between these affinitive influences leads him in and out of various states of self-coherence, where integration tends to be associated with capital and temperance, disintegrative tendencies with alcohol, sexuality, time, death, the city, sickness, poverty, market dependency, crime, prison, shame, singing, and pleasure. "How delicious everything seemed!"

At the end of *Franklin Evans*, Whitman summarizes the moral of the story: "I would warn that youth whose eye may scan over these lines, with a voice which speaks to him, not from idle fear, but the sad knowledge of experience, how bitter are the consequences attending these musical drinking-shops ... pestilent places, where the mind and the body are both rendered effeminate together."[21] It's not difficult to hear attraction here. Something that cannot be openly avowed is nevertheless coming to expression. Modern bourgeois culture gets a lot of things done this way, but nowhere more visibly than in the literature of addiction, to which *Franklin Evans* belongs. Addiction literature is marked by a dialectic: no sooner do scenes of self-abandonment conjure up the necessity of self-mastery than this instrumental self-relation in turn gives way to the possibility of self-contemplation, of an abandonment newly regarded as expressive. Though the theme is addiction, it's hard not to hear some reference to the emergent same-sex subculture of New York in the following passage, which describes a lower Manhattan theater of exactly the sort where that subculture flourished:

> The Demon of Intemperance had taken possession of all our faculties, and we were his alone.
>   A wretched scene! Half-a-dozen men, just entering the busy scenes of life, not one of us over twenty-five years, and there we were, benumbing our faculties, and confirming ourselves in practices which ever too surely bring the scorn of the world, and deserved disgrace to their miserable victims! It is a terrible sight, I have often thought since, to see *young men* beginning their walk on this fatal journey! ... To know that the blood is poisoned, and that the strength is to be broken down, and the bloom banished from the cheek, and the lustre of the eye dimmed, and all for a few hours' sensual gratification, now and then — is it not terrible! ... [It] saps the foundations, not only of the body's health, but places a stigma for the future on their worldly course, which can never be wiped out, or concealed from the knowledge of those about them.[22]

Alcohol discriminates finely; it assaults young blood, manly strength, blooming cheeks, and bright eyes. Its symptoms, scarcely distinguishable from those associated with onanism in the mass reform literature of the time, appear in whole numbers of men at once. Seeing such men in public, you recognize them by an epistemology of stigma. This is where they hang out. I have often thought about it.

Alcohol becomes a figure for self-incoherence in general; any "Demon" that has "taken possession of all our faculties" will do. "I sicken as I narrate this part of my story," he says at another point. "The recollection comes of the sufferings of my poor wife, and of my unkindness to her. I paid no attention to her comforts, and took no thought for her subsistence. I *think* I never proceeded to any act of violence — but God only knows what words I spoke in my paroxysms of drunken irritation."[23] Franklin has problems of self-characterization: "God only knows what words I spoke." Whitman heightens his difficulty with autonarration by a number of odd voicing devices: the first scene, for example, is told in the omniscient third person until the narrator says of the main character, "Reader, I was that youth" — a device later repeated in the interpolated tales. Drunkenness, however, allows or requires Franklin to treat his problems of self-characterization as part of his self-characterization. He is a person subject to "paroxysms," self-sickenings, involuntary amnesias, alien thrills of retrospection. These forms of internal heteronomy take on special significance because they contrast with the confessional performance of the narration itself, which is organized by a metalanguage of choice, responsibility, and association through affinity and self-characterization rather than through kinship and status.

At the end of the novel, when Whitman strives for closure within the voluntarist rhetoric, Franklin's internal recognition problems suddenly find an equivalent in his double. He sees in the street a "tipsy loafer" begging, "going through his disgusting capers":

> Pausing a moment, and looking in the man's face, I thought I recollected the features. A second and a third glance convinced me. It was

Colby, my early intimate, the tempter who had led me aside from the paths of soberness. Wretched creature! ... His apparel looked as though it had been picked up in some mud hole; it was torn in strips and all over soiled. His face was bloated, and his eyes red and swollen. I thought of the morning when I awoke upon the dock, after my long fit of intemperance: the person before me was even more an object of pity than myself on that occasion.[24]

Since Franklin's friendship with Colby had been the paradigmatic instance of affinitive, voluntary association in the novel, Franklin can only repudiate him at some cost, leading him rather inconsistently to say, in the penultimate paragraph, "I would advise every young man to marry as soon as possible, and have a home of his own."[25]

The later Whitman's perverse self-characterization is not so far removed from the bourgeois propriety of the temperance novel as one might expect. Nor is his insistence on bringing sexuality into public view, given the peculiar nature of *Franklin Evans*'s public. Whitman's commitment to voluntarist culture never completely relaxed. Like *Franklin Evans*, *Leaves of Grass* imagines a stateless society, constituted in the public sphere through performative discourse. The significant difference is that the poetry imagines this associational style as yoked to — and explicated by — the contemplative or self-abandoning moment in the dialectic of individualism rather than its instrumental or self-mastering moment. Where *Franklin Evans* had imagined civil-society association as organized by voluntarity and self-mastery, condensed in the image of a pledging association, Whitman in the 1850s and 1860s imagined non-state association as called into being by desire, by contemplative recognition, by the imperfect success of selfing.

Unfortunately, this difference has been obscured by the central tradition of Whitman criticism. With its obsessive discourse about Whitman's so-called self, Whitman criticism has provided the most extreme instance I know of the ideology of self analyzed by Vincent Crapanzano. Crapanzano has argued that pragmatic features of discourse tend to be perceived, in middle-class American culture, in a referential language of character. These texts are no exception, since their pragmatics are uniformly taken as indices of Whitman's "self" and their peculiarities are taken to be peculiarities of that self. (Sometimes with a great deal of unintended comedy, as when Malcolm Cowley explains that Whitman had an abnormally developed sense of touch.) "Self" seems to be a concept without which it is impossible to do Whitman criticism. In a long tradition of Whitman criticism, from Quentin Anderson's *Imperial Self* to recent essays by Doris Sommer and Philip Fisher, Whitman has been regarded as a prophet of "the liberal self," a self that regards itself as universal, that does not "recognize difference." In my view, this reading of Whitman gets almost everything wrong, though it's a misreading partly developed by the late Whitman, as it were, himself.

Whitman's writing thematizes a modern phenomenology of self everywhere: "I celebrate myself and sing myself." But it almost always does so in order to make the pragmatics of selfing a mess: "And what I assume you shall assume." The second line can be taken as elaborating the indicatively modern and liberal problem of the other, the problem of mutuality — a problem frequently enough taken up by Whitman, as, for example, in "Crossing Brooklyn Ferry." But it can also be taken as thematizing the pragmatics of self-attribution. It announces that "I" and "you" bear no relation to content, action, choice, self-knowledge or mutual knowledge, the attribution of traits, the reciprocal confirmation of identity through action, or any other condition of selfing: "what I assume you shall assume."

Moreover, the impossibility of selfing is driven home in the way the line parrots interpersonal drama while deploying the special discursive conventions of print-mediated publicity. Whitman's poetry, more than any other body of writing I know, continually exploits public-sphere-discourse conventions as its condition of utterance. In this case, it relies on a discourse context defined by the necessary anonymity and mutual nonknowledge of writer and reader, and therefore on the definitional impossibility of intimacy. Assuming what I assume, you have neither an identity together with me, mediated as we are by print, nor apart from me, since neither pronoun attributions nor acts of assuming manage to distinguish us.

From the first word of "Song of Myself" ("I") to the last ("you"), in every major poem he wrote, Whitman tries out an enormous range of strategies for frustrating the attempt to "self" his language, both by thematic assertion — "I resist anything better than my own diversity" — and by attribution problems: "My voice is the wife's voice, the screech by the rail of the stairs." I interpret the metadiscursive queerness of the poems as a provocation against the ideology of self-characterization. "To a Stranger," for example, invokes the communicative medium of intimacy — the medium to which character attribution is most indispensable — in a way that toys with the nonintimate, depersonalizing conventions of print publication:

> Passing stranger! you do not know how longingly I look upon
> you,
> You must be he I was seeking, or she I was seeking, (it comes
> to me as of a dream,)
> I have somewhere surely lived a life of joy with you,
> All is recall'd as we flit by each other, fluid, affectionate,
> chaste, matured,
> You grew up with me, were a boy with me or a girl with me,

I ate with you and slept with you, your body has become not
    yours only nor left my body mine only,
You give me the pleasure of your eyes, face, flesh, as we pass,
    you take of my beard, breast, hands, in return,
I am not to speak to you, I am to think of you when I sit alone
    or wake at night alone,
I am to wait, I do not doubt I am to meet you again, I am to
    see to it that I do not lose you.[26]

When the speaker says "you do not know how longingly I look upon you," we know that Whitman is not looking longingly upon us, that we cannot possibly *be* the self addressed in second-person attributions. But we also cannot simply fictionalize either the speaker or the scene of address, in the manner of Robert Browning's "My Last Duchess," because the speaker himself indicates the genericizing conventions of publication. It is addressed "to a stranger," and that we certainly are. He is not to speak to us, he says, and that he certainly does not. When the speaker says in the last line "I am to see to it that I do not lose you," we are able to recognize his sense of difficulty simultaneously as (a) his personal commitment to me, whom he loves; and (b) his attempt to acknowledge our anonymity, our mutual nonknowledge, our mediation by print.

The same tension marks all the lines that grope for particularity: "You grew up with me, were a boy with me or a girl with me." You can imagine that one of these recognizes you in particular, but the effort of imagination involved in being recognized both ways serves to remind you that this "you" is, after all, not you but a pronominal shifter, addressing the in-principle anonymous and indefinite audience of the print public sphere. At the same time, you know that you are not being addressed by a complacently generic you, of the kind I am using to address you in this sentence. In "To a Stranger," while we remain on notice about our place in non-intimate public discourse, we are nevertheless solicited into an intimate recognition exchange. Like so much of Whitman's poetry, "To a Stranger" mimes the phenomenology of cruising.

Now, the first thing I want to say about this is that it connects with the contemplative, expressive side of individualism, which Whitman in the 1850s radicalized out of the dialectic visible in the 1842 novel. The language of *Leaves of Grass* presents challenges for the pragmatics of selfing in a way that bears out the speaker's talk of inner divisions, shifting personal boundaries, cross-identifications, and so on. And this erratically selfed language frequently announces an erotics or even ethics of contemplative self-abandonment. Whitman's poetry may in fact be the earliest instance of a theme that has come to be taken for granted in Euro-American culture: the idea of sexuality as an expressive capacity of the individual.

The second thing I want to say about the poem is that it links its erotics of self-abandonment to its own perverse publicity, to its use of a print public-sphere mode of address. A more famous example would be these lines, with which Whitman began the second poem of his 1855 *Leaves of Grass*, a poem later given the title "Song for Occupations":

Come closer to me,
Push close my lovers and take the best I possess,
Yield closer and closer and give me the best you possess.

This is unfinished business with me.... how is it with you?
I was chilled with the cold types and cylinder and wet paper
between us.

I pass so poorly with paper and types.... I must pass with the
contact of bodies and souls.

If I were to read these lines to you, you would know that I was quoting rather than soliciting; that would have been clear, if you hadn't already recognized the passage, when I got to the reference to paper and types. If you were to read the lines on the page, however, you would recognize a certain fictionality in the scenario from the first line, "Come closer to me," since the deictics of that line indicates exactly the kind of embodied sociality that modern public-print discourse negates. Reading the passage, you might be drawn into its erotic fantasy — pubic hairs on the ink rollers and so on — but you would still realize that the speaker references the speech situation itself in a way that is manifestly wrong, that there is no question of coming closer to this speaker *or not*, that part of what makes the passage kinky is not just that Ballard-like image of cold lead on skin, pre-come on the platen, but also the parasitic relation of one discourse context to another, a cultivated perversity at the metadiscursive level. In this as in so many other passages, Whitman wants to make sex public, and doing so involves jarring conventions of representation.

There are of course other poems that fictionalize their own discursive status. In a work like Browning's "My Last Duchess," the reader is expected to suspend recognition of the publication context of the poem in order to construct the fictional scenario of the duke's embodied speech, which includes several deictic phrases that, like "Come closer to me," are impossible references in the print context: "That's my last Duchess painted on the wall"; "Will't please you rise?"; "We'll go / Together down, sir," and so on. Whitman's method is different because he does not suspend awareness of the publication context, which therefore becomes the ground of his perversity.*

---

*In "To a Stranger," the effect of metadiscursive perverseness was heightened in revision. Where the published version ends with "I am to see to it that I do not

288

In sections 27 and 28 of "Song of Myself," the dialectic of sexual expressivism becomes explicit, as it does also in section 5, where Whitman turns a fictive internal I/you scenario — the soul's speech to the body — into an erotic relation: "the other I am must not abase itself to you." As in Thoreau, the self-relation of expressive individualism takes the form of a self-other relation, which is also to say that selfing becomes problematic even as the phenomenology of self is radically broadened. As in Thoreau, the internal problematics of the expressive self become difficult to distinguish from the paradigmatically liberal erotic dilemmas of recognition and mutuality. And, like Thoreau's, Whitman's interest in those dilemmas is strongest when they are not stabilized by heterosexuality, which is to say, by the modern ideology that interprets gender difference as the form of self-other difference.[27]

The distinctive pragmatics of Whitman's poetry refigure the conventions of temperance fiction in a number of ways that are equally relevant to the valuation of sexuality. Whitman takes voluntarist culture as a context in which internal dissonances of appetite, the involuntary, or amnesia can be read simultaneously as expressive of a self *and* as selfing problems. What had been internal heteronomy in the addiction rhetoric of the novel becomes both the other of self-contemplation and a limit to the responsibilizing language of self. This dialectic is the core of the Whitmanian sublime.

---

lose you," the manuscript had continued with two more lines:

I listen to the different voices, winding in and out, striving, contending
with fiery vehemence to excel each other in emotion,

I do not think the performers know themselves — But now I think I begin
to know them.

By eliminating this referencej to the speech-mediated scene of the street, Whitman focused the reader's own impossible insertion in the poem.

Notes

INTRODUCTION

1. See, for example, Leon Mayhew, *The New Public: Professional Communication and the Means of Social Influence* (Cambridge, UK: Cambridge University Press, 1997).

2. Michael Warner, *The Trouble with Normal: Sex, Politics, and the Ethics of Queer Life* (New York: The Free Press, 1999).

CHAPTER ONE: PUBLIC AND PRIVATE

1. Diogenes Laertius, *Lives of Eminent Philosophers*, quoted in Michel Foucault, *The History of Sexuality*, vol. 2: *The Use of Pleasure*, trans. Robert Hurley (New York: Pantheon, 1985), p. 54.

2. *Ibid.*

3. *Letters on the Difficulty of Religion*, quoted in Larry Ceplair, ed., *The Public Years of Sarah and Angelina Grimké: Selected Writings, 1835–1839* (New York: Columbia University Press, 1989), p. 138. On Beecher, see the classic study by Kathryn Kish Sklar, *Catharine Beecher: A Study in American Domesticity* (New Haven, CT: Yale University Press, 1973); and Jeanne Boydston, Mary Kelley, and Anne Margolis, eds., *The Limits of Sisterhood: The Beecher Sisters on Women's Rights and Woman's Sphere* (Chapel Hill: University of North Carolina Press, 1988).

4. An example of this kind of analysis can be found in Rosalyn Deutsche, "Men in Space," *Artforum* 28 (Feb. 1990), pp. 21–23.

5. Laura Graham, "A Public Sphere in Amazonia?" *American Ethnologist* 40.4 (1993), pp. 717–41.

6. On these rival paradigms for public and private in American Constitutional law, see Kendall Thomas, "Beyond the Privacy Principle," *Columbia Law Review* 92 (1992), pp. 1359–1516, especially pp. 1444–47.

7. This list amplifies remarks by Nancy Fraser, "Rethinking the Public Sphere: A Contribution to a Critique of Actually Existing Democracy," in Craig Calhoun, ed., *Habermas and the Public Sphere* (Cambridge, MA: MIT Press, 1992), pp. 109–42. The definition from Hannah Arendt appears in *The Human Condition* (Chicago: University of Chicago Press, 1958), p. 52.

8. See Thomas, "Beyond the Privacy Principle"; Janet Halley, *Don't: A Reader's Guide to the Military's Anti-Gay Policy* (Durham, NC: Duke University Press, 1999); and Janet Halley, "The Politics of the Closet: Towards Equal Protection for Gay, Lesbian, and Bisexual Identity," in Jonathan Goldberg, ed., *Reclaiming Sodom* (New York: Routledge, 1994), pp. 145–204. Goldberg also reprints the text of *Bowers*.

9. Michelle Zimbalist Rosaldo, "Woman, Culture, and Society: A Theoretical Overview," in Michelle Zimbalist Rosaldo and Louise Lamphere, eds., *Woman, Culture, and Society* (Stanford, CA: Stanford University Press, 1974), pp. 17–42.

10. Jean Bethke Elshtain, *Public Man, Private Woman: Women in Social and Political Thought* (Princeton, NJ: Princeton University Press, 1981).

11. Carol Pateman, "Feminist Critiques of the Public/Private Dichotomy," in *The Disorder of Women: Democracy, Feminism, and Political Theory* (Stanford, CA: Stanford University Press, 1989), p. 118.

12. Catharine MacKinnon, "Privacy v. Equality," in *Feminism Unmodified: Discourses on Life and Law* (Cambridge, MA: Harvard University Press, 1987), p. 100.

13. Pateman, *Disorder of Women*, p. 135.

14. For the context, see Alice Echols, *Daring to Be Bad: Radical Feminism in America, 1967–1975* (Minneapolis: University of Minnesota Press, 1989).

15. Eli Zaretsky, "Identity Theory, Identity Politics: Psychoanalysis, Marx-

ism, Post-Structuralism," in Craig Calhoun, ed., *Social Theory and the Politics of Identity* (Oxford, UK: Blackwell, 1994), p. 206.

16. Joan Wallach Scott, *Gender and the Politics of History* (New York: Columbia University Press, 1988), p. 26.

17. A notable irony in claims to break down the "binary" of public and private is that most major theorists of the terms — notably Hannah Arendt, Jürgen Habermas, and Richard Sennett — argued that the conditions of mass society were already dissolving the potential for both public action and real privacy. For Arendt and Habermas, see below. For Sennett, see *The Fall of Public Man* (New York: Knopf, 1977).

18. Jane Addams's dictum "A city is enlarged housekeeping" represents an early version of this remapping. "From the beginning of tribal life," Addams writes, "women have been held responsible for the health of the community, a function which is not represented by the health department; from the days of the cave dwellers, so far as the home was clean and wholesome, it was due to their efforts, which are now represented by the bureau of tenement-house inspection; from the period of the primitive village, the only public sweeping performed was what they undertook in their own dooryards, that which is now represented by the bureau of street cleaning." Quoted in Eli Zaretsky, "Hannah Arendt and the Meaning of the Public/Private Distinction," in Craig Calhoun and John McGowan, eds., *Hannah Arendt and the Meaning of Politics* (Minneapolis: University of Minnesota Press, 1997), pp. 224–25.

19. Fraser, "Rethinking the Public Sphere," p. 110.

20. See, for example, Mary P. Ryan, *Women in Public: Between Banners and Ballots, 1825–1880* (Baltimore, MD: Johns Hopkins University Press, 1990).

21. On this history within feminism, see the excellent account by Mary Dietz, "Feminist Receptions of Hannah Arendt," in Bonnie Honig, ed., *Feminist Interpretations of Hannah Arendt* (University Park: Pennsylvania State University Press, 1995), pp. 17–50.

22. This history is traced for an American context by Sean Wilentz, *Chants Democratic* (New York: Oxford University Press, 1984); Paul Johnson, *A Shopkeeper's Millennium: Society and Revivals in Rochester, New York, 1815–1837* (New

York: Hill and Wang, 1978); and Eli Zaretsky, *Capitalism, the Family, and Personal Life*, rev. ed. (New York: Harper and Row, 1986).

23. On this subject, there is a large and growing literature. See especially Mary Kelley, *Public Woman, Private Stage* (New York: Oxford University Press, 1984).

24. Classic studies of this history include Quentin Skinner, *The Foundations of Modern Political Thought*, 2 vols. (Cambridge, UK: Cambridge University Press, 1978); and C.B. Macpherson, *The Political Theory of Possessive Individualism* (Oxford, UK: Oxford University Press, 1962).

25. Albert Hirschman, *The Passions and the Interests: Arguments for Capitalism Before Its Triumph* (Princeton, NJ: Princeton University Press, 1977).

26. See the multivolume history of this subject in Europe, Philippe Ariès and Georges Duby, eds., *A History of Private Life*, especially vol. 3, *Passions of the Renaissance*, ed. Roger Chartier, trans. Arthur Goldhammer (Cambridge, MA: Harvard University Press, 1989).

27. Fraser discusses the concept of bracketing in "Rethinking the Public Sphere"; the "veil of ignorance" version is in John Rawls, *A Theory of Justice* (Cambridge, MA: Harvard University Press, 1989).

28. See Joan Wallach Scott, *Only Paradoxes to Offer: French Feminists and the Rights of Man* (Cambridge, MA: Harvard University Press, 1996).

29. *Letters on the Equality of the Sexes and the Condition of Woman* (1837), in Ceplair, ed., *The Public Years of Sarah and Angelina Grimké*, p. 195.

30. *Ibid.*, p. 217.

31. See Katherine Henry, "Angelina Grimké's Rhetoric of Exposure," *American Quarterly* 49.2 (June 1997), pp. 328–55.

32. Zaretsky, "Identity Theory, Identity Politics," p. 201.

33. Andrew Sullivan, *Virtually Normal: An Argument About Homosexuality* (New York: Knopf, 1995), p. 171.

34. The vicissitudes of this political tradition, and the ironies by which its central ideas have migrated from right to left and vice versa in twentieth-century politics, are traced in Alan Brinkley, *Liberalism and Its Discontents* (Cambridge, MA: Harvard University Press, 1998).

35. The indispensable reference here is J.G.A. Pocock, *The Machiavellian Moment* (Princeton, NJ: Princeton University Press, 1975). Pocock has been criticized by many historians for overstating the incompatibility of republican and liberal traditions. For recent treatments with somewhat different views, see Joyce Appleby, *Liberalism and Republicanism in the Historical Imagination* (Cambridge, MA: Harvard University Press, 1992), and Isaac Kramnick, *Republicanism and Bourgeois Radicalism: Political Ideology in Late Eighteenth-Century England and America* (Ithaca, NY: Cornell University Press, 1990).

36. In addition to *A Theory of Justice*, see John Rawls, *Political Liberalism* (New York: Columbia University Press, 1996).

37. John Christian Laursen, "The Subversive Kant: The Vocabulary of 'Public' and 'Publicity,'" in James Schmidt, ed., *What Is Enlightenment? Eighteenth-Century Answers and Twentieth-Century Questions* (Berkeley: University of California Press, 1996), pp. 253–69.

38. Immanuel Kant, "An Answer to the Question: What Is Enlightenment?" trans. Schmidt, in Schmidt, ed., *What Is Enlightenment?*, pp. 58–64.

39. *Ibid.*, p. 61. There is a useful discussion of this passage in Roger Chartier, *The Cultural Origins of the French Revolution*, trans. Lydia Cochrane (Durham, NC: Duke University Press, 1991), pp. 20–37.

40. See Laursen, "Subversive Kant," pp. 258–61.

41. Jürgen Habermas, *The Structural Transformation of the Public Sphere: An Inquiry into a Category of Bourgeois Society*, trans. Thomas Burger (Cambridge, MA: MIT Press, 1989). See also his "The Public Sphere: An Encyclopedia Article," *New German Critique* 1.3 (Fall 1974), pp. 49–55.

42. Habermas, Structural Transformation, p. 4.

43. *Ibid.*, p. 23.

44. *Ibid.*, p. 27.

45. *Ibid.*, p. 106.

46. Calhoun, introduction to *Habermas and the Public Sphere*, p. 7.

47. Quoted in Habermas, *Structural Transformation*, p. 125.

48. *Ibid.*, p. 128.

49. *Ibid.*, p. 136.

50. See, for example, Joan Landes, *Women and the Public Sphere in the Age of the French Revolution* (Ithaca, NY: Cornell University Press, 1988); and the essays by Mary Ryan, Nancy Fraser, and Geoff Eley in Calhoun, ed., *Habermas and the Public Sphere*. On Landes's claim that the public sphere was "essentially, not just contingently, masculinist," see Keith Michael Baker's astute discussion in "Defining the Public Sphere in Eighteenth-Century France," in Calhoun, ed., *Habermas and the Public Sphere*, pp. 181–211.

51. Habermas, *Structural Transformation*, p. 195.

52. *Ibid.*, p. 157.

53. See Oskar Negt and Alexander Kluge, *Public Sphere and Experience* (Minneapolis: University of Minnesota Press, 1993), especially the introduction by Miriam Hansen; and Lauren Berlant and Michael Warner, "Introduction to 'Critical Multiculturalism,'" in David Theo Goldberg, ed., *Multiculturalism: A Critical Reader* (Oxford, UK: Basil Blackwell, 1994), pp. 107–13.

54. For a critique of this turn, see Benjamin Lee, "Textuality, Mediation, and Public Discourse," in Calhoun, ed., *Habermas and the Public Sphere*, pp. 402–20.

55. Eve Kosofsky Sedgwick, *The Epistemology of the Closet* (Berkeley: University of California Press, 1990).

56. Halley, *Don't*.

57. See Zaretsky, "Identity Theory, Identity Politics"; and John Brenkman, *Straight Male Modern* (New York: Routledge, 1993), especially pp. 109–28.

58. This misreading can be found in the essays by Fraser and Eley in Calhoun, ed., *Habermas and the Public Sphere*. It is an easy reading to make, and appears even in that close and scrupulous reader of Habermas, Craig Calhoun, in his "Nationalism and the Public Sphere," in Jeff Alan Weintraub and Krishnan Kumar, eds., *Public and Private in Thought and Practice: Perspectives on a Grand Dichotomy* (Chicago: University of Chicago Press, 1997), p. 84. What supports it is Habermas's strong emphasis on the way the public is thought to derive an implied unity from its critical opposition to the state and the legislative power.

59. Habermas, *Structural Transformation of the Public Sphere*, p. 244

60. On this subject, see Michael Warner, *The Letters of the Republic: Publica-*

tion and the Public Sphere in Eighteenth-Century America (Cambridge, MA: Harvard University Press, 1990).

61. See Warner, "The Mass Public and the Mass Subject," and Berlant and Warner, "Sex in Public," below chapters 4 and 5.

62. Anne Phillips, quoted in Dietz, "Feminist Receptions of Hannah Arendt," p. 18.

63. Bonnie Honig, "Toward an Agonistic Feminism: Hannah Arendt and the Politics of Identity," in Honig, ed., *Feminist Interpretations of Hannah Arendt*, pp. 135–66.

64. This point has been the subject of some dispute between Honig and Seyla Benhabib. It will be seen that I follow Honig's reading here. For a contrasting reading of Arendt, see Seyla Benhabib, "Feminist Theory and Hannah Arendt's Concept of Public Space," *History of the Human Sciences* 6 (1993), pp. 97–114, and "The Pariah and Her Shadow: Hannah Arendt's Biography of Rahel Varnhagen," in Honig, ed., *Feminist Interpretations of Hannah Arendt*, pp. 83–104.

65. See, for example, Arendt, *Human Condition*, pp. 27–28. On the relation between *The Human Condition* and *The Origins of Totalitarianism*, see Zaretsky, "Hannah Arendt and the Meaning of the Public/Private Distinction."

66. This point is made by Zaretsky in "Hannah Arendt and the Meaning of the Public/Private Distinction," particularly in reference to *The Origins of Totalitarianism*. A sticking point in many contemporary debates about Arendt is that in the classical conception, as she interprets it, the private is almost entirely without value, even without content. That, she emphasizes, is the point: the private is privative, a negative category, a state in which one is deprived of context for realizing oneself through action and in free interaction with others. The most private person is the slave. The life of the polis is opposed to all that is one's own (*idion*) — hence a merely private or idiosyncratic person would be an idiot. That Arendt was capable of seeing the expression of a strong value in such a vacuous — or rather, evacuating — conception of the private is testament to the imaginative strength of her interpretation; but it is not a site of nostalgia or phallocentric commitment, as some feminist critics contend. Privacy for Arendt does have one valuable dimension, however: the sense of rootedness, of place in the world,

provided by the classical conception of property as a transgenerational estate. But this sense of the private is unrecoverable in a capitalist economy and in an age with no secular orientation to immortality, and Arendt writes that "the intimate is not a very reliable substitute" for it (*Human Condition*, p. 70).

67. Arendt, *Human Condition*, p. 57.

68. *Ibid.*, p. 58.

69. An excellent illustration of the latter point is to be found in Lauren Berlant, "Poor Eliza," *American Literature* 70.3 (Sept. 1998), pp. 635–68. Berlant, analyzing the women's culture of sentimentality, shows that it has some counterpublic features but that these are distorted. "When sentimentality meets politics," Berlant writes, "it uses personal stories to tell of structural effects, but in so doing it risks thwarting its very attempt to perform rhetorically a scene of pain that must be soothed politically. Because the ideology of true feeling cannot admit the nonuniversality of pain, its cases become all jumbled together and the ethical imperative toward social transformation is replaced by a civic-minded but passive ideal of empathy. The political as a place of acts oriented toward publicness becomes replaced by a world of private thoughts, leanings, and gestures. Suffering, in this personal-public context, becomes answered by survival, which is then recoded as freedom. Meanwhile, we lose the original impulse behind sentimental politics, which is to see the individual effects of mass social violence as *different from* the causes, which are impersonal and depersonalizing" (p. 641).

CHAPTER TWO: PUBLICS AND COUNTERPUBLICS

1. An instructive review of the methodological problems can be found in Robert O. Carlson, ed., *Communications and Public Opinion: A "Public Opinion Quarterly" Reader* (New York: Praeger, 1975); see especially Floyd D. Allport, "Toward a Science of Public Opinion," pp. 11–26, and Harwood Childs, "By Public Opinion I Mean – ," pp. 28–37.

2. The critique of polling appears in a number of contexts in Bourdieu's work; see especially "Opinion Polls: A 'Science' Without a Scientist," in *In Other Words: Essays Towards a Reflexive Sociology*, trans. Matthew Adamson (Stanford, CA: Stanford University Press, 1990), pp. 168–76.

3. This ancient exotic is the kind of stranger that Georg Simmel has in mind in his much-cited 1908 essay "The Stranger," in *On Individuality and Social Forms* (Chicago: University of Chicago Press, 1971). Simmel fails to distinguish between the stranger as represented by the trader or the Wandering Jew and the stranger whose presence in modernity is unremarkable, even necessary to the nature of modern polities. One of the defining elements of modernity, in my view, is normative stranger sociability, of a kind that seems to arise only when the social imaginary is defined not by kinship (as in non-state societies) or by place (as in state societies until modernity) but by discourse.

4. Louis Althusser, "Ideology and Ideological State Apparatuses," in *Lenin and Philosophy and Other Essays* (New York: Monthly Review Press, 1971), pp. 127–86.

5. For example, Patricia Spacks, *Gossip* (New York: Knopf, 1985), especially pp. 121–46; and James C. Scott, *Weapons of the Weak: Everyday Forms of Peasant Resistance* (New Haven, CT: Yale University Press, 1985).

6. "The right to gossip about certain people," Max Gluckman writes in a classic essay, "is a privilege which is only extended to a person when he or she is accepted as a member of a group or set. It is a hallmark of membership." Moreover, this kind of membership tends to presuppose others, such as kin groups, equally distant from stranger sociability. "To be a Makah [the Northwest Amerindian group discussed by Gluckman] you must be able to join in the gossip, and to be fully a Makah you must be able to scandalize skillfully. This entails that you know the individual family histories of your fellows; for the knowledgeable can hit at you through your ancestry." Max Gluckman, "Gossip and Scandal," *Current Anthropology* 4 (1963), pp. 313 and 311.

7. Virginia Jackson, *Dickinson's Misery: A Theory of Lyric Reading* (Stanford, CA: Stanford University Press, forthcoming), MS pp. 127–28.

8. Quoted in *ibid.*, p. 128.

9. Quoted in *ibid.*, p. 129.

10. It would be interesting to pursue the implications of this history for lyric; at the very least, it would be a productive context in which to reread Adorno's classic essay "On Lyric Poetry and Society," in Theodor Adorno, *Notes*

to Literature, vol. 1, trans. Rolf Tiedemann (New York: Columbia University Press, 1991), pp. 37–54.

11. I have given what must seem a reductive and overly schematic description of a very complex history. Yet I believe it would be a useful framework for rereading such detailed analyses as Douglas Patey, "'Aesthetics' and the Rise of Lyric in the Eighteenth Century," *Studies in English Literature* 33.3 (1993), pp. 587–608.

12. Many texts could be said to exploit the very difficulty of hybridizing public and lyric modes of address. For a notable example, see Shelley's sonnet "England in 1819," usefully analyzed in James Chandler's book of the same title (Chicago: University of Chicago Press, 1998).

13. Michael Warner, ed., *American Sermons: The Pilgrims to Martin Luther King* (New York: Library of America, 1999), pp. 101–102.

14. Quoted in Charles E. Hambrick-Stowe, "The Spiritual Pilgrimage of Sarah Osborn (1714–1796)," *Church History* 61 (Dec. 1992), pp. 408–21; reprinted in Jon Butler and Harry S. Stout, eds., *Religion in American History: A Reader* (New York: Oxford University Press, 1998), pp. 130–41, at p. 132.

15. Harry S. Stout, "Religion, Communications, and the Ideological Origins of the American Revolution," *William and Mary Quarterly* 34 (1977), pp. 519–41; reprinted in Butler and Stout, eds., *Religion in American History*, pp. 89–108, at p. 93. See also Harry S. Stout, *The New England Soul: Preaching and Religious Culture in Colonial New England* (New York: Oxford University Press, 1986).

16. A number of scholars have emphasized the importance of print and news in organizing the revivals; the most extensive study is Frank Lambert, *Inventing the "Great Awakening"* (Princeton, NJ: Princeton University Press, 1999). The importance of strangers to itinerant preaching, and the sense of scandal that resulted, is argued by Stout in "Religion, Communications, and the Ideological Origins of the American Revolution."

17. See, for example, Stout, "Religion, Communications, and the Ideological Origins of the American Revolution." Stout, in an otherwise perceptive and innovative essay, falls prey to an especially reductive distinction between orality and literacy, derived from Jack Goody, Walter Ong, and others. I have argued

against this crude dichotomy in *The Letters of the Republic: Publication and the Public Sphere in Eighteenth-Century America* (Cambridge, MA: Harvard University Press, 1990), chap. 1.

18. These are described in Paul Conkin, *Cane Ridge: America's Pentecost* (Madison: University of Wisconsin Press, 1990).

19. Walter Lippmann, *The Phantom Public* (1927; reprint, New Brunswick, NJ: Transaction, 1993), pp. 4–5 and 10–11.

20. *Ibid.*, pp. 54–55.

21. For an example of a promising and rich analysis marred by this misapprehension, see Nina Eliasoph, *Avoiding Politics: How Americans Produce Apathy in Everyday Life* (Cambridge, UK: Cambridge University Press, 1998). As I argue in the following chapter, Eliasoph's stated but unexamined ideal is that of a continuity of *discussion* from small-scale interaction to the highest organizing levels of politics.

22. Quoted in Harold Love, *Scribal Publication in Seventeenth-Century England* (Cambridge, UK: Cambridge University Press, 1993), pp. 20–21.

23. On the necessity of any public's being metatopical, see Charles Taylor, "Modern Social Imaginaries," forthcoming in *Public Culture* (2002).

24. Alexandre Beljame, *Men of Letters and the English Public in the Eighteenth Century, 1660–1744: Dryden, Addison, and Pope* (London: K. Paul, Trench, Trubner, 1948), p. 130.

25. Warner, *Letters of the Republic*.

26. Jane Feuer, "The Concept of Live Television: Ontology as Ideology," in E. Ann Kaplan, ed., *Regarding Television: Critical Approaches–An Anthology* (Los Angeles: Greenwood Press, 1983), pp. 12–22. "Television," writes Feuer, "becomes a continuous, never-ending sequence in which it is impossible to separate out individual texts.... Indeed the 'central fact' of television may be that it is designed to be watched intermittently, casually, and without full concentration" (p. 15).

27. Joan Dejean, *Ancients Against Moderns: Culture Wars and the Making of a Fin de Siècle* (Chicago: University of Chicago Press, 1997), pp. 31–77. Dejean (in my view mistakenly) thinks her argument contradicts Habermas's history: "In

the case of *le public* . . . the terminology was not, as the Habermasian view would have it, primarily evocative of a 'medium of political confrontation' constructed 'against the public authorities themselves' for the purpose of generating 'debate over . . . the sphere of commodity exchange and social labor.' Instead, the modern vocabulary of public exchange was initially most remarkable for its connotations of a sphere in which a socially and sexually diverse audience debated for the first time the meaning and the function of public culture" [p. xv].

28. *Ibid.*, p. 58.

29. Abbé du Bos, *Réflexions critiques sur la peinture et sur la poésie* (1719), quoted in *ibid.*, p. 64. Antoine Furetière's *Dictionnaire universel des arts et des sciences* (1690) already has the sense of a public not just as an audience or theatrical public but as a public of readers. "An author gives his works to the public when he has them printed" (quoted in *ibid.*, p. 36).

30. Robert Darnton, "Paris: The Early Internet," *New York Review of Books*, June 29, 2000, p. 43.

31. Eyal Amiran discusses the temporality of electronic media, in a way that differs substantially from mine, in his "Electronic Time and the Serials Revolution," *Yale Journal of Criticism* 10.2 (1997), pp. 445–54.

32. It is difficult to assess this change not simply because the effects of change in the medium have yet to become visible but because the infrastructure of the medium is itself changing. On this, the best account I know is Lawrence Lessig, *Code and Other Laws of Cyberspace* (New York: Basic Books, 1999). Lessig's book, though focused on the legal regulation of cyberspace, raises important topics for the more general discussion of new media and their social implications.

33. Not a weekly, as Habermas mistakenly asserts.

34. Kathryn Shevelow, *Women and Print Culture: The Construction of Femininity in the Early Periodical* (London: Routledge, 1989). Shevelow treats reader correspondence and "audience production of the text" at pp. 37–42, the development of "audience-building" at pp. 61–66, and the importance of anonymity at pp. 71–74.

35. For a somewhat different analysis along these lines, see Scott Black, "Social and Literary Form in the *Spectator*," *Eighteenth-Century Studies* 33.1

(1999), pp. 21–42. I have also found much insight in Michael G. Ketcham, *Transparent Designs: Reading, Performance, and Form in the Spectator Papers* (Athens: University of Georgia Press, 1985). Other relevant treatments of the *Spectator* can be found in Edward A. Bloom and Lillian D. Bloom, eds., *Addison and Steele, the Critical Heritage* (London: Routledge & K. Paul, 1980); and Edward A. Bloom and Lillian D. Bloom, *Joseph Addison's Sociable Animal: In the Market Place, on the Hustings, in the Pulpit* (Providence, RI: Brown University Press, 1971).

36. Donald F. Bond, ed., *The Spectator*, 5 vols. (Oxford, UK: Oxford University Press, 1965), vol. 1, p. 144.

37. Ketcham describes this phenomenon in *Transparent Designs*, p. 130.

38. Patricia Winters Lauro, "Advertising: America's Asking Whassup?" *New York Times*, Feb. 16, 2001. "After being beamed up to an alien spaceship, a family pet takes off his dog suit to reveal that he is an alien creature himself. 'What have you learned?' his leader asks. The creature pauses to think, then responds 'Whassup?' with his tongue lolling out of his mouth.... The Whassup campaign has won practically every award in advertising, including the prestigious international Grand Prix.... And, most important to Anheuser-Busch, the nation's largest brewer, the campaign has helped it sell more beer, not just Budweiser but its light beer, Bud Light. The company's worldwide sales grew by 2.4 million barrels, to 99.2 million barrels last year, according to Beer Marketer's Insights, a trade newsletter in Nanuet, N.Y." Note, by the way, the *Times*'s headline to the story. The idea that all this circulation can be heard as "America" talking is the distinctive contribution made by news media in the layering of reflexivity on a circulation in which, after all, the *Times* story is otherwise merely one more example.

39. Paula McDowell, in her otherwise excellent study *The Women of Grub Street: Press, Politics, and Gender in the London Literary Marketplace, 1678–1730* (Oxford, UK: Oxford University Press, 1998), goes so far as to depict the representational conventions of the *Spectator* as a strategy for displacing and silencing the female authors with whom Addison and Steele were in competition — an interpretation that has some force but in my view misses the distinctive features of the public as a form and shows the limiting effect of our conception of politics as strategic.

40. See "Public and Private," note 50.

41. M.M. Bakhtin, *The Dialogic Imagination*, ed. Michael Holquist, trans. Caryl Emerson and Michael Holquist (Austin: University of Texas Press, 1981), p. 289.

42. *Ibid.*, p. 296.

43. Bond, ed., *Spectator*, vol. 2, p. 345.

44. *Ibid.*, vol. 2, p. 346.

45. *Ibid.*, vol. 1, p. 21.

46. *Ibid.*, vol. 2, p. 346.

47. *Ibid.*, vol. 2, p. 346.

48. *Ibid.*, vol. 2, p. 346.

49. See Rictor Norton, *Mother Clap's Molly House: The Gay Subculture in England, 1700–1830* (London: Gay Men's Press, 1992).

50. Even if the address is indirect. The most insightful study I know of the tight relation between a public form and a mode of life is an example of indirect implication of a reception context by a form that refuses to address it outright: I am thinking of D.A. Miller's *Place for Us: An Essay on the Broadway Musical* (Cambridge, MA: Harvard University Press, 2000).

51. In all the literature on the history of reading, the development of this ideology remains an understudied phenomenon. Adrian Johns makes a significant contribution in *The Nature of the Book: Print and Knowledge in the Making* (Chicago: University of Chicago Press, 1998), especially pp. 380–443. Johns's study suggests that the idea of reading as a private act with replicable meaning for strangers dispersed through space emerged in the very period that gave rise to publics in the modern form analyzed here; support for this conjecture can also be found in Kevin Sharpe, *Reading Revolutions: The Politics of Reading in Early Modern England* (New Haven, CT: Yale University Press, 2000); Guglielmo Cavallo and Roger Chartier, eds., *A History of Reading in the West* (Amherst: University of Massachusetts Press, 1999); and James Raven, Helen Small, and Naomi Tadmore, eds., *The Practice and Representation of Reading in England* (Cambridge, UK: Cambridge University Press, 1996).

52. Nancy Fraser, "Rethinking the Public Sphere: A Contribution to the

Critique of Actually Existing Democracy," in Craig Calhoun, ed., *Habermas and the Public Sphere* (Cambridge, MA: MIT Press, 1992), pp. 122–23.

53. *Ibid.*, 123.

54. *Ibid.*, 123.

55. For an interesting limit case, see Charles Hirschkind, "Civic Virtue Within Egypt's Islamic Counter-Public," *Cultural Anthropology* 16.1 (2001), forthcoming. Hirschkind analyzes complex modes of commentary and circulation in contemporary Egypt; what remains unclear is the degree to which this emergent and reactive discourse culture can still be called a public.

56. Michael Warner, *The Trouble with Normal: Sex, Politics, and the Ethics of Queer Life* (New York: The Free Press, 1999), especially ch. 2.

CHAPTER THREE: STYLES OF INTELLECTUAL PUBLICS

1. George Orwell, *1984* (New York: Signet, 1981), p. 10.

2. *Ibid.*, pp. 26–27.

3. James Miller, "Is Bad Writing Necessary?" *Lingua Franca*, Dec./Jan. 2000, p. 38.

4. George Orwell, "Politics and the English Language," in *A Collection of Essays* (New York: Harcourt, Brace, 1981), p. 169.

5. Henry David Thoreau, *Walden* (New York: Library of America, 1985), pp. 580–81.

6. Theodor Adorno, *Minima Moralia: Reflections from Damaged Life,* trans. E.F.N. Jephcott (London: Verso, 1978), p. 101.

7. *Ibid.*, p. 101.

8. Judith Butler, "A 'Bad Writer' Bites Back," *New York Times*, March 20, 1999. Butler's op-ed piece responds to an earlier article by Dinitia Smith, "When Ideas Get Lost in Bad Writing," *New York Times*, Feb. 27, 1999.

9. Miller, "Is Bad Writing Necessary?" p. 37.

10. *Ibid.*, p. 41.

11. *Ibid.*, p. 36.

12. Theodor Adorno, "Scientific Experiences of a European Scholar in America," trans. Donald Fleming, in Donald Fleming and Bernard Bailyn, eds.,

The Intellectual Migration: Europe and America, 1930–1960 (Cambridge, MA: Harvard University Press, 1969), pp. 338–70.

13. Miller, "Is Bad Writing Necessary?" p. 43.

14. The issues enumerated in this sentence pervade Adorno's writing, but a few key texts can serve as examples, in addition to *Minima Moralia*: *The Stars Down to Earth and Other Essays on the Irrational in Culture* (New York: Routledge, 1994); *Introduction to the Sociology of Music* (New York: Continuum, 1989); and "Freudian Theory and the Pattern of Fascist Propaganda," in Andrew Arato and Eike Gebhardt, eds., *The Essential Frankfurt School Reader* (New York: Continuum, 1987), pp. 118–37.

15. Martha Nussbaum, "The Professor of Parody," *New Republic*, Feb. 22, 1999, pp. 37–45.

16. John Guillory, "Literary Critics as Intellectuals: Class Analysis and the Crisis of the Humanities," in Wai-chee Dimock and Michael T. Gilmore, eds., *Rethinking Class: Literary Studies and Social Formations* (New York: Columbia University Press, 1994), p. 117.

17. Nina Eliasoph, *Avoiding Politics: How Americans Produce Apathy in Everyday Life* (Cambridge, UK: Cambridge University Press, 1998).

18. "Polemics, Politics, and Problematizations: An Interview with Michel Foucault," in Michel Foucault, *Ethics: Subjectivity and Truth*, ed. Paul Rabinow (New York: New Press, 1997), pp. 111–20.

19. *Ibid.*, p. 111.

20. *Ibid.*, p. 111–12.

21. Didier Eribon, *Michel Foucault et ses contemporains* (Paris: Fayard, 1994), pp. 310–11.

22. "Polemics, Politics, and Problematizations," p. 114.

23. For these, see Graham Burchell, Colin Gordon, and Peter Miller, eds., *The Foucault Effect: Studies in Governmentality* (Chicago: University of Chicago Press, 1991). On Foucault's relation to Habermas, a very useful essay is to be found in Thomas McCarthy, *Ideals and Illusions* (Cambridge, MA: MIT Press, 1991), pp. 43–75.

CHAPTER FOUR: THE MASS PUBLIC AND THE MASS SUBJECT

1. Claude Lefort, "The Image of the Body and Totalitarianism," in *The Political Forms of Modern Society: Bureaucracy, Democracy, and Totalitarianism*, ed. John B. Thompson (Cambridge, MA: MIT Press, 1986), p. 306.

2. J. G. Ballard, *Love and Napalm: Export U.S.A.* (New York: Grove Press, 1972), pp. 149–51.

3. The arguments condensed here can be found in full form in Michael Warner, *The Letters of the Republic: Publication and the Public Sphere in Eighteenth-Century America* (Cambridge, MA: Harvard University Press, 1990).

4. [Richard Steele], *Spectator*, no. 555, in Angus Ross, ed., *Selections from the Tatler and the Spectator* (New York: Penguin, 1982), p. 213.

5. Lauren Berlant, "National Brands/National Body: Imitation of Life," in Hortense Spillers, ed., *Comparative American Identities* (New York: Routledge, 1990), pp. 110–40.

6. Jürgen Habermas, *The Structural Transformation of the Public Sphere: An Inquiry into a Category of Bourgeois Society*, trans. Thomas Burger (Cambridge, MA: MIT Press, 1989), p. 43.

7. The point here about the character of gender difference has been a common one since Simone de Beauvoir's *The Second Sex* (1949); its more recent extension to an analysis of the bourgeois public sphere is in Joan Landes, *Women and the Public Sphere in the Age of the French Revolution* (Ithaca, NY: Cornell University Press, 1988).

8. Pier Paolo Pasolini, *Lutheran Letters*, quoted in Douglas Crimp, "Strategies of Public Address: Which Media, Which Publics?" in Hal Foster, ed., *Discussions in Contemporary Culture* (Seattle, WA: Bay Press, 1987), vol. 1, p. 33.

9. Timothy Breen, "Baubles of Britain," *Past and Present* 119 (May 1988), pp. 73–104.

10. Lefort, "Image of the Body," p. 303.

11. *Ibid.*, pp. 304–6.

12. Habermas, *Structural Transformation of the Public Sphere*, p. 8.

13. *Ibid.*, p. 201. The MIT Press translation reads "whose" where I have corrected the text to "which."

14. "F.D.R., Anyone?" *Nation*, May 22, 1989, p. 689.

15. For a critique of the still-popular notion of media manipulation, see Hans Magnus Enzensberger, "Constituents of a Theory of the Media," in *Critical Essays* (New York: Continuum, 1982), pp. 46–76.

16. John Waters, *Shock Value* (New York: Dell, 1981), p. 24.

17. Jacques Lacan, "Aggressivity in Psychoanalysis," in *Ecrits*, trans. Alan Sheridan (New York: Norton, 1977), p. 19.

18. Waters, *Shock Value*, p. 26.

19. Simon Watney, *Policing Desire: Pornography, AIDS, and the Media* (Minneapolis: University of Minnesota Press, 1987), pp. 83–84 and passim.

20. Jan Zita Grover, "AIDS: Keywords," *October* 43 (1987), p. 23. This issue has since been reprinted as Douglas Crimp, ed., *AIDS: Cultural Analysis, Cultural Activism* (Cambridge, MA: MIT Press, 1988).

21. Susan Stewart, "Ceci Tuera Cela: Graffiti as Crime and Art," in John Fekete, ed., *Life After Postmodernism: Essays on Value and Culture* (New York: St. Martin's, 1987), pp. 175–76.

22. *Ibid.*, p. 163.

CHAPTER FIVE: SEX IN PUBLIC

1. On "public sex" in the standard sense, see Pat Califia, *Public Sex: The Culture of Radical Sex* (Pittsburgh, PA: Cleis Press, 1994). On " identities and acts," see Janet Halley, "The Status/Conduct Distinction in the 1993 Revisions to Military Antigay Policy: A Legal Archaeology," *GLQ* 3 (1996), pp. 159–252.

2. The classic political argument for sexual derepression as a condition of freedom is put forth in Herbert Marcuse, *Eros and Civilization: A Philosophical Inquiry into Freud* (Boston: Beacon Press, 1966). In contemporary pro-sex thought inspired by Michel Foucault's *History of Sexuality*, vol. 1 (New York: Vintage, 1978), the denunciation of "erotic injustice and sexual oppression" is situated less in the freedom of individuals than in analyses of the normative and coercive relations between specific "populations" and the institutions created to manage them (Gayle Rubin, "Thinking Sex," in *Pleasure and Danger: Exploring Female Sexuality* [Boston: Pandora Press, 1984], p. 275).

3. By heteronormativity we mean the institutions, structures of understanding, and practical orientations that make heterosexuality seem not only coherent — that is, organized as a sexuality — but also privileged. Its coherence is always provisional, and its privilege can take several (sometimes contradictory) forms: unmarked as the basic idiom of the personal and the social; or marked as a natural state; or projected as an ideal or moral accomplishment. It consists less of norms that could be summarized as a body of doctrine than of a sense of rightness produced in contradictory manifestations — often unconscious, immanent to practice or to institutions. Contexts that have little visible relation to sex practice, such as life narrative and generational identity, can be heteronormative in this sense, while in other contexts forms of sex between men and women might *not* be heteronormative. Heteronormativity is thus a concept distinct from heterosexuality. One of the most conspicuous differences is that it has no parallel, the way heterosexuality organizes homosexuality as its opposite. Because homosexuality can never have the invisible, tacit, society-founding rightness that heterosexuality has, it would not be possible to speak of "homonormativity" in the same sense. See Michael Warner, "Fear of a Queer Planet," *Social Text* 29 (1991), pp. 3–17.

4. *Time*, special issue, 142.21 (Fall 1993). This analysis reworks materials in Lauren Berlant, *The Queen of America Goes to Washington City: Essays on Sex and Citizenship* (Durham, NC: Duke University Press, 1997), pp. 200–208.

5. For a treatment of the centrality of "blood" to U.S. nationalist discourse, see Bonnie Honig, *No Place Like Home: Democracy and the Politics of Foreignness* (Princeton, NJ: Princeton University Press, 1998).

6. See, for example, William Bennett, *The De-Valuing of America: The Fight for Our Culture and Our Children* (New York: Simon and Schuster, 1992); Peter Brimelow, *Alien Nation: Common Sense About America's Immigration Disaster* (New York: Random House, 1995); William A. Henry III, *In Defense of Elitism* (New York: Doubleday, 1994).

7. On the family form in national rhetoric, see Jay Fliegelman, *Prodigals and Pilgrims: The American Revolution Against Patriarchal Authority, 1750–1800* (Cambridge, UK: Cambridge University Press, 1982); and Shirley Samuels, *Romances of the Republic: Women, the Family, and Violence in the Literature of the Early*

American Nation (New York: Oxford University Press, 1996). On fantasies of genetic assimilation, see Robert S. Tilton, *Pocahontas: The Evolution of an American Narrative* (Cambridge, UK: Cambridge University Press, 1994), pp. 9–33; and Elise Lemire, "Making Miscegenation" (Ph.D. diss., Rutgers University, 1996).

8. The concept of welfare-state governmentality has a growing literature. For a concise statement, see Jürgen Habermas, "The New Obscurity: The Crisis of the Welfare State and the Exhaustion of Utopian Energies," in *The New Conservatism: Cultural Criticism and the Historians' Debate*, trans. Shierry Nicholsen (Cambridge, MA: MIT Press, 1990), pp. 48–70. Michael Warner has discussed the relation between this analysis and queer culture in "Something Queer About the Nation-State," below chapter 6.

9. *Congressional Record*, 1st sess., 1989, vol. 135, no. 134, S12967.

10. Political geography in this way produces systematic effects of violence. Queers are forced to find each other in untrafficked areas because of the combined pressures of propriety, stigma, the closet, and state regulation such as laws against public lewdness. The same areas are known to gay bashers and other criminals. And they are disregarded by police. The effect is to make both violence and police neglect seem natural hazards, voluntarily courted by queers. As the 1996 documentary film *Licensed to Kill* illustrates, antigay violence has been difficult to combat by legal means; victims are reluctant to come forward in any public and prosecutorial framework, while bashers can appeal to the geographic circumstances to implicate the victims themselves. The legal means has helped to produce the violence it is called on to remedy.

11. Eve Kosofsky Sedgwick, *The Epistemology of the Closet* (Berkeley: University of California Press, 1992).

12. Gay and lesbian theory, especially in the humanities, frequently emphasizes psychoanalytic or psychoanalytic-style models of subject formation, the differences among which are significant and yet all of which tend to block out the difference between the categories male/female and the process and project of heteronormativity. Three propositional paradigms are relevant here: those that propose that human identity itself is fundamentally organized by gender identifications that are hardwired into infants; those that equate the clarities of

gender identity with the domination of a relatively coherent and vertically stable "straight" ideology; and those that focus on a phallocentric Symbolic order that produces gendered subjects who live out the destiny of their positioning in it. The psychoanalytic and philosophical insights and limits of these models (which, we feel, underdescribe the practices, institutions, and incongruities of heteronormativity) require further engagement. For the time being, these works stand in as the most challenging relevant archive: Judith Butler, *Bodies That Matter: On the Discursive Limits of "Sex"* (New York: Routledge, 1993); Luce Irigaray, *Speculum of the Other Woman* (Ithaca, NY: Cornell University Press, 1985) and *The Sex Which Is Not One* (Ithaca, NY: Cornell University Press, 1985); Teresa de Lauretis, *The Practice of Love* (Bloomington: Indiana University Press, 1995); Kaja Silverman, *Male Subjectivity at the Margin* (New York: Routledge, 1992); Monique Wittig, *The Straight Mind and Other Essays* (Boston: Beacon Press, 1992). Psychoanalytic work on sexuality does not always latch acts and inclinations to natural or constructed "identity"; see, for example, Leo Bersani, *Homos* (Cambridge, MA: Harvard University Press, 1995) and "Is the Rectum a Grave?" in Douglas Crimp, ed., *AIDS: Cultural Analysis, Cultural Activism* (Cambridge, MA: MIT Press, 1988).

13. The notion of metaculture we borrow from Greg Urban; see his *Toward a Discourse-Centered Approach to Culture* (Austin: University of Texas Press, 1991) and *Noumenal Community: Myth and Reality in an Amerindian Brazilian Society* (Austin: University of Texas Press, 1996). On normalization, see Michel Foucault, *Discipline and Punish*, trans. Alan Sheridan (New York: Vintage, 1979), pp. 184–85; and *The History of Sexuality*, vol. 1, trans. Robert Hurley (New York: Vintage, 1980), p. 144. Foucault derives his argument here from the revised version of Georges Canguilhem, *The Normal and the Pathological*, trans. Carolyn Fawcett (New York: Zone Books, 1991).

14. Here we are influenced by Eli Zaretsky, *Capitalism, the Family, and Personal Life*, rev. ed. (New York: Harper and Row, 1986), and Stephanie Coontz, *The Social Origins of Private Life: A History of American Families, 1600–1900* (London: Verso, 1988), though heteronormativity is a problem not often made visible in Coontz's work.

15. On privatization and intimacy politics, see Berlant, *Queen of America*, pp. 1–24, and "Feminism and the Institutions of Intimacy," in E. Ann Kaplan and George Levine, eds., *The Politics of Research* (New Brunswick, NJ: Rutgers University Press, 1997); Honig, *No Place Like Home*; Rosalind Pollack Petchesky, "The Body as Property," in Faye D. Ginsburg and Rayna Rapp, eds., *Conceiving the New World Order: The Global Politics of Reproduction* (Berkeley: University of California Press, 1995). On privatization and national capitalism, see David Harvey, *The Condition of Postmodernity* (Oxford: Blackwell, 1989); and Mike Davis, *City of Quartz: Excavating the Future in Los Angeles* (New York: Verso, 1992).

16. This language for community is a problem for gay historiography. In otherwise fine and important studies such as Esther Newton's *Cherry Grove, Fire Island: Sixty Years in America's First Gay and Lesbian Town* (Boston: Beacon Press, 1993), or Elizabeth Lapovsky Kennedy and Madeline D. Davis's *Boots of Leather, Slippers of Gold: The History of a Lesbian Community* (New York: Routledge, 1993), or even George Chauncey's *Gay New York: Gender, Urban Culture, and the Making of the Gay Male World, 1890–1940* (New York: Basic Books, 1994), community is imagined as whole-person, face-to-face relations — local, experiential, proximate, and saturating. But queer worlds seldom manifest themselves in such forms. Cherry Grove — a seasonal resort depending heavily on weekend visits by New Yorkers — may be typical less of a "gay and lesbian town" than of the way queer sites are specialized spaces in which transits can project alternative worlds. John D'Emilio's *Sexual Politics, Sexual Communities: The Making of a Homosexual Minority in the United States, 1940–1970* (Chicago: University of Chicago Press, 1983) is an especially interesting example of the imaginative power of the idealization of local community for queers. The book charts the separate tracks of political organizing and local scenes such as bar life, showing that when the "movement" and the "subculture" began to converge in San Francisco, the result was a new formation with a new utopian appeal: "A 'community,'" D'Emilio writes, "was in fact forming around a shared sexual orientation" (p. 195). D'Emilio (wisely) keeps quotation marks around "community" in the very sentence declaring it to exist in fact.

17. David M. Halperin, "Sex Before Sexuality: Pederasty, Politics, and Power in Classical Athens," in Martin Bauml Duberman, Martha Vicinus, and George Chauncey, eds., *Hidden from History: Reclaiming the Gay and Lesbian Past* (New York: New American Library, 1989), p. 49. The list Halperin cites is from Artemidorus, *Oneirocritica* 1.2 (pp. 8.21–9.4 Pack).

18. Studies of intimacy that do not assume this "web of mutuality," either as the self-evident nature of intimacy or as a human value, are rare. Roland Barthes's *A Lover's Discourse*, trans. Richard Howard (New York: Farrar, Straus and Giroux, 1978), and Niklas Luhmann's *Love As Passion*, trans. Jeremy Gaines and Doris Jones (Cambridge, MA: Harvard University Press, 1986), both try, in very different ways, to describe the production of intimacy analytically. More typical is Anthony Giddens's attempt to theorize intimacy as "pure relationship" in *The Transformation of Intimacy: Sexuality, Love, and Eroticism in Modern Societies* (Stanford, CA: Stanford University Press, 1992). There, ironically, it is "the gays who are the pioneers" in separating the "pure relationship" of love from extraneous institutions and contexts such as marriage and reproduction.

19. See our "What Does Queer Theory Teach Us About *X*?" *PMLA* 110.3 (May 1995), pp. 343–49.

20. William Bennett, quoted in *New York Times*, Oct. 26, 1995, p. A25.

21. Biddy Martin, "Extraordinary Homosexuals and the Fear of Being Ordinary," *Differences* 6.2/3 (1994), pp. 122–23.

22. In some traditions of social theory, the process of world making as we describe it here is seen as common to all social actors. See, for example, Alfred Schutz's emphasis on the practices of typification and projects of action involved in ordinary knowledge of the social, in *The Phenomenology of the Social World*, trans. G. Walsh and F. Lehnert (Evanston, IL: Northwestern University Press, 1967). Yet in most contexts, the social world is understood not as constructed by reference to types or projects but as an instantiated whole in a form capable of reproducing itself. The family, the state, a neighborhood, the human species, or institutions such as schools and churches — such images of social being share an appearance of plenitude seldom approached in contexts of queer world making. However much the latter might resemble the process of world construction

in ordinary contexts, queer worlds do not have the power to represent a taken-for-granted social existence.

23. See, for example, Alan Bray, "Homosexuality and the Signs of Male Friendship in Elizabethan England," *History Workshop Journal* (Spring 1990), pp. 1–19; Laurie J. Shannon, "Emilia's Argument: Friendship and 'Human Title' in *The Two Noble Kinsmen*," *ELH* 64.3 (Fall 1997); and Roger Chartier, ed., *Passions of the Renaissance*, trans. Arthur Goldhammer, vol. 3 of *A History of Private Life*, eds. Philippe Ariès and Georges Duby (Cambridge, MA: Harvard University Press, 1989).

24. On the relation between Foucault and Habermas, we take inspiration from Tom McCarthy, *Ideals and Illusions* (Cambridge, MA: MIT Press, 1991), pp. 47–75.

25. Jürgen Habermas, *The Structural Transformation of the Public Sphere: An Inquiry into a Category of Bourgeois Society*, trans. Thomas Burger (Cambridge, MA: MIT Press, 1989), pp. 49 and 46.

26. On the centrality of semipublic spaces like tearooms, bathrooms, and bathhouses to gay male life, see Chauncey, *Gay New York*; Lee Edelman, "Tearooms and Sympathy, or, Epistemology of the Water Closet," in Andrew Parker, Mary Russo, Doris Sommer, and Patricia Yaeger, eds., *Nationalisms and Sexualities* (New York: Routledge, 1992), pp. 263–84. The spaces of both gay and lesbian semipublic sexual practices are investigated in David Bell and Gill Valentine, eds., *Mapping Desire: Geographies of Sexualities* (New York: Routledge, 1994).

27. Douglas Crimp, "How to Have Promiscuity in an Epidemic," *October* 43 (Winter 1987), p. 253.

28. The notion of a demand for recognition has recently been advanced by a number of thinkers as a way of understanding multicultural politics. See, for example, Axel Honneth, *The Struggle for Recognition* (Cambridge, UK: Polity Press, 1995); and Charles Taylor, *Multiculturalism* (Princeton, NJ: Princeton University Press, 1994). We are suggesting that although queer politics does contest the terrain of recognition, it cannot be conceived as a politics of recognition *as opposed to* an issue of distributive justice; this is the distinction proposed in Nancy Fraser, "From Redistribution to Recognition? Dilemmas of

Justice in a 'Postsocialist' Age," *New Left Review* 212 (July/Aug. 1995), pp. 68–93, reprinted in her *Justice Interruptus: Critical Reflections on the 'Postsocialist' Condition* (New York: Routledge, 1997).

29. See Sedgwick, *Epistemology of the Closet*; and Yvonne Zipter, *Diamonds Are a Dyke's Best Friend: Reflections, Reminiscences, and Reports from the Field on the Lesbian National Pastime* (Ithaca, NY: Firebrand Books, 1988).

30. Such a politics is increasingly recommended within the gay movement. See, for example, Andrew Sullivan, *Same-Sex Marriage, Pro and Con* (New York: Vintage, 1997); Michelangelo Signorile, *Life Outside* (New York: HarperCollins, 1997); Gabriel Rotello, *Sexual Ecology: AIDS and the Destiny of Gay Men* (New York: Dutton, 1997); William N. Eskridge, *The Case for Same-Sex Marriage: From Sexual Liberty to Civilized Commitment* (New York: The Free Press, 1996); Robert Baird and Stuart Rosenbaum, eds., *Same-Sex Marriage: The Moral and Legal Debate* (Amherst, NY: Prometheus Books, 1996); and Mark Strasser, *Legally Wed: Same-Sex Marriage and the Constitution* (Ithaca, NY: Cornell University Press, 1997).

31. The phrase "the right to the city" is Henri Lefebvre's, from his 1968 *Le Droit à la ville*, trans. Eleonore Kofman and Elizabeth Lebas, in Henri Lefebvre, *Writings on Cities* (Oxford, UK: Blackwell, 1996). See also Manuel Castells, *The City and the Grassroots* (Berkeley: University of California Press, 1983).

32. On "deadness" as an affect and aspiration of normative social membership, see "Live Sex Acts," in Berlant, *Queen of America*, pp. 59–60 and 79–81.

33. The argument against the redemptive sex pastoralism of normative sexual ideology is classically made in Bersani, "Is the Rectum a Grave?"; on redemptive visions more generally, see his *The Culture of Redemption* (Cambridge, MA: Harvard University Press, 1990).

CHAPTER SIX: SOMETHING QUEER ABOUT THE NATION-STATE

1. See Lisa Duggan, "Making It Perfectly Queer," *Socialist Review* 22.1 (1992), pp. 11–32; and Lauren Berlant and Elizabeth Freeman, "Queer Nationality," in Michael Warner, ed., *Fear of a Queer Planet* (Minneapolis: University of Minnesota Press, 1993), pp. 193–229.

2. On this point, Michelangelo Signorile is especially vivid; see his *Queer in America* (New York: Random House, 1993).

3. Often the implication has been that queerness supersedes lesbian and gay identity, either because of its superior sophistication or because of its putatively greater inclusiveness. The argument from inclusiveness seems especially damaging to me because it involves the assumption that group inclusion is synonymous with democracy. Like "subversion" or "nondiscrimination" or "transgression," it's a political formalism — a formal relation that appears to guide political judgments but that holds a place for more substantive norms that remain covert. In this case, those norms are suspect not only because they are so disguised but because they are so unreflectively communitarian. The argument that queer rhetoric is more inclusive has an additional flaw: there are a lot of people — visibly, actively, impressively lesbian and gay — who do not find a home in queerness. Whatever the new term does, it does not simply replace or expand the old ones. It competes with them and, if taken literally, will rule out many of the people whom the revaluation of the term was meant to serve.

4. This identitarian culture has left its mark on queer theory as well. Part of my point here is that the history and promise of queer politics can be captured only imperfectly in personological theory, either in its positive liberationist variant or in its negative postmodern variant. Theorizing this historical moment in the language of identity and post-identitarian subjectivity once again returns our understanding of sexuality to the frame of the psyche — just at the moment and with just the language that had opened us onto an analysis of conflicting contexts for discourse. Queer theory inherits this predisposition from psychoanalytic identification theory, from Althusserian interpellation theory, from the uneasy graft of Gramscian deconstruction, from the American reception of Foucault, from the entire program of cultural studies in which it is imagined that "the construction of subjectivity" is the ultimate problem of the political. Given the limitations of that program, conditions were ripe for an overinvestment in the referential flexibility of queerness.

5. Jürgen Habermas, "The New Obscurity: The Crisis of the Welfare State and the Exhaustion of Utopian Energies," in the *The New Conservatism: Cultural*

316

Criticism and the Historians' Debate (Cambridge, MA: MIT Press, 1989), p. 59.

6. *Ibid.*, pp. 58.

7. Hannah Arendt, *The Human Condition* (Chicago: University of Chicago Press, 1958), p. 28.

8. *Ibid.*, pp. 41–42.

9. Henry David Thoreau, "Resistance to Civil Government," in *Reform Papers*, ed. Wendell Glick (Princeton, NJ: Princeton University Press, 1973), p. 86.

10. *Ibid.*, p. 80.

11. Henry David Thoreau, "Resistance to Civil Government," in *Reform Papers*, ed. Wendell Glick (Princeton, NJ: Princeton University Press, 1973), p. 79.

12. Henry David Thoreau, *Walden* (Princeton, NJ: Princeton University Press, 1973), p. 318.

CHAPTER SEVEN: A SOLILOQUY "LATELY SPOKEN AT THE AFRICAN THEATRE"

1. Early mentions of the African Theatre appear in Laurence Hutton, *Curiosities of the American Stage* (New York: Harper, 1891); and George O. Seilhamer, *History of the American Theatre: During the Revolution and After*, 3 vols. (Philadelphia: Globe Printing House, 1889). Most accounts of the theater, however, derive from George C.D. Odell, *Annals of the New York Stage* (New York: Columbia University Press, 1927–1941), taking from Odell some points of confusion along with valuable documentary material. After Odell, for example, the troupe is generally called "the African Grove Theater." ("The African Grove" was the name of the ice-cream garden that later gave rise to a theater and was not used as the name of the theater itself.) In this essay, we use the name "African Theatre," since this is the name that came to be established both in local usage and in the troupe's publicity.

Later texts discussing the episode include James Weldon Johnson, *Black Manhattan* (New York: Knopf, 1930); Frederick W. Bond, *The Negro and the Drama: The Direct and Indirect Contribution Which the American Negro Has Made to Drama and the Legitimate Stage, with the Underlying Conditions Responsible*

(Washington, DC: Associated Publishers, 1940); Edith J.R. Isaacs, *The Negro in the American Theatre* (New York: Theatre Arts, 1947); Glenn Hughes, *A History of the American Theatre, 1700–1950* (New York: Samuel French, 1951); Mary C. Henderson, *The City and the Theatre: New York Playhouses from Bowling Green to Times Square* (Clifton, N.J: James T. White & Co., 1973); Yvonne Shafer, "Black Actors in the Nineteenth Century American Theatre," *College Language Association Journal* 20.3 (March 1977), pp. 387–400; Jonathan Dewberry, "The African Grove Theatre and Company," *Black American Literature Forum* 16.4 (Winter 1982), pp 128–31; Bernard L. Peterson, ed., *Early Black American Playwrights and Dramatic Writers: A Biographical Directory and Catalog of Plays, Films, and Broadcasting Scripts* (Westport, CT: Greenwood Press, 1990); Thelma Wills Foote, "Crossroads or Settlement? The Black Freedmen's Community in Historic Greenwich Village, 1644–1855," in Rich Beard and Leslie Cohen Berlowitz, eds., *Greenwich Village: Culture and Counterculture* (New Brunswick, NJ: Rutgers University Press, 1993), pp. 120–33; Samuel A. Hay, *African American Theatre: A Historical and Critical Analysis* (Cambridge, UK: Cambridge University Press, 1994); Bernard L. Peterson, ed., *The African American Theatre Directory, 1816–1960: A Comprehensive Guide to Early Black Theatre Organizations, Companies, Theatres, and Performing Groups* (Westport, CT: Greenwood Press, 1997); Shane White and Graham White, eds., *Stylin': African-American Expressive Culture from Its Beginnings to the Zoot Suit* (Ithaca, NY: Cornell University Press, 1998); and Edwin Burrows and Mike Wallace, *Gotham: A History of New York City to 1898* (New York: Oxford University Press, 1998).

Much new information is to be found in George Thompson, *A Documentary History of the African Theatre* (Evanston, IL: Northwestern University Press, 1998). The authors wish to thank George Thompson for generously sharing his manuscript for this work. (The findings of the present article are summarized by Thompson on pp. 220–21.) Thanks are also due to Marvin McAlister, who shared thoughts about the theater based on research for his dissertation at Northwestern University.

2. *St. Tammany's Magazine* 4 (Dec. 4, 1821).

3. *St. Tammany's* turns up in neither Frank Luther Mott, *A History of Ameri-*

can *Magazines*, 5 vols. (Cambridge, MA: Harvard University Press, 1930–1968), nor in Edward Chielens, *American Literary Magazines: The Eighteenth and Nineteenth Centuries* (New York: Greenwood, 1986). It also seems to be unknown to the twentieth-century scholarship on early national literary culture in New York City. All seven issues can be found in the Special Collections room at the New York Public Library, the source for the text here.

4. All of the "Negro Melodies" texts are reprinted in the journal version of this essay, in *American Literature* 73.1 (March 2001), pp. 1–46.

5. See "Memoir of Robert C. Sands," in *The Writings of Robert C. Sands in Prose and Verse*, 2 vols. (New York: Harper & Brothers, 1834), vol. 1, pp. 3–30. Verplanck writes, no doubt mistaking the year, that in 1823–1824 Sands and his friends "published seven numbers of a sort of mock-magazine, entitled the St. Tammany Magazine. Here he gave the reins to his most extravagant and happiest humour, indulging in parody, burlesque, and grotesque satire, thrown off in the gayest mood and with the greatest rapidity, but as good-natured as satire and parody could well be" (pp. 16–17). Verplanck exaggerates the satiric character of *St. Tammany's*, much of which was quite serious, but he is clearly describing the same magazine. This brief comment was repeated, including the mistake about the dates, by several nineteenth-century sources, before the record of the magazine was lost in the twentieth century. See entries on Sands in S. Austin Allibon, comp., *A Critical Dictionary of English Literature and British and American Authors*, 3 vols. (Philadelphia: Lippincott, 1858–1871); *Appelton's Cyclopedia of American Biography* (New York: Appleton, 1888); and E. Vale Blake, *History of the Tammany Society, or Columbian Order, from Its Origin to the Present Time* (New York: Souvenir Publishing Co., 1901).

6. See Robert C. Sands, "Ghosts of the Stage," in *The Talisman*, a gift book he coedited with William Cullen Bryant, and discussed by Verplanck in *Writings of Robert C. Sands*, p. 15n.

7. The second issue of *St. Tammany's*, in fact, carried the first installment of a long satiric poem called "Nicholas," in which a black slave speaks a kind of folk wisdom. The poem goes out of its way to account for Nicholas's knowledge, given his illiteracy:

Tho' learning never to our hero's eyes,

Rich with the spoils of time, unrolled her page,

He made on outward things reflections wise,

which would not have disgraced an ancient sage.

This is very far from putting learned eloquence into the mouth of a black speaker. When Nicholas speaks, he speaks in dialect.

8. For example, a stage adaptation of *Oroonoko* by Thomas Southerne (London, 1785) gives Oroonoko the following speech:

Hard fate, and whips, and chains may overpow'r

The frailer flesh, and bow my body down:

But there's another, nobler part of me,

Out of your reach, which you can never tame. (p. 19)

Both the erudite literariness of the poems and the anthropological element in the first text link the series particularly to the tradition of Anglophone West Indian poetry. See, for a comparable example, *Poems, on Subjects Arising in England and the West Indies* (London, 1783), by the Rector of St. John's, Nevis. One especially interesting poem from this volume, "The Field Negroe; or, The Effect of Civilization," is reprinted in Myra Jehlen and Michael Warner, eds., *The English Literatures of America, 1500–1800* (New York: Routledge, 1997).

9. These comments are not meant to deny the development of a distinctive tradition; the point is simply that the conditions in which that distinctiveness would be seen as necessary or valuable might not have been in place for all African-American writers. A similar question has been raised on the inappropriateness of modern assumptions about "voice" and ethnic self-designation to some indigenous peoples; see Greg Urban, *Metaphysical Community* (Austin: University of Texas Press, 1997), especially pp. 47–49. Nor is it necessary to assume that the absence of a racially distinctive voice must be read as a sign of censorship or oppression, a position that has been developed with some subtlety in the case of Wheatley by Kirstin Wilcox, "The Body into Print: Marketing Phillis Wheatley," *American Literature* 71.1 (March 1999), pp. 1–29.

10. On the Maroons, see R.C. Dallas, *The History of the Maroons*, 2 vols. (New York: Frank Cass, 1968), and Abigail Bakan, *Ideology and Class Conflict in*

Jamaica: The Politics of Rebellion (Montreal: McGill-Queens University Press, 1990).

11. William Earle, *Obi; or, The History of Three-Fingered Jack. In a Series of Letters from a Resident in Jamaica to His Friend in England* (London: Earle & Hemet, c. 1800; reprinted by Isaiah Thomas, Worcester, MA, 1804).

12. The earliest extant stage version, a two-act pantomime by Fawcett, consists of a descriptive account of Obeah, followed only by notes and song lyrics for the pantomime. (The manuscript is in the Henry Huntington Library.) Another version survives from a Philadelphia production of 1810; it, too, merely outlines the plot, adding glosses on Obeah and lyrics for songs. Burdett's version of *Obi*, similarly, offers no dialogue at all. It comprises a fifty-page history of the practice of Obeah in Jamaica and related slave uprisings in 1760 and a ten-page script. This brief section consists of scene headings that function as plot summary. *Life and Exploits of Mansong, commonly called Three-Finger'd Jack, the Terror of Jamaica, with a particular account of the Obi, being the only true one of that celebrated and fascinating mischief, so prevalent in the West Indies. On which is founded the popular pantomimical Drama of "Obi; or, The Three-Finger'd Jack"; by William Burdett, many years overseer of a plantation in Jamaica* (Sommerstown [London]: A. Neil, 1800).

13. Thompson, *Documentary History of the African Theatre*, pp. 131–35.

14. On Taft, see *ibid.*, pp. 75–81. Thompson believes that contemporary reports of Taft playing Othello are mistaken; the evidence is discussed below. The most famous actor associated with the theater was Ira Aldridge; but the evidence of this connection is unclear. See the discussion in Thompson, *ibid.*, pp. 46–47.

15. Meredith McGill, "The Matter of the Text: Commerce, Print Culture, and the Authority of the State in American Copyright Law," *American Literary History* 9.1 (1997), pp. 21–59.

16. These descriptions are reprinted in Thompson, *Documentary History of the African Theatre*, pp. 114 and 94, respectively.

17. Earle, *Obi*.

18. This point is well illustrated by Thomas Krise, "True Novel, False History: Robert Robertson's Ventriloquized Ex-Slave in *The Speech of Mr. John Talbot Campo-Bell* (1736)," *Early American Literature* 30.2 (1995), pp. 152–64.

19. This can be inferred from Simon Snipe [pseud.], *Sports of New York, Containing an Evening at the African Theatre. Also a Trip to the Races and Two Songs* (New York, 1823). Snipe describes going to "The American, or in plainer words, Negro Theatre" as a diversion. The text is reprinted in Thompson, *Documentary History of the African Theatre*, pp. 114–16.

20. Snipe, *Sports of the New York*, p. 4.

21. *Ibid.*, pp. 6–10 and 13–14.

22. This play was advertised as *The Drama of King Shotaway*, probably a misprint for Chatoyer. See the discussion in Thompson, *Documentary History of the African Theatre*, pp. 88 and 136–39.

23. For a description of Taft, see *ibid.*, pp. 79–80.

24. This appears from an 1823 playbill in the Library of Congress, reprinted and discussed in *ibid.*, pp. 126–27.

25. Mathews gave his performance in London and did not repeat it in America until 1834; but Hewlett either heard from someone or read the account published in Charles Mathews, *Mr. Mathews's Trip to America* (London: J. Duncombe, 1824). Hewlett denied having performed Hamlet; Mathews evidently took large liberties. On Mathews's practicing black dialect, see Thompson, *Documentary History of the African Theatre*, p. 122, quoting Anne Jackson Mathews, *Memoirs of Charles Mathews, Comedian* (London: Richard Bentley, 1839), vol. 3, pp. 449–50.

26. *National Advocate*, May 8, 1824, reprinted in Thompson, *Documentary History of the African Theatre*, pp. 147–48. Thompson, following some rather doubtful evidence in remarks by Martin Delany (who refers to the actor as "Ulett"), suggests that Hewlett might have been assisted in writing the letter (p. 149).

27. For the context, see DeAlva Stanwood Alexander, *A Political History of the State of New York*, vol 1: 1774–1832 (1909; reprint, Port Washington, NY: Ira J. Friedman, 1969); John Anthony Casais, "The New York State Constitutional Convention of 1821 and Its Aftermath" (Ph.D. diss., Columbia University, 1967); Alvin Kass, *Politics in New York State, 1800–1830* (Syracuse, NY: Syracuse University Press, 1967); Chilton Williamson, *American Suffrage from Property to Democracy, 1760–1860* (Princeton, NJ: Princeton University Press, 1960).

28. *National Advocate*, Aug. 3, 1821. The entire column is reprinted in Thompson, *Documentary History of the African Theatre*, pp. 87–88.

29. Thompson, *Documentary History of the African Theatre*, pp. 64–66.

30. Hay, *African American Theatre*, pp. 5–14.

31. Mordecai Noah (1785–1851) is a fascinating figure in his own right, and his complex profile makes it difficult to assess his role in the theater affair. He had been editor of the *National Advocate*, a paper founded by the Tammany Hall Democrats, since 1817. He continued there until 1826, a reliable opponent to Governor DeWitt Clinton and a voice for the Bucktail wing of the party. He then established the *New York Enquirer*, which merged in 1829 with the *Morning Courier*. Noah's plays were among the most popular American dramas of the first half of the century. See Simon Wolf, *Mordecai M. Noah: A Biographical Sketch* (Philadelphia: The Levytype Co., 1897); Abraham B. Makover, *Mordecai M. Noah, His Life and Work from the Jewish Viewpoint* (New York: Bloch Publishing, 1917); Isaac Goldberg, *Major Noah: American-Jewish Pioneer* (Philadelphia: The Jewish Publication Society of America, 1936); Jonathan D. Sarna, *Jacksonian Jew: The Two Worlds of Mordecai M. Noah* (New York: Holmes and Meier, 1981); and Craig Kleinman, "Pigging the Nation, Staging the Jew in M.M. Noah's *She Would Be a Soldier*," *American Transcendental Quarterly* 10.3 (1996), pp. 201–17.

32. The 1822 riot is discussed in Thompson, *Documentary History of the African Theatre*; and in Paul Gilje, *The Road to Mobocracy: Popular Disorder in New York City, 1763–1834* (Chapel Hill: University of North Carolina Press, 1987), pp. 156–57.

33. *National Advocate*, July 14, 1821. The reference is to Addison's *Cato*, I.iv.

34. Despite the impression given by Noah's editorials, however, African-Americans were actually declining as a percentage of the overall population in the 1820s, from 8.8 percent to 6.9 percent, owing to the even greater influx of other immigrants. See Burrows and Wallace, *Gotham*, p. 479. See also Edgar McManus, *A History of Negro Slavery in New York* (Syracuse, NY: Syracuse University Press, 1966); Roi Ottley and William J. Weatherby, eds., *The Negro in New York: An Informal Social History* (New York: New York Public Library, 1967);

Daniel Perlman, "Organizations of the Free Negro in New York City, 1800–1860," *Journal of Negro History* 56 (1971), pp. 18–97; Shane White, *Somewhat More Independent: The End of Slavery in New York City, 1770–1810* (Athens: University of Georgia Press, 1991); and Shane White, "'We Dwell in Safety and Pursue Our Honest Callings': Free Blacks in New York City, 1783–1810," *Journal of American History* 75 (1988), pp. 445–70.

35. Charles Sellers contends that the black vote was a pivotal bloc in New York City elections; see his *The Market Revolution* (New York: Oxford University Press, 1991). His source for this claim is Dixon Ryan Fox, "The Negro Vote in Old New York," *Political Science Quarterly* 32 (1917), pp. 252–75. But Fox claims only that the freedmen were significant in the 1813 election, and that claim rests on the assertions of Erastus Root in the 1821 convention. Root and others seem to have been afraid of the African-American vote, but little scholarship has been done on the grounds of their anxiety. Fox, in fact, claims that the free black vote became significant only after 1830. See also Dixon Ryan Fox, *The Decline of Aristocracy in the Politics of New York* (New York: Harper Torchbooks, 1965); and Shaw Livermore, *The Twilight of Federalism* (Princeton, NJ: Princeton University Press, 1962). The general context of state constitutional revision is discussed in Laura J. Scalia, *America's Jeffersonian Experiment: Remaking State Constitutions, 1820–1850* (De Kalb: Northern Illinois University Press, 1999).

36. Washington Irving, *Letters*, ed. Ralph M. Aderman et al. (Boston: Twayne, 1978), vol. 1, pp. 231–32. See also Michael Warner, "Irving's Posterity," *ELH* 67.3 (Fall 2000), pp. 773–99.

37. Nathaniel Carter and William Stone, *Reports of the Proceedings and Debates of the Convention of 1821* (Albany, NY: E. and E. Hosford, 1821), p. 134.

38. *National Advocate*, Sept. 21, 1821; reprinted in full in Thompson, *Documentary History of the African Theatre*, pp. 61–62.

39. *National Advocate*, Sept. 29, 1821; reprinted in Thompson, *Documentary History of the African Theatre*, p. 69.

40. *New-York Commercial Advertiser*, Jan. 16, 1822; reprinted in Thompson, *Documentary History of the African Theatre*, pp. 87–88.

41. See Jerome Mushkat, *Tammany: The Evolution of a Political Machine*

(Syracuse, NY: Syracuse University Press, 1971); and Blake, *History of the Tammany Society*.

42. Very little scholarly information exists on Van Winkle. He is known primarily as the author of *The Printer's Guide* (New York: Van Winkle, 1818), long the standard work of reference for the printer's trade in America. His significance for Irving's tale has never been discussed. According to a descendant in 1945, family lore had it that Van Winkle was angry over Irving's use of his name. (William Mitchell Van Winkle, "A Note on *The Printer's Guide*," *Walpole Society Note Book* [1945].) But this cannot be true. For many years after he published *The Sketch Book*, Van Winkle continued to court Irving for later titles and often reprinted earlier ones such as *The History of New York*. *St. Tammany's Magazine* would alone refute the story, since it shows Van Winkle conducting a publicity campaign on behalf of Irving, defending him at length from charges of plagiarism over "Rip Van Winkle." In his partnership with John Wiley, Van Winkle had been associated with Irving at least since 1814, when he was the New York publisher of the *Analectic Magazine*, which Irving then edited. One curious fact about Van Winkle emerges from Gilje, *The Road to Mobocracy*, where his name appears in a list of those arrested in an 1812 riot against the religious mountebank Amos Broad (p. 218).

43. *St. Tammany's Magazine* 5 (Dec. 17, 1821), pp. 70–71.

44. Frances Wright, *Views of Society and Manners in America*, ed. Paul R. Baker (Cambridge, MA: Harvard University Press, 1963). First published in London in 1821, the book recounts Wright's visit to America from 1818 to 1820.

45. *St. Tammany's Magazine* 5 (Dec. 17, 1821), pp. 71–72.

46. Of special relevance is letter no. 3, which treats patriotic sentiment among the lower classes: "It is truly interesting to listen to an intelligent American when he speaks of the condition and resources of his country, and this, not merely when you find him in the more polished circles of society, but when toiling for his subsistence with the saw or spade in his hand. I have never yet conversed with the man who could not inform you upon any fact regarding the past history and existing institutions of his nation, with all the readiness and accuracy with which a schoolboy, fresh from his studies, might reply to your queries upon the laws of Lycurgus or the twenty-seven years' war of the Peloponnesus"

(Wright, *Views*, p. 18). This is almost certainly the reference when the "Journal" describes deckhands reading Thucydides. The dream vision refers to letter no. 4, with its digression on women's rights and education: "A new race, nurtured under the watchful eye of judicious mothers and from them imbibing in tender youth the feelings of generous liberty and ardent patriotism, may evince in their maturity an elevation of sentiment which now to prognosticate of any nation on the earth might be accounted the dream of an idle theorist or vain believer in the perfectibility of his species" (p. 23).

47. The narrator claims to have arrived on the *Phoebe Ann*, but a search of the marine lists for the latter half of 1821 turns up no ship by that name.

48. The *New-York Commercial Advertiser* reported on January 16, 1822, that the African Theatre was to stage *The Fortress of Sorrento*.

49. Thompson, *Documentary History of the African Theatre*, p. 80, reproduces this short notice.

50. At least two accounts describe performances of *Othello* in 1822. They are reproduced in *ibid.*, pp. 113–16.

51. *New-York City-Hall Recorder*, 6:10 (Nov. 17, 1821), p. 88; in *ibid.*, p. 79.

52. In *ibid.*, p. 78.

53. *St. Tammany's Magazine* 2 (Nov. 17, 1821), p. 26.

54. On scientific racism, see William Stanton, *The Leopard's Spots: Scientific Attitudes Toward Race in America, 1815–59* (Chicago: University of Chicago Press, 1960).

55. Carter and Stone, *Reports*, p. 365.

56. *Ibid.*, p. 188.

57. *Ibid.*, p. 191.

58. A large body of recent scholarship is relevant here, much of it following Stuart Hall's general call for studies of ethnicity that acknowledge "the place of history, language, and culture in the construction of subjectivity" (David Morley and Kuan-Hsing Chen, eds., *Stuart Hall: Critical Dialogues in Cultural Studies* [New York: Routledge, 1996], p. 446). See especially David Roediger, *The Wages of Whiteness: Race and the Making of the American Working Class* (London: Verso, 1991); Alexander Sexton, *The Rise and Fall of the White Republic: Class Politics*

and *Mass Culture in Nineteenth-Century America* (London: Verso, 1990); and Dale T. Knobel, *Paddy and the Republic: Ethnicity and Nationality in Antebellum America* (Middletown, CT: Wesleyan University Press, 1986).

59. Noah was probably the most prominent Jew in New York and in 1818 had put out a pamphlet calling for a Jewish settlement in America — published, ironically, by Cornelius Van Winkle! "Here, no inequality of privileges — no asperity of opinion — no invidious distinctions exist; dignity is blended with equality, justice administered impartially: merit alone is a fixed value; and each man is stimulated by the same laudable ambition — an ambition of doing his duty and meriting the good will of his fellow citizens" (*Discourse, delivered at the consecration of the Synagogue of KK Shirit Yisroel in the City of New York . . .* [New York: C.S. Van Winkle, 1818], p. 19).

60. On the concept of a counterpublic, see chapters 1 and 2 above.

61. James Fenimore Cooper, *The Spy: A Tale of the Neutral Ground* (New York: Wiley, 1821). The quotation is found in Wayne Franklin's edition (New York: Penguin, 1997) at p. 37, but Franklin uses the later, modified text.

62. Cooper, *The Spy*, pp. 167–69.

63. *Ibid*, p. 249.

64. "It was printed as it was written, and a copy of the first volume, *bound*, lay about my house, several weeks, before a line of the second volume was thought of. At length the 'beginning of the end' was undertaken. Still, our progress was desultory and slow. Wiley began to fancy the book would be made too long for profit; to set his heart at ease, the last chapter was printed and *paged*, before several of the preceding chapters were even conceived." Quoted in James H. Pickering, introduction to *The Spy* (Schenectady, NY: New College and University Press, 1971), p. xvi.

65. See, for example, Cooper's letter of September 6, 1821, to John Jay, discussing the convention.

66. Cooper, *The Spy*, p. 10.

67. *Ibid*, p. 333.

68. *Ibid*. On the African-American holiday known as Pinkster, see Stephen Nissenbaum, *The Battle for Christmas* (New York: Knopf, 1998).

69. Cooper, *The Spy*, p. 339.

70. See Herbert Marshall and Mildred Stock, *Ira Aldridge: The Negro Trage-dian* (Washington, DC: Howard University Press, 1993).

71. W. T. Lhamon, *Raising Cain: Black Performance from Jim Crow to Hip Hop* (Cambridge, MA: Harvard University Press, 1998), p. 8.

72. *Ibid*, pp. 3–55.

73. Burrows and Wallace, *Gotham*, p. 480.

74. The print, from the collection of the New-York Historical Society, is reproduced in *ibid*, p. 490.

75. Simon Snipe [pseud.], *The Sports of New York, by Simon Snipe, Esq; Con-taining a Peep at the Grand Military Ball, "Hewlett at Home,"...* (New York, 1824). Thompson, who reproduces this excerpt, notes that the author of this pamphlet seems to write in a different style and with a different stance from the "Simon Snipe" of the 1823 *Sports of New York*; Thompson, *Documentary History of the African Theatre*, pp. 150–51.

76. Bond, *Negro and the Drama*, p. 18.

CHAPTER EIGHT: WHITMAN DRUNK

1. Charles Sellers, *The Market Revolution* (New York: Oxford University Press, 1991), p. 265.

2. Walt Whitman, *Franklin Evans*, in *The Early Poems and the Fiction*, ed. Thomas L. Brasher (New York: New York University Press, 1963), p. 152.

3. *Ibid.*, p. 153–54; italics in original. Brasher's edition reads "have" instead of "lave."

4. The rhetorical weight accorded to mere italicization in that last phrase, "such a scene of *pleasure*" — like the conclusion's emphasis on the voice that speaks to the reader in these lines, or like the women's ability through "war-bling" to lave Evans in happiness — indicates Whitman's characteristic (and char-acteristically faggy) attachment to voice as a limit case both of embodied self-mastery and of boundary problems.

5. Jonathan Edwards, *Freedom of the Will*, ed. Paul Ramsey (New Haven, CT: Yale University Press, 1957), p. 139.

6. Whitman, *Franklin Evans*, p. 179.

7. These three quotations appear in *ibid.*, p. 180.

8. Eve Kosofsky Sedgwick, "Epidemics of Will," in *Tendencies* (Durham, NC: Duke University Press, 1993), pp. 133–34.

9. Whitman, *Franklin Evans*, pp. 222–23.

10. Floyd Stovall, *The Foreground of Leaves and Grass* (Charlottesville: University Press of Virginia, 1974), p. 36.

11. Horace Traubel, *With Walt Whitman in Camden*, 9 vols. (1905–99; New York: Rowman and Littlefield, 1961), vol. 1, p. 93.

12. Herbert Ross Brown, *The Sentimental Novel in America, 1789–1860* (Durham, NC: Duke University Press, 1940), p. 201.

13. Whitman, *Franklin Evans*, pp. 126–27.

14. Alexis de Tocqueville, *Democracy in America*, 2 vols. (New York: Knopf, 1945), vol. 1, pp. 198–99.

15. Henry David Thoreau, "Resistance to Civil Government," in *Reform Papers*, ed. Wendell Glick (Princeton, NJ: Princeton University Press, 1973), p. 79.

16. Whitman, *Franklin Evans*, p. 212.

17. *Ibid.*, p. 232.

18. *Ibid.*, p. 230.

19. *Ibid.*, p. 151.

20. *Ibid.*, p. 219.

21. *Ibid.*, p. 239.

22. *Ibid.*, pp. 167–68.

23. *Ibid.*, p. 175.

24. *Ibid.*, p. 234.

25. *Ibid.*, p. 263.

26. Walt Whitman, *Poetry and Prose* (New York: Library of America, 1982), p. 280.

27. This reading of Thoreau I have elaborated in "Thoreau's Bottom," *Raritan* 11.3 (Winter 1992): pp. 53–79; and "Walden's Erotic Economy," in Hortense Spillers, ed., *Comparative American Identities: Race, Sex and Nationality in the Modern Text* (New York: Routledge, 1991), pp. 157–74.

Index

Zone Books series design by Bruce Mau
Type composed by Archetype
Printed and bound by Maple Press